# ILLUSTRATED
# ENGLISH SOCIAL HISTORY

*Works by*
*George Macaulay Trevelyan, O.M.*

ENGLISH SOCIAL HISTORY

ILLUSTRATED ENGLISH SOCIAL HISTORY
> VOLUME I *Chaucer's England and the Early Tudors*
> VOLUME II *The Age of Shakespeare and the Stuart Period*
> VOLUME III *The Eighteenth Century*
> VOLUME IV *The Nineteenth Century*

HISTORY OF ENGLAND

BRITISH HISTORY IN THE NINETEENTH CENTURY
> AND AFTER (1782–1919)

ENGLAND UNDER QUEEN ANNE:
> *Blenheim*
> *Ramillies and the Union with Scotland*
> *The Peace and the Protestant Succession*

ENGLAND IN THE AGE OF WYCLIFFE

GREY OF FALLODON

GARIBALDI'S DEFENCE OF THE ROMAN REPUBLIC

GARIBALDI AND THE THOUSAND

GARIBALDI AND THE MAKING OF ITALY

LORD GREY OF THE REFORM BILL, THE LIFE OF
> CHARLES, SECOND EARL GREY

CLIO, A MUSE, AND OTHER ESSAYS

AN AUTOBIOGRAPHY AND OTHER ESSAYS

CARLYLE: AN ANTHOLOGY

A LAYMAN'S LOVE OF LETTERS

ILLUSTRATED HISTORY OF ENGLAND

SELECTED POETICAL WORKS OF GEORGE MEREDITH

I. Queen Elizabeth—' a shrewd, learned and moderate young woman '

# ILLUSTRATED
# ENGLISH SOCIAL HISTORY

VOLUME TWO

*The Age of Shakespeare and
the Stuart Period*

by

## G. M. TREVELYAN, O.M.

*Master of Trinity College, 1940-1951
Formerly Regius Professor of Modern
History in the University of Cambridge*

*ILLUSTRATIONS SELECTED BY*
*RUTH C. WRIGHT*

## DAVID McKAY COMPANY, INC.
New York

BIBLIOGRAPHICAL NOTE
*First published in U.S.A. and Canada* 1942
*First published in Great Britain* 1944

ILLUSTRATED EDITION IN FOUR VOLUMES
*First published* 1949–1952
*Issued as a set of four volumes,*
*bound in leather,* 1954
*New impressions* 1962, 1964, 1965, 1967 *and* 1969

SBN 582 11352 0

*Lithographic plates printed by*
JARROLD & SONS LTD. NORWICH

*Colour plates printed by*
W. P. GRIFFITH LTD.
and LOWE & BRYDONE LTD.

*Text printed in Great Britain by*
SPOTTISWOODE, BALLANTYNE & CO. LTD.
*London & Colchester*

# PREFATORY NOTE TO THE ILLUSTRATIONS

THE choice of illustrations for this volume has been guided by the same principles as in Volume I, that is to say, they have been drawn as far as possible from English work (or from that of foreign artists working in England), and from sources as nearly contemporary as possible with the scenes they represent.

There has, perforce, been a change in the type of sources used; whereas MSS. supplied the greater part of the illustrative commentary for the mediaeval and early Tudor period in Volume I, printed books and engravings, ballads, broadsides and tracts largely provide the material for the late Sixteenth and Seventeenth Centuries.

I have found it necessary to use such foreign books as the *Civitates Orbis Terrarum* and Agricola's *De Re Metallica*, the former, with its detailed maps and plans, because it provides unrivalled views of English city layout in the Sixteenth Century, and the latter, because it is the only source known to me of Sixteenth-Century mining scenes and appropriate in that German mining practice was applied in England at this date. Similarly, I have let de Bry's engravings speak for Virginia (§ 57) and Augustine Ryther's for the Armada (§ 52, 53), both being based on English drawings.

Artists working in a country not their own often bring to their work an interestingly different view of the people or scenes they are depicting, and so I have used as frontispiece Zuccaro's crayon drawing of Elizabeth, where the simplicity of effect serves to concentrate the interest in the Queen's face and personality, rather than in her jewels and royal trappings.

As in Volume I, later drawings and modern photographs have been freely used to illustrate places as distinct from social scenes, but care has been taken to distinguish and specify in the descriptive notes any features of a later date that occur—thus in Two-penny's drawing of the Great Gallery at Powys Castle (§ 17), reference to the note will show that while the rich decoration of the plaster ceiling and frieze is original work of 1592–93, the panelling, furniture and busts belong to varying and later dates. Grimm's sketches of Portland stone quarrying have been used though they belong to the Eighteenth Century, but neither the method of quarrying nor transport had changed very radically since Wren's time.

Air photographs have played an important part in this volume in making it possible to exhibit the layout of the great houses of the period or the features of a whole area—Montacute and Moreton Old Hall (§ 13, 14) can thus contrast their style and setting, the Cheviots (§ 8) lay bare their almost primaeval wildness, and the floods of 1947 allow a momentary glimpse of the watery solitudes and oozy islands of the mediaeval fen (§ 5). For the rest, contemporary printed books, etchings and engravings have been used to illustrate as many sides as possible of English life and activities, while portraits record for us at least some of those who left the imprint of their thoughts or discoveries upon their times.

Detailed notes as in Volume I will be found at the end of the book, giving sources of the illustrations, their authorship and present ownership, and pointing out any noteworthy features, either in the illustrations themselves or in their history.

I should like to take this opportunity to thank Sir Henry Hake, Director of the National Portrait Gallery and his Assistant, Mr. C. K. Adams, for their advice and guidance in the selection of the earliest or most authentic portraits of the people illustrated in this volume, and also Miss Hamilton Jones, Librarian of Aerofilms, Ltd., who has been indefatigable in her efforts to secure the air photographs I wanted.

RUTH C. WRIGHT
*Illustrations Editor.*

## ACKNOWLEDGMENTS

THE publishers' grateful thanks are due to all those who have given permission for photographs to be taken of the MSS., printed books, pictures or antiquities in their care or ownership, or have allowed photographs in their possession to be reproduced. Full details of such ownership, etc., will be found in the descriptive notes for each item.

# CONTENTS

*Prefatory Note to the Illustrations*

*Introduction*

CHAPTER                                                          PAGE

I SHAKESPEARE'S ENGLAND. 1. THE TOWNS. THE
COUNTRYSIDE. CLASSES AND MODES OF LIFE.
WALES. THE NORTHERN COUNTIES. ELIZABETHAN
HOMES. INNS. SOCIAL RELATIONSHIPS. MILITIA.
LAW. J.P.S. POOR LAW                         1

II SHAKESPEARE'S ENGLAND. 2. RELIGION AND UNI-
VERSITIES. THE SOCIAL POLICY OF THE ELIZA-
BETHAN STATE. INDUSTRY AND SEAFARING.
SHAKESPEARE                                33

III THE ENGLAND OF CHARLES AND CROMWELL. THE
BEGINNING OF COLONIAL EXPANSION. EAST
INDIA COMPANY. FEN DRAINING. SOCIAL CON-
DITIONS AND CONSEQUENCES OF THE GREAT
REBELLION. HOUSEHOLD LIFE              65

IV RESTORATION ENGLAND.                   111

DESCRIPTIVE NOTES TO THE ILLUSTRATIONS     153

INDEX                                         197

# ILLUSTRATIONS

## Colour Plates

I QUEEN ELIZABETH — 'A SHREWD, LEARNED AND MODERATE YOUNG WOMAN'  *Frontispiece*

II MINIATURE OF A YOUNG MAN BY NICHOLAS HILLIARD  *facing p.* 20

III THE PAINTED ROOM AT OLD WILSLEY, KENT (C. 1680)  ,, 106

IV SIR CHRISTOPHER WREN  ,, 146

## Litho Plates

§§ 1–17  *Between pp.* 16–17

§§ 18–42  ,, 32–33

§§ 43–59  ,, 64–65

§§ 60–80  ,, 112–113

§§ 81–105  ,, 128–129

§§ 106–124  ,, 144–145

*Illustrations in the text on pp.* 3, 48, 58, 61, 71, 95–97, 109
*Map of Late Tudor and Early Stuart London pp.* 150–151

# INTRODUCTION

THIS second volume of the Illustrated Edition of my *English Social History* covers both the Elizabethan and the Stuart eras. Although the latter half of the period witnessed a series of political revolutions, the economic and social aspects of life as here described are characterized by fruition and steady growth. There are no such rapid changes as those which began in the following century and are called the 'Industrial Revolution.' The harmony of the economic and social structure in the Stuart era was certainly one reason why England was able to survive the violent political and religious strife of the period, and arrive at a peaceable adjustment of these quarrels at the end of the Seventeenth Century. If the struggle of King and Parliament for power had not been settled before we were involved in the economic and social upheavals of the Industrial Revolution, we should not have got through so well, as the later history of France, Germany and Russia suggests.

## Chapter One

### SHAKESPEARE'S ENGLAND [1564-1616]

1. *The Towns. The Countryside. Classes and modes of life. Wales. The
Northern counties. Elizabethan homes. Inns. Social relationships.
Militia. Law. J.P.s. Poor Law.*
*(Queen Elizabeth, 1558-1603. The Armada, 1588).*

AFTER the economic and religious unrest of the middle
Tudor period, followed the golden age of England. Golden
ages are not all of gold, and they never last long. But Shakespeare
chanced upon the best time and country in which to live, in order
to exercise with least distraction and most encouragement the
highest faculties of man. The forest, the field and the city were
there in perfection, and all three are needed to perfect the poet.
His countrymen, not yet cramped to the service of machines, were
craftsmen and creators at will. Their minds, set free from mediaeval trammels, were not yet caught by Puritan or other modern
fanaticisms. The Elizabethan English were in love with life, not
with some theoretic shadow of life. Large classes, freed as never
before from poverty, felt the upspring of the spirit and expressed
it in wit, music and song. The English language had touched its
moment of fullest beauty and power. Peace and order at last
prevailed in the land, even during the sea-war with Spain.
Politics, so long a fear and oppression, and soon in other forms
to be a fear and oppression again, were for a few decades simplified
into service paid to a woman, who was to her subjects the symbol
of their unity, prosperity and freedom.

The Renaissance, that had known its springtime long ago in
its native Italy, where biting frosts now nipped it, came late to
its glorious summer in this northern isle. In the days of Erasmus,
the Renaissance in England had been confined to scholars and to
the King's Court. In Shakespeare's day it had in some sort
reached the people. The Bible and the world of classical antiquity
were no longer left to the learned few. By the agency of the
grammar schools, classicism filtered through from the study into

the theatre and the street, from the folio to the popular ballad which familiarized the commonest auditories with *The Tyranny of Judge Appius* and *The Miserable state of King Midas* and the other great tales of Greece and Rome. The old Hebrew and the Graeco-Roman ways of life, raised from the grave of the remote past by the magic of scholarship, were opened to the general understanding of Englishmen, who treated them not as dead archaeological matter, but as new spheres of imagination and spiritual power, to be freely converted to modern use. While Shakespeare transformed Plutarch's *Lives* into his own *Julius Caesar* and *Antony,* others took the Bible and fashioned out of it a new way of life and thought for religious England.

And during these same fruitful years of Elizabeth, the narrow seas, amid whose tempests English mariners had for centuries been trained, expanded into the oceans of the world, where romance and wealth were to be won by adventurous youth, trading and fighting along newly discovered shores. Young, light-hearted England, cured at last of the Plantagenet itch to conquer France, became conscious of herself as an island with an ocean destiny, glad, after that Armada storm, to feel the safety and freedom that the guarded seas could give, while the burden of distant Empire was not yet laid upon her shoulders.

There is, of course, another side to all this, as there is to every picture of human well-being and well-doing. The cruel habits of centuries past were not easily or quickly to be shed. The overseas activity of the Elizabethans paid no regard to the rights of the negroes whom they transported into slavery, or the Irish whom they robbed and slaughtered: some even of the noblest English, like John Hawkins on the Gold Coast and Edmund Spenser in Ireland, failed to see what dragons' teeth they were helping to sow. At home, the woman hunted by her neighbours as a witch, the Jesuit missionary mounting the scaffold to be cut to pieces alive, the Unitarian burning at the stake, the Puritan dissenter hanged or 'laden with irons in dangerous and loathsome gaols,' had little joy of the great era. But in Elizabeth's England such victims were not numerous, as elsewhere in Europe. We escaped the pit of calamity into which other nations were being thrust— the Spanish Inquisition and the vast scale of martyrdom and massacre that turned the Netherlands and France into a shambles in the name of religion. Looking across the Channel and seeing these things, the English rejoiced that they were islanders and that wise Elizabeth was their Queen.

As the tour of Henry VIII's England was made and recorded by the antiquary Leland, so the tour of Elizabeth's happier kingdom was made and recorded by the greatest of all our antiquaries, William Camden, in his *Britannia*. [See § 34.] And just before him William Harrison, the parson, and just after him Fynes Moryson, the traveller, left us pictures of the English life of their

Religious Persecution

day, which it is a pleasure to collate with the more vivid glimpses in Shakespeare. [Cf. also § 33.]

It is probable that the population of England and Wales at the end of the Queen's reign had passed four millions, about a tenth of its present size. More than four-fifths lived in the rural parts; but of these a fair proportion were engaged in industry, supplying nearly all the manufactures required by the village, or, like the clothiers, miners and quarrymen, working for a more general market. The bulk of the population cultivated the land or tended sheep.

Of the minority who inhabited towns, many were engaged, at least for part of their time, in agriculture. A provincial town of average size contained 5000 inhabitants. The towns were not overcrowded, and had many pleasant gardens, orchards and farmsteads mingled with the rows of shops. Some smaller towns and ports were in process of decay. The recession of the sea, the silting up of rivers (which gradually put Chester on the Dee out of action as a port), the increase in the size of ships demanding larger harbours, the continued migration of the cloth and other manufactures in rural villages and hamlets, were all causes of the decline of some of the older centres of industry or commerce.

Yet the town population was on the increase in the island taken as a whole. York, the capital of the North; Norwich, a great centre of the cloth trade, welcoming skilled refugees from Alva's Netherlands; Bristol with mercantile and inland trade of its own wholly independent of London—these three were in a class by themselves, with perhaps 20,000 inhabitants each. [See § 2, 3.] And the new oceanic conditions of trade favoured other port towns in the West, like Bideford.

But, above all, London, absorbing more and more of the home and foreign commerce of the country at the expense of many smaller towns, was already a portent for size in England and even in Europe. When Mary Tudor died it may have had nearly 100,000 inhabitants; when Elizabeth died it may already have touched 200,000. It was spreading most rapidly in the 'liberties' outside its old walls; in the heart of the City there were small open spaces, and houses with gardens, courtyards and stables. In spite of the recurrent visits of the Plague (the old Black Death) and the novel visitation of the 'sweating sickness,' Tudor London was relatively healthy and deaths were fewer than births. It was not yet as congested as it became in the early Eighteenth Century, when its still vaster population was more closely packed in slums, further removed from access to the country, and more unhealthy, although the Plague had by that time disappeared, to give place to smallpox and typhus. [See § 4.]

The London of Queen Elizabeth, by its size, wealth and power, was the most formidable unit in the Kingdom. Socially, intellectually and politically it exercised an influence that went far to secure the success of the Protestant revolution in the Sixteenth Century and of the Parliamentary revolution in the Seventeenth. The area of the City was now the fortress of a purely civic and mercantile community, unchallenged within its own borders by any rival influence. The great monasteries and convents of mediaeval London had disappeared; the laity were supreme, and refashioned their religion in the City churches and in their own homes after the Protestant and individual patterns of their preference. Neither monarchy nor aristocracy had any strongholds within the City boundaries. The royal power lay outside in

Whitehall and Westminster on one flank, and in the Tower upon the other. Even the great nobles were leaving their mediaeval quarters in the City and migrating to mansions in the Strand or in the neighbourhood of Court and Parliament at Westminster. The power and privilege of the Mayor and citizens, with their formidable militia, formed a State within the State—a society that was purely bourgeois, inside the larger England that was still monarchical and aristocratic. And the leaven of London worked throughout the land. [See § 23, 24.]

The feeding of Tudor London governed the agricultural policy of the home counties, and the same influence was felt in varying degrees further afield. Food was wanted in the capital, in vast quantity for the population, and of the best quality for the richest tables of the kingdom. Kent with its enclosed fields, already called 'the garden of England,' was specifically London's fruit-garden, rich with 'apples beyond measure and also with cherries.' The barley of East Anglia, coming through brewing towns like Royston, quenched the daily thirst of the Londoner; while Kent and Essex were learning to train hops to flavour his beer. For the rest, the wheat and rye that made London's bread, were grown all over the south-eastern counties.

Thus the great market of the capital helped to change agricultural methods, by inducing districts best fitted for one particular crop to specialize on that. Near London, Norden the topographer noticed 'another sort of husbandman, or yeoman rather, who wade in the weeds of gentlemen, . . . who having great feedings for cattle,' sell their fat stock at Smithfield, 'where also they store themselves with lean. There are also those that live by carriage for other men, and to that end they keep carts and carriages, carry milk, meal and other things to London, whereby they live very gainfully.' In regions so fortunately situated, the pressure to enclose the land was strong.

Besides London, there were other markets for agricultural produce. Few towns, if any, could grow all the food they required in the 'town fields' without need to purchase outside. And even in the country, if one rural district had a bad season, it could buy the surplus of other districts through middlemen, unless the harvest had been poor all over England, when, perhaps once in a decade, there might be considerable importation from abroad. In normal years some English corn was exported.

Huntingdonshire, Cambridgeshire and other regions of the Ouse valley, sent great quantities of wheat through Lynn and the Wash to Scotland, Norway and the cities of the Netherlands. Much food came to Bristol and the Western towns from the granary of central England, the open fields of south-eastern Warwickshire, the 'Feldon' lying between the Avon and Edgehill. But the other half of Warwickshire lying north-west of Avon, as Leland and Camden both noted, was deep woodland, thinly studded with pastoral settlements; it was the Forest of Arden. Thus the winding Avon, spanned by Stratford's famous bridge of 'fourteen arches of stone,' divided the lonely forest from the populous cornlands. One born and bred in the town upon its banks saw, in his boyhood's rambles, what was best in wild nature on one side of the river, and what was most characteristic of man upon the other.

Until the Eighteenth Century with its highly capitalized farming, it was not possible to ripen enough wheat to feed the whole population. Oats, wheat, rye and barley were all grown, some more, some less, according to the soil and climate. Oats prevailed in the North; wheat and rye in most parts of England, except the south-west where rye was little grown. Everywhere barley abounded, and much of it went into beer. The West, with its apple orchards, drank cider; and the pears of Worcestershire gave perry, which Camden condemned as 'a counterfeit wine, both cold and flatulent.' In all parts of England the village grew a variety of crops for its own use, and its bread was often a mixture of different kinds of grain. Fynes Moryson, who knew the chief countries of Europe well, wrote, shortly after Queen Elizabeth's death—

'The English husbandmen eat barley and rye brown bread, and prefer it to white bread as abiding longer in the stomach, and not so soon digested with their labour ; but citizens and gentlemen eat most pure white bread, England yielding all kinds of corn in plenty.[1]

'The English have abundance of white meats, of all kinds of flesh, fowl and fish and of things good for food. In the seasons of the

---

[1] Harrison, writing a generation earlier (circa 1577) says the same thing :
'The bread throughout our land is made of such grain as the soil yieldeth, nevertheless the gentility commonly provide themselves sufficiently of wheat for their own tables, whilst their household and poor neighbours in some shires are forced to content themselves with rye or barley, yea and in time of dearth many with bread made out of beans, peason or oats and some acorns among.'

year the English eat fallow deer plentifully, as bucks in summer and does in winter, which they bake in pasties, and this venison pasty is a dainty, rarely found in any other kingdom.   England, yea perhaps one County thereof, hath more fallow deer than all Europe that I have seen.   No kingdom in the world hath so many dove-houses. Likewise brawn is a proper meat to the English, not known to others. English cooks, in comparison with other nations, are most commended for roasted meats.'

This experienced traveller goes on to praise our beef and mutton as the best in Europe, and our bacon as better than any except that of Westphalia.

'The English inhabitants [he continues] eat almost no flesh commoner than hens, and for geese they eat them in two seasons, when they are fatted upon the stubble after harvest and when they are green about Whitsuntide.  And howsoever hares are thought to nourish melancholy, yet they are eaten as venison both roast and boiled.  They have also great plenty of conies [rabbits] the flesh whereof is fat, tender and more delicate than any I have eaten in other parts.  The German conies [our traveller declares] are more like roasted cats than the English conies.'

Meat and bread were the chief foods.   Vegetables were little eaten with meat; cabbages helped to make the pottage.  Potatoes were just beginning to come in to some garden plots, but were not yet grown as a crop in the fields.

Puddings and stewed fruit did not yet play so great a part in the Englishman's table as in later centuries, though sugar was already obtained in moderate quantities from Mediterranean lands.   The time of dinner, the chief meal, was at eleven or twelve, and supper some five hours later. [See § 1, 27.]

Since the English village, whether in the western lands of old enclosure or in the 'champion' regions of the open field, still grew its own food, 'subsistence agriculture' was the basis of English life.  But, as we have seen, the self-supplying village also grew wool and food-stuffs for some special market at home or abroad. 'Industrial crops' were also coming much into use; flax grew well in some parts of Lincolnshire; woad, madder and the great fields of saffron in Essex (whence 'Saffron Walden' already had taken its name) supplied the dyers of cloth, who had previously depended on foreign imports.

Such specialization for the market demanded enclosure and

7

private methods of farming. The new lands won from forest, marsh and waste, were now always enclosed with hedges and farmed on the individualist system. The area of open field and common pasture did not increase as the total area under cultivation increased. The bleak open fields, though not much reduced in acreage, were relatively a smaller part of the farmlands of the Kingdom than they had formerly been.

It was the low-lying clay districts that produced the surplus corn for the home and foreign market. The sheep, that supplied the wool and cloth trades, fed on the thin upland pastures which alternate with the clay valleys in the geographic structure of the island. The chalk downs and the wolds—the Chilterns, the Dorset Heights, the Isle of Wight, the Cotswolds, the Lincoln and Norfolk ridges, and many moorlands of the North, had always produced the best wool. On such hillsides, foreign and native travellers in Tudor England marvelled at the number and size of the flocks, unparalleled elsewhere in Europe. The sheep on the less fertile lands were often half starved, but their fleeces were the most valuable in the world, owing to some quality latent in the soil.

The increased demand for sheep and cattle in Tudor times caused, as we have seen, some highly unpopular enclosures of arable clay-land for pasture. The valley sheep were fatter, but their wool proved less good than that of their leaner brethren of the uplands. Yet the new lowland pastures were not unprofitable: though their fleeces were less fine, the demand for coarser wools was also on the increase, and larger supplies of mutton and beef were consumed by a prosperous and hospitable generation, whose carnivorous habits amazed foreign visitors accustomed to a more farinaceous diet. The Midlands therefore continued in Elizabeth's reign to add sheep and cattle to corn. Rugby 'abounded in butchers.' The cattle fairs of Leicestershire and Northamptonshire were famous. The great quantities of cattle in the island helped all leather industries; the southern English walked on leather, and disdained the 'wooden shoes' that foreigners were fain to wear. Clogs, however, were very generally worn in the thrifty North, and Scots lads and lasses went barefoot.

The breeding of horses had to keep pace with an ever-increasing demand. The horse was very gradually replacing the ox at cart and plough; [1] and the general prosperity of the country demanded more riding-horses, as in good years we demand more motor-cars. In many parts of Yorkshire and on the grass moors of the turbulent Border country, the breeding of horses and cattle was more important than the sheep-farming which prevailed there in later and more settled times. It was not sheep but cattle that the Mosstroopers drove off in their midnight raids.

Though sheep and cattle were now reared in such abundance in England, they were, by our modern standards, small and thin until the era of the Eighteenth Century improvements. For as yet there were only very inadequate means of feeding them during the winter months.

> 'From Christmas to May
> Weak cattle decay'

sang Thomas Tusser, the poet of Elizabethan agriculture. And the open-field system, still prevalent in half the country, afforded neither sufficient shelter nor sufficient grazing for beasts.

One region of England was still a world by itself, the great fen that stretched from Lincoln to Cambridge, from King's Lynn to Peterborough. Already in the later years of Elizabeth there were projects debated in Parliament, to drain Fenland as the Dutch had drained Holland, and so reclaim its watery, reedy solitudes to rich cornfields and pasture. But the great design was not carried out till an age when more capital was to be had for such ventures—in Stuart times for the south half of the fen, and in Hanoverian times for the north. Meanwhile the fenmen continued to dwell round its shores and on its innumerable oozy islands—living an amphibious life, and varying their traditional occupations with the changing seasons of the year. [See § 5.]

'The upper and north part of Cambridgeshire [Camden writes] is all over divided into river isles, which all summer long afford a most delightful green prospect, but in winter time are almost all laid under water, farther every way than a man can see, and in some sort resembling the sea itself. The inhabitants of this and the rest of the fenny country (which reaches 68 miles from the borders of Suffolk to Wainfleet in Lincolnshire) are a sort of people (much like the place)

---

[1] The process was very gradual, from Tudor to Hanoverian times; persons now living have seen oxen ploughing in Victoria's England.

of brutish, uncivilized tempers, envious of all others, whom they call *Upland men*; and usually walking aloft upon a sort of stilts they all keep to the business of grazing, fishing and fowling. All this country in the winter time, and sometimes for the greatest part of the year, is laid under water by the rivers Ouse, Grant (Cam), Nen, Welland, Glene and Witham, for want of sufficient passages. But when they once keep to their proper channels, it so strangely abounds with rich grass and rank hay (by them called *Lid*) that when they've mown enough for their own use, in November they burn up the rest to make it come again the thicker. About which time a man may see all the moorish country round about of a light fire, to his great wonder. Besides it affords great quantity of turf and sedge for firing, reeds for thatching. Elders also and other watershrubs, especially willows, either growing wild, or else set on the banks of rivers to prevent their overflowing; which being frequently cut down come again with a numerous offspring. 'Tis of these that baskets are made.' (Camden's *Britannia,* p. 408, Gibson's edition.)

The taking of wild fowl for the market was conducted by the fenmen on an immense scale. The wild geese and duck were captured hundreds at a time, being driven or lured into long cages of netting called 'decoys.' Rents were paid largely in fixed quantities of eels, counted by the thousand.

It may perhaps be doubted whether the Fenmen had such 'brutish uncivilized tempers' as the 'upland men' told Camden. In any case it is a mistake to suppose, as many writers have done, that because their life was amphibious, because they herded their cattle and sheep on stilts, and because they went about in boats, fishing, fowling and reed cutting, that therefore they were any more 'lawless' than the farmer who carted his corn on dry land. Recent research (H. C. Darby, *The Mediaeval Fenland,* 1940) has shown that throughout the Middle Ages, from the time of Domesday Book and beyond, the laws and customs of the Manorial system held good throughout Fenland; that rents and services were regularly paid to the great Abbeys and to their successors after the Dissolution; that the most complicated laws, rules and divisions of proprietary and fishing rights were observed among the fenmen; that the most elaborate system of embankment and 'sewerage' was maintained by constant labour and skill, without which the great waterways would have become unnavigable, and Lincoln, Lynn, Boston, Wisbech, Cambridge, St. Ives, Peterborough and the lesser towns of the region would have lost most of their trade and communications. 'Almost every stream and bank in Fenland,' writes Dr. Darby, 'had, in one way or another, someone who was held responsible for it.' In short, the Fenland, before its reclamation by the great drainage operations of Stuart and Hanoverian times, was indeed an amphibious region, but with a highly specialized economic system of its own. [See § 6.]

In the midst of these scenes of wild nature, Ely Cathedral had for centuries floated like an ark upon the waters, its two towers and two long shining roofs far seen on distant horizons. In its shadow lay the Palace where the Bishop held his court. [See § 7.] He still exercised remnants of the authority which his mediaeval predecessors had enjoyed in the so-called 'County Palatine' of Ely Isle. But in fact the Reformation had reduced the independent power of the Clergy. The State now held the Church in check, sometimes with an arrogant disregard of spiritual interests. Queen Elizabeth compelled Bishop Cox to surrender Ely Place in Holborn, London, and its famous fruit-gardens to her favourite, Sir Christopher Hatton. And when Cox died she kept the see vacant for eighteen years for the benefit of the Crown. Yet whenever a Bishop of Ely was allowed to exist, he was the chief ruler of Fenland—till first Oliver Cromwell and then the draining Dukes of Bedford acquired in the region an influence more than episcopal.

Besides Fenland, two other regions, the Principality of Wales and the Northern Border, differed from the social and economic structure of the rest of Elizabethan England. But they were approximating to the general pattern, and of the two, Wales had recently moved furthest along the road leading to modern life.

Throughout the Middle Ages, Wales had been the seat of military and social conflict between the wild Welsh, nursing their ancient tribal ways in the high places of the hills, and the 'Marcher Lords,' champions of English feudalism in their castles along the valleys. During the Wars of the Roses, the Marcher Lords had turned eastwards to play leading parts in the dynastic strife of England, with the happy result that their independent power was extinguished. By the end of the Fifteenth Century their principal castles and estates had passed into the King's hands.

Here then was an opportunity for the amalgamation of Wales with England under the Crown, provided only that the operation were affected without wronging and exacerbating the national feeling and traditions of the Welsh, as the sentiment of the Irish was so disastrously alienated by Tudor policy. Fortunately in Wales the circumstances were more propitious. No religious difference arose to divide the old inhabitants from the English, and there was no movement to 'colonize' the Principality by robbing the natives of their land. By good chance, Bosworth Field placed a Welsh dynasty on the throne of England, thereby making loyalty to the Tudors a point of national pride with all the inhabitants of Wales.

Under these happy auspices Henry VIII effected the legal, parliamentary and administrative union of the two countries. The English county system, the rule of the Justices of the Peace, and the body of English law were extended all over the Principality, and the leading Welsh gentry were flattered by representing their counties in the Parliament at Westminster. The Council of Wales, a court of monarchial power analogous to the Star Chamber and the Council of the North, usefully enforced order during the long period of transition from old to new. Feudalism in the valleys had been extinguished with the Marcher Lords, and tribalism in the hills now also disappeared, without any violent conflict such as marked its end in the Scottish Highlands two centuries later. In Elizabeth's reign Wales was in process of settling down as a part of England. Already the structure of government, and to a large extent the form of society had been adapted to the English model. But Wales retained her native language, poetry and music. Her soul was still her own.

The Welsh gentry, an amalgam of former tribal chiefs, former Marcher Lords, and 'new men' of the type so well known in that era, were well content with the Tudor rule, which gave their class the same advantages in Wales as in England. Some of them were already accumulating great estates under the recently introduced English land-laws, and these properties swelled to vast size in years to come. But in Elizabeth's reign and for some time afterwards there was also a numerous class of Welsh gentry of smaller wealth and pretension. Major General Berry reported to Oliver Cromwell from his command in Wales—'You can sooner find fifty gentlemen of £100 a year than five of £500.' Most of them, like the corresponding class of small squires in England, flourished in Tudor and early Stuart times, but disappeared in the course of the Eighteenth Century, leaving Wales a land of great estates.

But the essential part of the Welsh people was to be sought not among the landowners but among the small tenant farmers. Large farms of the commercial type did not grow up in Wales to the same extent as in England. Nor, on the other hand, were the farms divided and sub-divided to excess as among the unfortunate peasantry of Ireland. The sound basis of modern Welsh society was laid in tenant farms of the peasant and family type, small, but not too small to maintain the cultivators in hardy self-respect. Their relation to the landlords, who undertook improvements and repairs, resembled the system of agricultural England, rather than the less happy relationship of the impoverished tenant to the exploiting landlord in Ireland or the Scottish Highlands.

The Dissolution of the Monasteries had been carried through in Wales in the same way and with the same social consequences as in England. There had been no revolt against it, like the northern Pilgrimage of Grace. The Welsh upper class found their advantage in the Reformation, and the peasantry accepted it with indifference born of ignorance. If they did not understand the Prayer Book and Bible in the foreign tongue of England, neither had they understood the Latin Mass. As yet religion passed them by. Early in Elizabeth's reign the Welsh peasantry were in a state of intellectual torpor and educational neglect, compatible indeed with all that is good in country life and old tradition, but certain ere long to be disturbed by some outside influence. What would it be? The Jesuit missionaries, who might have broken the virgin soil, left Wales alone. At length, in the last decades of Elizabeth's reign the Established Church began to do its duty, and brought out a Welsh translation of Bible and Prayer Book. The foundations were thereby laid for popular Welsh Protestantism, and for the great educational and religious movements of the Eighteenth Century.

Under the Tudor Kings the life of England north of the Trent bore a character of its own. The constant troubles of the Scottish border, the poverty of the whole region except the clothing valleys and the mining districts, the greater strength of old feudal loyalties and pretensions, and the greater popularity of the monasteries and the old religion differentiated it from the rest of England in the reign of Henry VIII, and to a less extent under Elizabeth.

In the early years of Henry, the Border was still ruled by its fighting families, particularly the Percies and Nevilles, of whom the Earls of Northumberland and Westmorland were the heads. Among the armed farmers of these pastoral shires, a fierce spirit of personal independence was combined with loyalty to the hereditary chiefs who led them to war, not only against occasional Scottish invasion and frequent cattle raiding, but sometimes against the Tudor government itself. The Pilgrimage of Grace (1536) was made in defence of monasteries, and also in defence of the quasi-feudal power of the noble families of the Border against the intruding force of the new Monarchy. Henry seized the opportunity of the suppression of that rising to crush feudalism, and to extend the royal power, governing Yorkshire and the Border Counties through Wardens of the Marches dependent on the Crown's commission instead of their own hereditary influence. Much of Henry's work was never undone, particularly in Yorkshire. But Northumberland and Cumberland were seldom really at rest. The policy of Henry VIII and Edward VI was foolishly hostile to Scotland, and the occasional wars and perpetual illwill between the two nations prolonged the disturbed state of the border shires. Under Mary the Roman Catholic influence was revived, and with it the power of the Percy family which Henry VIII had broken.

And so, when Elizabeth came to the throne, the battle between the old and the new religion, between the power of the Crown and the power of feudalism was not yet fully decided in the far North. Such was the state of things in the more civilized parts of the Border, the seaward plains of Northumberland on the East, and of Cumberland on the West. Between them lay the Middle Marches, the moors and hills of the Cheviot district, where a yet more lawless and primitive state of society survived in the regions of Redesdale and North Tyne. Those robber valleys, cut off by trackless wastes of grass 'bent,' heather and wet moss-hag from the more civilized lands round about, were inhabited by clans who paid little heed to the King's writ or even to the feudal power of the Percies, Nevilles and Dacres. Indeed, the only allegiance of the warriors of these wild regions was loyalty towards their own clans. Family feeling served, more than anything else, to protect culprits and defy the law. Stolen property could not be followed up and recovered in the thieving valleys, because each raider was protected by the revengeful jealousy of a warlike tribe. Small families came for protection under the rule of the Charltons who answered for North Tyne. The Halls, Reeds, Hedleys, Fletchers of Redesdale, the Charltons, Dodds, Robsons and Milbournes of North Tynedale, were the real political units within a society that knew no other organization. The Crown when it raised taxes, secured the tribute through the agency of the clan chiefs. [See § 8.]

The royal commissioners, reporting in 1542 and 1550 on the state of the Border (Hodgson's *Northumberland,* ii, pp.171–248), estimated that there were 1500 armed and able-bodied men in these two lawless valleys. The meagre soil could not yield food enough for their families, so, like the Scottish Highlanders, they eked out their living by raids on the cattle of their richer neighbours in the seaward plains to east and west. They were in close league with the robbers of Scottish Liddesdale, where a similar state of society existed. The Mosstroopers of either nation, when close pressed by the 'fray' of the men they had robbed, could slip over the Border and be safe till the danger had passed. But usually no English officer dared 'follow the fray' even into North Tyne or Rede, still less into Liddesdale. The robber strongholds, built of oak trunks, covered with turf to prevent the application of fire, were hid in unapproachable wildernesses, among treacherous mosses, through which no stranger knew the paths. Henry VIII's commissioners did not venture to suggest to their royal master the expense of conquering and occupying North Tyne and Rede, but only a better system of watch and ward against the raiders, and a stronger force of lances in Harbottle and Chipchase Castles on the edge of the lawless region, to bridle the constant invasion of the Lowlands.

Such was the society, much the same on both sides of the Border, which produced the popular poetry of the Border Ballads, transmitted by word of mouth from one generation to another. Many of the stanzas took the shape we know in the days of Elizabeth and Mary Queen of Scots. These ballads, almost always tragic, describe such incidents of life and death as were of daily occurrence in those regions. Utterly different from the songs and poetry of Shakespeare's more gentle England, are these rough outpourings of the sombre North. A pair of lovers in South English song or ballad run a fair chance of 'living happily ever afterwards.' But to assume the part of lover in a Border Ballad is a desperate undertaking. No father, mother, brother or rival will have pity before it is too late. Like the Homeric Greeks, the Borderers were cruel and barbarous men, slaying each other like beasts of the forest, but high in pride and honour and rough faithfulness; and they were also (what men no longer are) untaught natural poets, able to express in words of power the inexorable fate of man and woman, and pity for the cruelties they nevertheless constantly inflicted on one another.

In Elizabeth's reign political relations with Scotland were greatly and permanently bettered, because the governments of the two countries had now a common interest in defending the Reformation against its enemies at home and abroad. Border warfare between Scottish and English armies came to an end, and cattle raiding as between the two nations was at least diminished. But the English robbers of Redesdale and North Tyne continued to raid the farms of their more civilized fellow-countrymen. In the middle of Elizabeth's reign, Camden was unable to pay an antiquarian visit to Housesteads on the Roman Wall 'for fear of the Mosstroopers,' who occupied that region in force. And the Grahams of Netherby, a clan situated on the Esk near where it flows into Solway, were perpetually harrying the lands of their Cumbrian neighbours. The levy of blackmail and the abduction of men and women from their homes to be held to ransom, were common incidents of life till the end of the Queen's reign.

But although mosstrooping continued, the feudal power of the Percies, Dacres and Nevilles was wholly destroyed after the suppression of their rebellion in 1570. After that crisis, Northumberland and Cumberland were governed by noblemen loyal to government.

Early in the reign, Mass was still said in parish churches within thirty miles of the Border, under the protection of Catholic nobles and gentry. But Protestantism made progress among the people with the help of missionaries like Bernard Gilpin, 'the Apostle of the North.' The Bishops of Carlisle were zealous in the work of gradually enforcing uniformity, as the Queen's

§ 1 A royal picnic

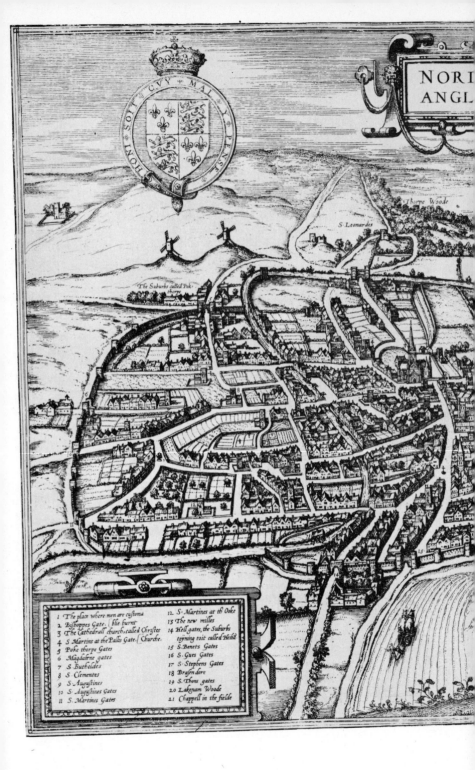

NOR
ANGL

1 The place where men are customa
2 Bisshoppes Gate. (hie burnt
3 The Cathedrall church, called Chrystes
4 S Martin at the Pallis Gate. (Churche.
5 Poke thorpe Gates
6 Magdalene gates
7 S Butholdes
8 S Clementes
9 S Augustines
10 S Augustines Gates
11 S Martines Gates
12 S Martines at th Ooke
13 The new milles
14 Hell gates, the Suburbs
   toyning toit called Heikt
15 S Benets Gates
16 S Gues Gates
17 S Stephens Gates
18 Brasen dore
19 S Tbons gates
20 Lakenam Woode
21 Chappell in the fielde

Thorpe Woode

S Leonardes

The Suburbs called Poke
thorpe

§2 Norwich—'a great centre of the cloth trade'

Great S. Augustin

Lycle S. Augustin

The Key

The marshe

BRIGHTSTOVVE, vul-
go; quondam venta, florē-
tissimum Angliae Em-
porium.

1. S. Peter.          9. S. Alhalowes.
2. S. Mary port.     10. S. Nycholas.
3. Christchurch.     11. S. Stephen.
4. S. Laurence.      12. S. Michael.
5. S. Tones.         13. S. Thomas.
6. S. Leonard.       14. The Temple.
7. S. Warbors.       15. S. James.
8. S. Alphius.

Ratcliffe

§3 Bristol—'with mercantile and inland trade'

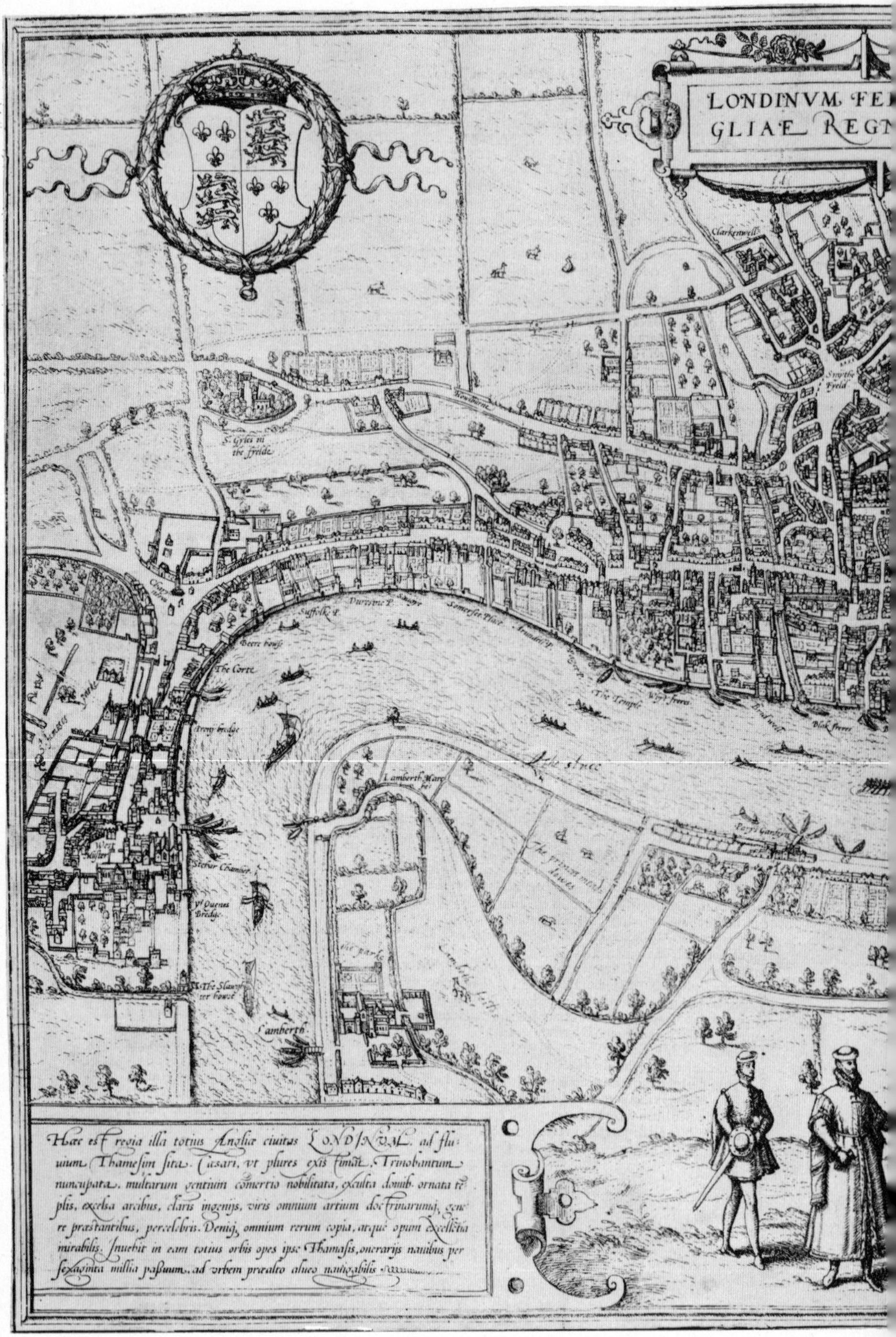

S. Gyles in
the fridde

Clarkenwell

Smythe
Feild

Cleye

Suffolck q.    Durveyes q.    Somerset Hous

Beere howse    Milford

The Corte    Fleet

Arundel Hous    Iroy bridge    Lambeth Mary    Fleet street    The Temple    Blackfryers

Strete Chamre

Y.e Quens
Bridge    The Fleming Lanes    Parris Garden

Y.e Slaughter Powel

Lambeth

Hæc est regia illa totius Angliæ ciuitas LONDINVM ad flu=
uium Thamesim sita, Cæsari, vt plures exis timāt, S. Trinobantum
nuncupata, multarum gentium comertio nobilitata, exculta domib. ornata tē
plis, excelsa arcibus, claris ingenijs, viris omnium artium doctrinarum�q, gene
re præstantibus, percelebris. Deni�q, omnium rerum copia, at�q. opum excellētia
mirabilis, fruebit in eam totius orbis opes ipse Thamasis, onerarijs nauibus per
sexaginta millia passuum, ad vrbem præalto alueo nauigabilis

§ 4 London

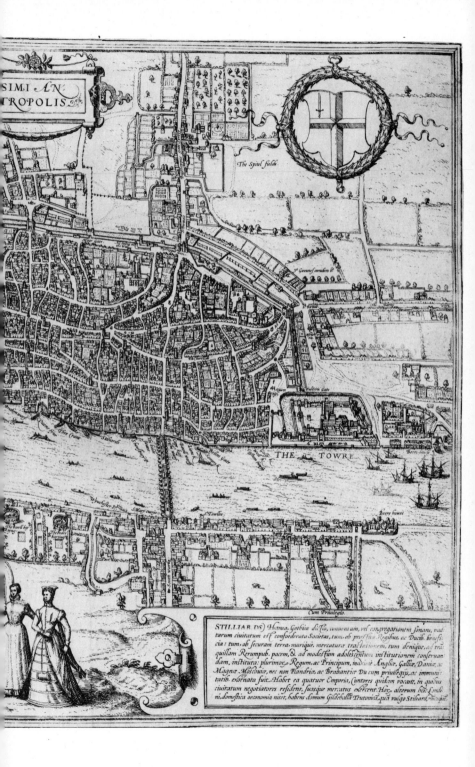

SIMI AN
TROPOLIS

The Spitel fields

THE TOWRE

Cum Priuilegio.

§ 5 'The oozy islands of the Fen.' Air view of Crowland, Lincolnshire, during the floods of 1947

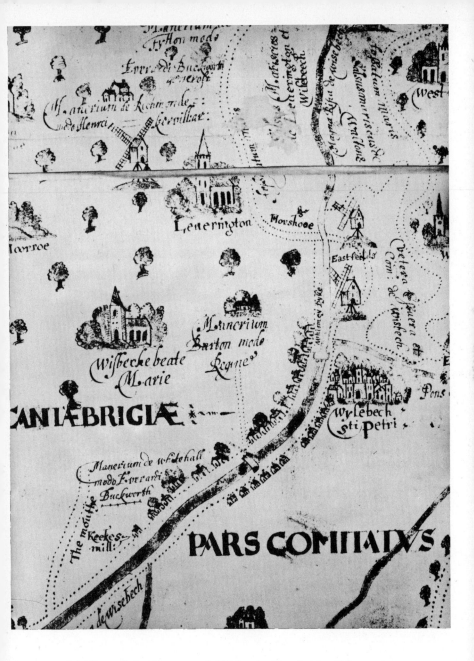

§6 Map of the Fen round Wisbech, Cambridgeshire, 1597

§7 Ely Cathedral—'like an ark upon the waters'

§8 The Cheviots—
'trackless wastes of
grass "bent", heather
and wet moss hag'

§9 Newark Castle, Selkirkshire, fifteenth century

§10 Darnick Tower (near Melrose), built in 1569

# 'THE ENGLAND OF ELIZABETH . . . THE LAND
# OF MANOR HOUSES'

§11 Stokesay Castle, Shropshire, a thirteenth-century manor with
Elizabethan gateway

§12 Charlecote Park, Warwickshire, 1558

§ 13 Montacute House, Somerset, 'in its glory of dull gold'

§ 14 Moreton Old Hall, Cheshire, 'of black and white half timber'

§15 Elizabethan needlework—detail from the Bradford table carpet

§16 The great hall, Montacute House, Somerset

§ 17 Powys Castle, Montgomeryshire
*Note the well-lit galleries and the elaboration of frieze and ceilings*

government grew stronger. But the warrior farmers of the 'riding' districts were not men to be coerced or easily led, either in religion or anything else. Change came slowly up that way.

Until the end of Elizabeth's reign many farmers of Cumberland and Northumberland held their land by rendering military service when called upon by the Wardens of the Marches. These light horsemen of the North, whether in the service of the government or of freebooting clans, wore leather coats and steel caps, were armed with a lance and bow or pistol, and rode surefooted nags of a local breed that knew their way through the mosses.

After the Union of the Crowns of England and Scotland on the head of James I (1603) co-operation became possible between the authorities on the two sides of the Border who were able at last to suppress the Mosstroopers and carry the King's peace into the heart of the thieving valleys. 'Belted Will Howard' of Naworth, though a Catholic recusant, loyally served King James as his Warden of the Western March. He hunted down the Grahams and the other mosstrooping clans, following them into their lairs with sleuth-hounds. North Tyne and Redesdale were gradually brought under the law. In the early years of the Seventeenth Century the gentlemen of Northumberland first ventured to build manor-houses instead of peel-towers and castles, as homes in which it was safe to live.

It is strange that the barbarous old-world life of the Border, as it still was in Queen Elizabeth's day, lay in close juxtaposition to the most forward-looking of industries, the coal-mining of the lower Tyne and East Durham. The winning of surface coal dated from before the Roman occupation; but now the pits were getting deeper and the work of the miner was beginning to approximate to that of his present-day successor. Newcastle, the centre of the great business of shipping the 'sea-coal' of London, was unique as a meeting-point of the feudal world of the Percies, the tribal world of the mosstrooper, and the coal trade not fundamentally different from that of to-day. (For the Border under the Tudors, see *Victoria County History,* Cumberland, Rev. J. Hodgson's *Hist. of Northumberland,* and Dr. Rachel Reid's *North Parts under the Tudors* in *Tudor Studies,* ed. Seton Watson, 1924.)

Everywhere, south of the still vexed Border with its grim stone castles and peel-towers, the England of Elizabeth was becoming *par excellence* the land of manor-houses, bewilderingly different from one another in size, material and style of architecture, but all testifying to the peace and economic prosperity of the age, its delight in display, in beauty and in the glory of man's life on earth. [See § 9–12.] Wealth and power, and with them the lead in architecture had passed from the Princes of the Church to the gentry. The great era of ecclesiastical building, after lasting for so many centuries, had at length come to an end. The new religion was the religion of the Book, the sermon and the psalm, rather than of the sacred edifice; there were already fine churches enough to satisfy the religious requirements of Protestant England.

Elizabethan architecture contained strong elements both of the Gothic and the classical, in other words, the old English and the new Italian. In the early part of the reign the more irregular and picturesque Gothic was most used, especially in converting old fortified manor-houses into more peaceful and splendid homes, such as Penshurst and Haddon Hall. But side by side with them, and increasingly as the reign went on, came in the more regular planning of the new private palaces in an Italianate or classical style, like Longleat, Audley End, Leicester's buildings at Kenilworth, and Montacute in its glory of dull gold— just a country gentleman's house in a remote district of Somerset, built in the local stone, yet certainly one of the most beautiful and magnificent homes in the world. [See § 13.]

In country houses of the new style like Audley End, and in public buildings like Gresham's Royal Exchange, intricate Renaissance ornament adorned the stone-work of the fabric and the woodwork of the interior. A fine and pure example is the Gate of Honour at Caius College, Cambridge (1575), and a later instance is found hard by in the roof and screen inside the hall of Trinity (1604–1605). The design and ornamentation of Elizabethan mansions were often carried out by Germans brought over for the purpose. As their taste and tradition were none of the best, it was fortunate that there were also many competent native builders and architects. [See § 18, 19.]

Besides the lordlier rural palaces, there were innumerable smaller manor-houses arising in every variety of style and material, some of stone, some of black-and-white half timber like Moreton Old Hall in Cheshire, and some of red brick in regions where neither stone nor timber were plentiful.[1] [See § 14.] Though the windows were not yet plate glass but lattice, they occupied a much larger area of the wall space than in former times, and let floods of light into the pleasant chambers and long Elizabethan galleries. Plain clear glass was now used in the lattices, which in early Tudor times had often been filled up with 'wicker or fine rifts of oak in chequerwise,' as Harrison tells us, 'but now only clearest glass is esteemed.'

Formerly the best glass had come from abroad, but early in Elizabeth's reign the industry in England was improved by foreign workmen from Normandy and Lorraine. Works in the Weald, Hampshire, Staffordshire and London supplied not only window glass but bottles and drinking-glasses, in imitation of the fashionable Venetian ware from Murano that only the wealthy could afford.

In rooms of the better kind the stucco work on the white-washed ceiling was often 'most expressed in fancy,' and its mouldings were sometimes picked out in colours or in gold. The walls were warmed and adorned with 'tapestry, arras work or painted cloth, wherein either diverse histories, or herbs, beasts and knots and such like are stained'; or else they are pannelled with 'oak of our own, or wainscot brought hither out of the east countries,' that is, the Baltic lands. (Harrison.) (See § 15, 16, 17.)

A less expensive way of decorating the walls, recommended by Falstaff to the Hostess, was to paint pictures on them:

HOSTESS: I must be fain to pawn both my plate and the tapestry of my dining-chambers.
FALSTAFF: Glasses, glasses, is the only drinking. And for thy walls,— a pretty slight drollery, or the story of the Prodigal, or the German hunting in the water-work, is worth a thousand of these bed-hangings and these fly-bitten tapestries.

Framed pictures, except family portraits, were few even in gentlemen's houses. But the more princely mansions had pictures

---

[1] Harrison (1577) writes,
'The ancient manors and houses of our gentlemen are yet, and for the most part, of strong timber, in framing whereof our carpenters have been and are worthily preferred before those of like science among all other nations. Howbeit such as be lately builded are commonly either of brick or of hard stone, or both, their rooms large and comely, and houses of office further distant from their lodgings.'

in the Venetian style. Thus the Lord's servants say to the be-wildered Christopher Sly

> 'Dost thou love pictures?   We will fetch thee straight
> Adonis painted by a running brook
> And Cytheraea all in sedges hid.'

The homes of common folk in town and village had changed less than the manor-houses of the rich. They were still the old-fashioned gabled and thatched cottages of timber—with clay, loam, rubble and wattle-work filling up the spaces between the uprights and crossbeams.

'Certes this rude kind of building [wrote Harrison] made the Spaniards in Queen Mary's days to wonder, but chiefly when they saw what large diet was used in many of these so homely cottages. In so much that one of no small reputation amongst them said after this manner— "These English (quoth he) have their houses made of sticks and dirt, but they fare commonly so well as the King." '

The greatness of the Elizabethan English in poetry, music and the drama was not equalled by their school of painting, though many competent portraits of the Queen and her courtiers were produced, on canvas. Nicholas Hilliard, son of a citizen of Exeter, founded the school of English miniature. [See Plate II.] There was much demand for this delicate and beautiful art, not only among courtiers ostentatiously vying with one another for the Queen's 'picture in little' at 'forty, fifty or a hundred ducats apiece,' but among all who desired mementoes of their family or friends. Miniature painting went on at a high level in England until the era of Cosway at the end of George III's reign, and indeed it was only killed by photography, as so many other arts have been killed by science.

The expense and fantasticalness of men's dress was a constant theme of satire. 'Fashions from proud Italy' and France were always being imitated, and the tailor played a great part in the life of the Elizabethan gentleman. [See Plate II.] Jewels, gold chains and costly trinkets of all sorts were worn by men as much as by women. Both sexes wore round the neck ruffs of various sizes and shapes. Such fashions were confined to the well-to-do—but all classes wore beards. ''Twas merry in hall when beards wagged all.'

Gentlemen had the privilege of wearing swords as part of their

II. Miniature of a young man by Nicholas Hilliard

full dress in civil life. The laws of the duel, endorsed by the code of honour, were beginning to replace the more savage 'killing affray,' the murder of an enemy by a man's retainers and serving-men. The fashions of fencing, whether in sport or earnest, were of foreign origin, when men of fashion quarrelled in print, by the book, 'on the seventh cause,' and fought with rapier and dagger, to cries of 'ah, the immortal *passado ! the punto reverso ! The hai !* '

With the continuous growth of commerce, land-development and general prosperity, the roads were more busy than ever with the passage of riders and pedestrians of all classes on business and pleasure. [See § 21, 22.] The mediaeval custom of Pilgrimage had helped to give people a taste for travel and sightseeing, which survived the religious custom of visiting shrines. The medicinal spa was taking the place of the holy well. Already, as Camden tells us, Buxton in distant Derbyshire was a fashion-able resort for 'great numbers of nobility and gentry,' who came to drink its waters, and were housed in fine lodgings erected by the Earl of Shrewsbury to develop the place. Bath was not yet in full fashion, for although its waters were famous its accom-modation was squalid.

The inns of Elizabethan England had a character of their own for individual attention accorded to travellers. Fynes Moryson, who had sampled the wayside hospitality of half Europe, wrote in the light of his experience:

'The world affords not such inns as England hath, either for food and cheap entertainment after the guests' own pleasure, or for humble attendance on passengers, yea even in very poor villages. For as soon as a passenger comes to an inn, the servants run to him, and one takes his horse, and walks him till he be cold, then rubs him and gives him meat [food], yet I must say that they are not much to be trusted in this last point, without the eye of the Master or his servant to oversee them. Another servant gives the passenger his private chamber, and kindles his fire; the third pulls off his boots and makes them clean. Then the host or hostess visit him; and if he will eat with the host, or at a common table with others, his meal will cost him sixpense, or in some places but four pence; yet this course is less honourable and not used by gentlemen. But if he will eat in his chamber, he com-mands what meat he will, yea the kitchen is open to him to command the meat to be dressed as he best likes. And when he sits down at table, the host or hostess will accompany him, or if they have many guests will at least visit him, taking it for courtesy to be bid sit down. While he eats, if he have company especially, he shall be offered music, which he may freely take or refuse. And if he be solitary, the musicians will give him good day with music in the morning. . . A man cannot more freely command in his own house than he may do in his inn. And at parting, if he give some few pence to the chamberlain and ostler, they wish him a happy journey.'

Unfortunately, behind all this hearty welcome, something sinister might be concealed. Shakespeare has given us the seamy side of inns as he knew them, in words muttered before dawn in the inn-yard at Rochester (1 H. IV, II, i), 'while Charles' wain is over the new chimney, and yet our horse not packed': the honest carriers, one learns, have not had such clean quarters, nor enjoyed so undisturbed a night as Fynes Moryson's gentleman. And they know the chamberlain for a rogue, who lives by betraying travellers to bolder thieves than himself.

Shakespeare is fully borne out by the account of the inns of that date given by William Harrison. He praises indeed the food, the wine, the beer, the scrupulously clean linen at bed and board, the tapestry on the walls, the key of his room given to every guest, and the freedom he enjoys as contrasted to the more tyrannous treatment of travellers on the Continent. But, alas, the willing servants and the jolly host himself are often in league with highwaymen. The obsequious attendance on the guest may cover a wish to learn what route he will take the next day and whether he is in charge of money. Before the days of cheques, large sums of gold and silver were carried along the roads in the ordinary way of business. The servants of the inn officiously handle every article of the traveller's baggage, to judge by its weight in hand if it contain coin. Then they pass on the result of their researches to confederates outside. The inn keeps its good name, for no robbery is done within its walls; the thieves spring out from a thicket some miles off upon the road.

This system, Harrison concludes, works 'to the utter undoing of many an honest yeoman as he journeyeth on his way.' Even so did the chamberlain of the Rochester inn betray to Falstaff's gang the 'franklin in the wild of Kent,' who 'brought three hundred marks with him in gold.'

But the inn was not the resort of wayfarers alone. It frequently happened that the inhabitants of the manor-house and their guests, after dining at home, would adjourn to the neighbouring hostelry, and spend long hours there in a privy chamber round the glasses and tankards; for in the difficult matter of foreign wine the squire was often more ready to trust mine host's cellar than his own. This custom continued among the smaller gentry for several generations after the death of Elizabeth. And in all ages the ale bench has been the social centre of the middling and lower classes of town, village and hamlet. [See § 25, 26, 27, 28.]

The study of the history and literature of Elizabethan England gives an impression of a greater harmony and a freer intercourse of classes than in earlier or in later times. It is not a period of peasants' revolts, of levelling doctrines, of anti-Jacobin fears, or of exclusiveness and snobbery in the upper class such as Jane Austen depicts in a later age. Class divisions in Shakespeare's day were taken as a matter of course, without jealousy in those below, or itching anxiety on the part of the 'upper and middling classes' to teach 'the grand law of subordination' to the 'inferior orders,' which is so painfully evident, in the Eighteenth and early Nineteenth Centuries, for example, in Charity School education. The typical unit of Elizabethan education was the Grammar School, where the cleverest boys of all classes were brought up together: the typical units of Eighteenth and Nineteenth Century education were the Charity School, the village school and the 'great Public School,' where the classes were educated in rigorous segregation. Elizabethans took the social world as they took everything else, naturally, and consorted together without self-consciousness or suspicion.

Class divisions, recognized without fuss on either side, were not rigid and were not strictly hereditary. Individuals and families moved out of one class into another by acquisition or loss of property, or by simple change of occupation. There is no such impassable barrier as used to divide the Lord of the manor from his peasantry in mediaeval England, or such as continued till 1789 to mark off the French *noblesse* as an hereditary caste separate from everyone else. In Tudor England such rigid lines were rendered impossible by the number and variety of men in intermediate classes and occupations, who were closely connected, in the business and amusement of daily life, with those above and those below them in social status. English society was based not on equality but on freedom—freedom of opportunity and freedom of personal intercourse. Such was the England known and approved by Shakespeare: men and women of every class and occupation were equally interesting to him, but he defended 'degree' as the necessary basis of human welfare.

The Peers of the Realm were a small section of the gentry enjoying great personal prestige and some invidious legal privileges, though not of exemption from taxation. They were expected to keep up great households and to extend munificent patronage to clients, which their estates could often ill support. The nobility had lost the independent military and political power which their order had exercised up till the Wars of the Roses. And the Tudors kept them few in number by abstaining from lavish creations. The acreage owned by members of the House of Lords was much smaller in Elizabethan than in Plantagenet or in Hanoverian times; the recent price revolution had hit them even harder than other landlords, and the process by which Peers like the Dukes of Bedford afterwards bought up the estates of small gentry and freeholders had not yet got under way. For all these reasons the House of Lords, especially after the mitred abbots had disappeared, was a less important body in Tudor times than it had been in the past and was to be again in the future. The old aristocracy had been pruned away, and the new aristocracy had not yet fully grown up to take its place.

But, if Elizabeth's reign was not a great age for the peerage, it was a great age for the gentry. Their numbers, wealth and importance had been increased by the decay of the old nobility that had stood between them and the Crown; by the distribution of the monastic estates; and by vitality of commerce and land-improvement in the new era. The squire in Tudor and Stuart times led by no means so isolated and bucolic a life as some historians have imagined. He was part of the general movement of an active society. Yeomen, merchants and lawyers who had made their fortunes, were perpetually recruiting the ranks of the landed gentry; while the younger sons of the manor-house were apprenticed into industry and trade. In these ways old families were kept in personal touch with the modern world, and the country was kept in touch with the town. No doubt there was more rural isolation in the West and North, the future Cavalier districts, than in the counties more closely associated with the trade of London; but the difference, though real, was only relative.

The sensible custom of apprenticing the younger sons of squires to trade became less common in Hanoverian times, partly because of the diminution (almost the disappearance) of the class of small squire. The contemptuous attitude affected by some gentlefolk in the Eighteenth and Nineteenth Centuries towards 'soiling the hands with trade,' was particularly absurd, because nearly all such families had risen wholly or in part by trade, and many were in fact still engaged in it though the smart ladies of the family may not have known much about it. But in Elizabeth's time there was much less of this snobbish nonsense. The London apprentices, as we read in Stow, were 'often children of gentlemen and persons of good quality,' who served their masters obediently, hoping to rise to a share in the business, but in their leisure time 'affected to go in costly apparel and wear weapons and frequent schools of dancing, fencing and music.'

'The Elizabethan and Jacobean monuments to be found in parish churches record the origin of many a squire's wealth in his prosperity as "Citizen and Mercer," "Citizen and Haberdasher" of London or some other town, in a way for which it would be hard to find parallels on the mural tablets of a later date.' (W. J. Ashley, *Economic Organization of England*, p. 131.)

While the landed gentry were thus closely intermingling with the commercial classes, the status of 'gentleman' was not supposed to be confined to landed proprietors. Harrison tells us how liberally and how loosely the matter was regarded in the days of Shakespeare's boyhood:

'Whosoever studieth the laws of the realm, whoso abideth in the University giving his mind to his book, or professeth physic and the liberal sciences, or beside his service in the room of a captain in the wars, or good counsel given at home whereby his commonwealth is benefitted, can live without manual labour, and thereto is able and will bear the port, charge and countenance of a gentleman, he shall be called "master," which is the title that men give to esquires and gentlemen, and be reputed a gentleman ever after. Which is so much the less to be disallowed of, for that the Prince doth lose nothing by it, the gentleman being so much subject to taxes and public payments as is the yeoman or husbandman, which he likewise doth bear the gladlier for the saving of his reputation.'

He is expected to tip largely, not to look too closely at a bill, and to remember that it is the privilege of a gentleman to get the worst of a bargain. On these terms his easy-going, obsequious countrymen will touch their caps to him and call him 'Master'— though behind his back they will say they remember his father, honest man, riding to market astride his sacks of corn. In that way everyone is pleased. As Professor Tawney has said, the gentry 'held a position determined, not by legal distinctions, but by common estimation. Mere caste had few admirers—fewer probably among the gentry militant of the early Seventeenth Century than among the gentry triumphant of the early Eighteenth. Common sense endorsed the remark that *gentility is nothing but ancient riches,* adding under its breath that they need not be very ancient.' (*Ec. Hist. Rev.* 1941, pp. 2–4.)

Harrison then passes on from the gentry to the citizens and merchants, and remarks on the expansion of the area of their trade:

'And whereas in times past their chief trade was into Spain, Portingall, France, Danske, Norwaie, Scotland and Iceland only, now in these days, as men not contented with these journeys, they have sought out the east and west Indies, and made voyages not only into the Canaries and New Spain, but likewise into Cathaia, Moscovia, Tartaria and regions thereabout, from whence (as they say) they bring home great commodities.'

The increasing importance of the merchant class is told in their monuments in parish churches with effigies worthy of noblemen, and bas-reliefs below of their sons and daughters in ruffs kneeling all in a row, and inscriptions commemorating the foundations of hospitals, alms-houses and schools. [See § 20.] Society is getting so mixed, that even a theatre manager, if he has made his money and settled down as a leading citizen in his native town, shall, when he dies, have his bust within the chancel.

After the merchants Harrison places the yeomen. Some of them are 'forty-shilling freeholders,' farming their own land and enjoying the Parliamentary franchise.

'But for the most part the yeomen are farmers to gentlemen; and with grazing, frequenting of markets and keeping of servants (not idle servants such as gentlemen do, but such as get their own and part of their master's living) so come to great wealth, in so much that many of them are able and do buy the lands of unthrifty gentlemen, and often setting their sons to the schools and to the Universities and to the Inns of Court; or otherwise leaving them sufficient lands whereupon they may live without labour, do make them by those means to become gentlemen.'

To-day the countryside, in almost every region of England, is full not only of Elizabethan mansions, but of more modest houses built in the Tudor or early Stuart type of architecture, now occupied by tenant farmers, which once were manor-houses of small gentry or seats of freehold yeomen on much the same economic level. Such houses remind us that from Elizabethan times down to the Restoration of 1660 the number of small gentry and yeomen freeholders was on the increase, while the great estates of the old feudal nobility were diminishing. It was a great age for the rural middle class.

After the merchants and yeomen came the 'fourth and last sort of people,' the wage-earning class of town and country.

'As for slaves and bondmen we have none,' Harrison says in a proud parenthesis, and boasts that by the privilege of our island every man who sets foot upon it becomes as free as his master. This principle, that to touch the soil of England in itself confers freedom, was two centuries later extended for the benefit even of negroes, by Lord Mansfield's celebrated judgment in the case of the runaway slave Somersett.

But the wage-earning class, though now free from all taint of servile position, 'have neither voice nor authority in the Commonwealth,' says Harrison; 'yet they are not altogether neglected, for in cities and corporate towns, for default of yeomen, they are fain to make up their inquests of such meaner people. And in villages they are commonly made churchwardens, sidesmen, aleconners, constables, and many times enjoy the name of headboroughs.' This principle of democratic self-government had subsisted even among the serf-farmers of mediaeval times. It was strong in the Court Leet, or Manor Court where petty justice was done: even so mean a member of village society as Christopher Sly could threaten to 'present' the hostess of the tavern 'at the Leet because she brought stone jugs and no sealed quarts.' And in the Leet Court, too, the agricultural policy to be pursued on the open field and the common pasture was discussed and decided by all. The English villager had not only rights but functions in the society of which he was member. Many were always very poor, and some were victims of oppression, but there was a spirit of independence running through all classes under the old system of land-tenure, before the Eighteenth Century enclosures broke up the village community.

Another sign of the self-respect and self-reliance of the English commonfolk was training for military service. It was only during the long period of peace and safety after Waterloo, that men began to regard it as part of English liberty not to be trained for defence. In all previous ages the opposite and more rational idea had prevailed. In the later Middle Ages the national skill in archery and the obligation to serve in the militia of town and country had fostered the spirit of popular independence which Froissart, Fortescue and other writers had noticed as peculiarly English. And so it still was under Elizabeth, though the long-bow was yielding to the caliver or hand-gun.

'Certes [writes Harrison] there is almost no village so poor in England (be it never so small) that it hath not sufficient furniture in a readiness to set forth three or four soldiers, as one archer, one gunner, one pike, and a billman at the least. The said armour and munition is kept in one several place appointed by the consent of the whole parish, where it is always ready to be had and worn within an hour's warning.'

A newly established County officer, the Lord Lieutenant, took the place in 1557 of the Sheriff as commander and organizer of the Militia of each Shire. He and his subordinates held frequent reviews of men, armour and munitions. The parsimony of Elizabeth's finance threw as much of the expense as possible on local and volunteer resources, but the system worked. The Rising of the Northern Earls was suppressed without a battle because 20,000 militiamen, ready armed and trained, took the field on the first alarm to defend the Queen and the Protestant religion. Twice as many were assembled when the Armada was off our shores, and more were mustering daily when that danger passed away before the wind. England had no regular army, but she was not defenceless. Each locality had to supply so many men trained and armed for the militia; each man of property had to find one or more men. Partly by volunteering, partly by compulsion the national duty was fulfilled.

For expeditions oversea such a system was gravely at fault; indeed the only English troops who won any credit upon the Continent between the Hundred Years' War and the time of Cromwell were the long-service regiments of Englishmen in Dutch or other foreign pay.

It was as well that the veterans of Spain did not effect a landing. For the English militia no longer had the superiority over other nations that the long-bow had once given. All through the Queen's reign the caliver or harquebus man was displacing the archer, in proportion as the gun, once so much inferior to the long-bow in an expert hand, increased in range, in rapidity of fire, and in force to penetrate plate-armour. At the beginning of the reign, most even of the well-appointed London militia were still bowmen, but the best companies already consisted of 'shot' and heavily armoured pikemen. After another generation had passed, not one of London's 6000 trained militiamen bore the bow during the alarm of the Armada, and it was the same in many Southern counties. A decade later, Shakespeare wrote a scene in which Falstaff is pressing Cotswold yokels by the authority of the Justices of the Peace; he is not seeking archers but only 'shot'; 'put me a caliver into Wart's hand, Bardolph.' In 1595 the Privy Council decreed that bows should never again be issued as weapons of war; and so a great chapter in English history came to its end.   [See § 29, 30, 31, 32.]

In sport the substitution of firearms for bows followed more slowly. As late as 1621 the Archbishop of Canterbury had the misfortune to aim at a buck and kill a gamekeeper with his cross-bow. But by that time many sportsmen used the 'long gun' especially in the stalking of wild fowl, though 'to shoot flying' was still regarded as something of a feat.

The good order preserved in Elizabeth's kingdom, in spite of religious differences and foreign dangers, was due to the power of the Crown exerted through the Privy Council, the real governing body of Tudor England, and the Prerogative Courts which represented the Council's judicial power. Those Courts—The Star Chamber, the Councils of Wales and of the North, the Chancery Court, the ecclesiastical Court of High Commission—were (all except Chancery) afterwards abolished in the Parliamentary Revolution of Stuart times, because they were the rivals of the Common Law Courts, and because they were a danger to individual liberty with their inquisitorial procedure and their avowed bias in favour of the Crown. Yet in the Tudor age it was precisely these Prerogative Courts that saved the liberties of Englishmen by enforcing respect for law, and saved the English Common Law by enabling and compelling men to administer it without fear or favour. The Privy Council and the Prerogative Courts stopped the terrorization of Judges and Juries by local mobs and local magnates; this restoration of the free working of the Jury system in ordinary cases was a service to society that far outweighed the Privy Council's occasional interference in cases of a political complexion. In this way the Common Law and its tribunals were saved by the very jurisdiction that was their rival. Moreover, the Prerogative Courts introduced many new principles of law suited to modern times, which were eventually absorbed into the law of the land.

In foreign countries the old feudal law was not so good a system as the Common Law of mediaeval England, and could not be adapted to the uses of modern society. And so the feudal law of Europe and with it the mediaeval liberties of Europe were swept away in this epoch, by the 'reception' of Roman law, which was a law of despotism. But in England the mediaeval law, fundamentally a law of liberty and private rights, was preserved, modernized, supplemented, enlarged, and above all enforced by the Council and Courts of the 'Tudor despotism,' so that both the old system of law and the old Parliament survived into a new age with a renewed vigour.

So, too, in the sphere of administration, the Tudor Privy Council blended the old with the new, local liberty with national authority. The will of the central power was imposed on the localities, not as in France by sending down bureaucrats and King's Intendents to govern the provinces in place of the local gentry, but by using the more influential local gentry themselves as the Queen's Justices of Peace. They were Elizabeth's maids of all work. They had not only to carry out her political and ecclesiastical policy, but to administer petty justice, and to execute all the ordinary functions of local government, including the new Poor Law, the Statute of Artificers and the regulation of wages and prices. These matters were neither left to adjust themselves on a principle of *laissez-faire,* nor abandoned to the whims of local authorities. They were regulated on nation-wide principles by Parliamentary Statutes, which it was the business of the J.P.s to enforce in every shire. If they were slack in performing these arduous duties, the vigilant eye of the Privy Council was upon them, and its long arm was soon extended. The J.P.s were not yet a law unto themselves, as they became in Hanoverian times. Squirarchical power and local interests were under the wholesome supervision of a central authority thinking for the whole nation.

Nothing is more characteristic of this aspect of the Elizabethan and early Stuart regime than the manner of providing for the poor and unemployed. Times were on the average better in that period (1559-1640) than during the earlier Tudor reigns, but there were recurrent periods of distress. Though complaints were less loud of agricultural troubles and depopulating enclosures, the growth of industries in the country districts was accompanied by periodic unemployment, especially under the domestic system then prevalent in most trades. Under the factory system, which was still in its infancy, a capitalist employer is often able and anxious to keep his works going as long as possible even in bad times, and to accumulate stock, which he hopes to get rid of when times improve. But the domestic worker was less able to carry on, if the demand for his goods grew slack. Whenever under Elizabeth there were bad times, as when a quarrel with the Spanish Governors of the Netherlands closed Antwerp to English goods, our cloth workers perforce left their looms idle as soon as the merchants ceased to buy their cloths or provide them with raw material. Periodic unemployment was a feature of the cloth trade, even during this period, which, taken as a whole, saw it greatly increase.

To meet such exigencies the Poor Law took shape in a long series of experiments and enactments. They were enforced locally by the J.P.s under the strict surveillance of the Privy Council; the Council had a real regard for the interests of the poor, with which the interests of public order were so closely involved. There were to be no more bands of 'sturdy beggars' such as had terrorized honest folk in the days of Henry VIII. A compulsory poor-rate was now levied with increasing regularity. From this fund, not only was poor relief given, but the Overseers of the Poor in every parish were compelled to buy material to provide work for the unemployed—'a convenient stock of flax, hemp, wool, thread, iron and other stuff to set the poor to work.' (Statute of 1601.)

So, too, in time of dearth, as during the series of bad harvests 1594-1597, the Privy Council, acting as always through the instrumentality of the J.P.s, controlled the price of grain, and saw that it was imported from abroad and distributed where famine was worst. No doubt both the Poor Law and the supply of food in time of dearth were imperfect, and more so in some districts than in others, but a compulsory national system existed both in theory and in fact; the provision for the poor was better than anything there had been in an older England, and better than anything there was to be for many generations to come in France and other European countries. (E. M. Leonard, *English Poor Relief*; W. J. Ashley, *Economic Organization of England*.)

The judicial, political, economic and administrative powers of the Justices of the Peace were so various and, taken together, so important that the J.P.s became the most influential class of men in England. They were often chosen for Parliament, where they could speak as experienced critics of laws and policies which they themselves administered. They were the Queen's servants, but they were not in her pay, or in her dependence. They were country gentlemen, living on their own estates and off their own rents. In the last resort what they valued most was the good opinion of their neighbours, the gentry and common folk of the shire. Whenever, therefore, as sometimes happened in Stuart times, the class of country gentlemen strongly opposed the King's political and religious policy, on such occasions the Crown had no instrument with which to govern the countryside. So it proved, for example, in 1688; but it was not so in 1588. Some of the gentry, especially in North and West, disliked Elizabeth's Reformation policy, but an increasingly large majority of their class favoured the new religion, and J.P.s of that persuasion could be used by government to restrain and occasionally to arrest their more recalcitrant neighbours. Such coercion if it had been exerted by paid officials sent down from London, would have been more resented by the opinion of the County— and would have been more expensive to the Queen's exchequer.

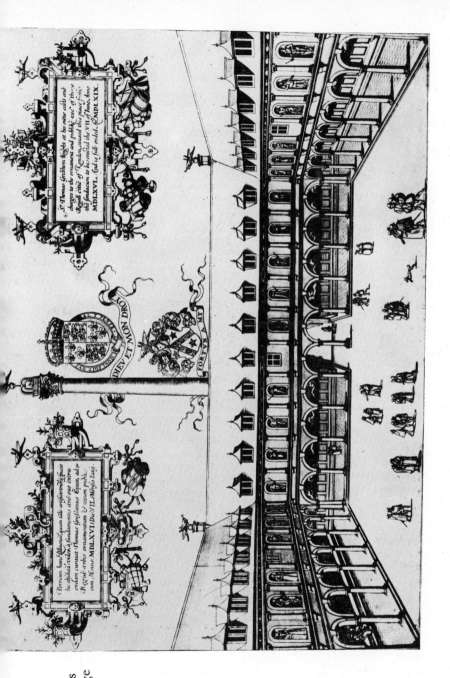

§18 Gresham's
Royal Exchange

§ 19 The Gate of Honour,
Gonville and Caius College, Cambridge

§ 20 The Skynner Monument, Ledbury Church, Herefordshire—
a cloth merchant's tomb

§ 21 A peasant woman riding to market

§ 22 Pillion riding

§ 23 The Lord Mayor of London

§ 24 The Lady Mayoress of London

§25 The ale-bench with minstrels

§26 A meal at the inn

§ 27 Dining at home

§ 28 A privy chamber with pipe and tankard

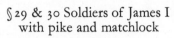

§ 29 & 30 Soldiers of James I with pike and matchlock

§31 The Art of Gunnery (1608)—concentration of fire

§32 Angle of fire

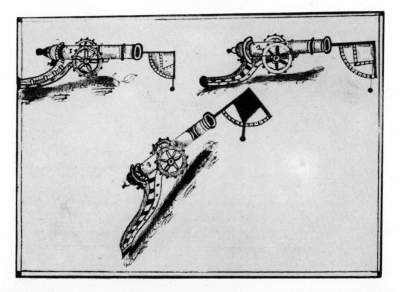

§ 33 Michael Drayton

§ 34 William Camden—
'the greatest of all our
antiquaries'

§35 Family worship in 1563

Come holy ghost eternall god, proceding from aboue,

both from the father & the son, y god of peace & loue.

isit our minds & into vs, thy heauēly grace inspire, that in all truth, and

lines, we may haue true desire.

A.ii.  Come

§36 An Elizabethan psalter—the contra tenor part of the *Veni Creator*

§37 A preaching at Old St. Paul's (*c.* 1616)

Marke 16. 10.

He that beleeueth, and is Baptiſed ſhall be ſaued. John 3. 5.
Verily, verily, I ſay vnto thee, except a man be borne of water and
of the Spirit, he cannot enter into the Kingdome of God. Hebrews 12
22. yee are come vnto mount Sion, and vnto the citty of the liuing God,
the heaunly Ieruſalem, and to an innumerable company of Angels 23. To
the generall aſſembly, and church of the firſt borne, which are written
in heauen: and to God the iudge of all; and to the ſpirits of iuſt men
made perfect. 24. And to Ieſus the mediatour of the new
couenant; and to the blood of ſprinckling that ſpea-
keth better things then that
of Abel.

§ 38 A christening in 1624

Hebrews 10. 19. 20.          Such by the Blood of Ieſus
may be bold to enter into (Heauen) the holieſt place: By a new and
liuing way thorough the vaile that is to ſay, his fleſh. 1 Corinth. 11. 28. 29.
30. Let euery man examine himſelfe, and ſoo let him eate of that bread, and
drincke of that Cupp: for he that eateth, and drinketh vnworthily eateth and
drinketh damnation to himſelfe, not diſcerning the Lords Body.
For this cauſe many are weake and sickly among you, and many
sleepe

§ 39 Holy Communion in 1624

OPPIDVM SEPTENTRIO CANTEBRIGIÆ
CANTEBRIGIA Vrbs celeberrima a Granta fluuio vicino, Cairgrant,
a primo non tam vrbis quam Academiæ conditore Cantabro, magni nominis Hispano,
Cantebrigia, a Saxonibus Grauntecestre, et Grantebrige iam olim nuncupata est. Fluuius ho-
die antiquum nomen retinens, flexuosis riparum anfractibus ab austro in aquilonem mari tenus
longissimo tractu protenditur. Vrbs uero conditoris nomen et memoriam sempiternam reddens
etiam Academiæ dignitatem multo quam olim fuit illustriorem conseruat. Muro fuisse cinc-
tam historiæ referunt sed eum pictis Danicis et Saxonicis bellis (ut et veterem vrbis faciem)
concidisse. Henricus tertius Angliæ Rex circa annū Dñi 1265 fossa et portis Cantebrigiam
muniuit. Quo tempore ibim contra exhæredatorū iniurias et excursiones, q Eliensem Insulam
occupabant se defendit. Muro etiam iam tum rursus cinxisset, nisi eo absente Londino a
Gilberto Clarensi duce occupato, nouæ calamitati pspicere fuisset coactus. Hui⁹ fossę q
ab eo tempore Regiæ nomen obtinuit vestigiū quoddam in hac charta cernitur. Sed q
ad vrbis ambitū et defensionē altissimis, fuit, et latissimis fossionibus primum apparata
expurgandis plateaṛū secib⁹, duendisq; in Grātā fluuiū sordib⁹ non male nunc inseruit. Qd
si Cantebrigienses cōiunctis opib⁹ efficerent vt q est ad vadū Trumpingtoniæ amniculus
fossam hanc allueret, non esset Cantebrigia vrbs vlla elegantior, tantiq; facti memoria non
tam posteris grata quam ipsis iucunda et fructuosa existeret.
HONI SOYT QVI MAL Y PENSE
Castell
Parochia omiū sanctorum ad Castrum
St Peters
MAT
CANT
St Giles
T
Magdalen Colledge
R
The Bridge
Bridge Warde
Bridge streate
St Clemen
The Kinges diche
N
St Pulchers
Jesus Colledge
Jesus lane
Gray Friers
Barnwell cawsey
Walles lane
St Johns Colledge
Trinitie Coll. Chap.
S
N
S

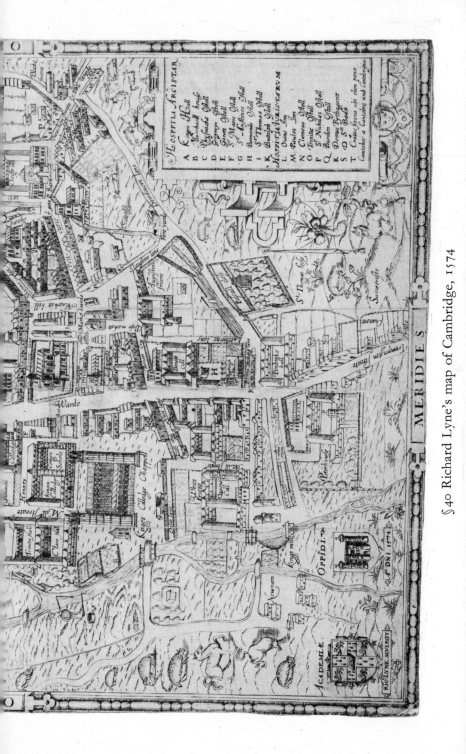

§ 40 Richard Lyne's map of Cambridge, 1574

§41 Oxford scholars (*c.* 1577)

§42 Minting coins in 1560

## Chapter Two

## SHAKESPEARE'S ENGLAND [1564-1616]

*2. Religion and Universities. The social policy of the Elizabethan State.
Industry and Seafaring. Shakespeare.
(Queen Elizabeth, 1558–1603. The Armada, 1588.)*

IN seafaring and discovery, in music, drama, poetry, and in many aspects of social life, we can speak with assurance of the golden age of Shakespeare's England, an age of harmony and creative power. But the religious life of the time seems on the face of it more obscure, less attractive and certainly less harmonious. Except 'the judicious Hooker,' there is no name of the first order that springs to the mind as connected with Elizabethan religion. Yet, if we consider the fate that in those years befell Spain, France, Geneva, Italy and the Netherlands on account of religion, we may see reason to be thankful that in England ecclesiastical feuds were so kept in check by the policy of the Queen and the good sense of the majority of her subjects, lay and clerical, that religious fanaticism never got loose to destroy or pervert the activities of Elizabethan man. Nor is that negative merit the only one to be attributed to religious life in the age of Shakespeare. He himself, and Edmund Spenser, were children of their time and breathed its religious atmosphere, just as the poets of other ages, Langland, Milton, Wordsworth and Browning were each the outcome and highest expression of a religious philosophy characteristic of their respective epochs. There were among Shakespeare's contemporaries many violent Puritans and Romanists and many narrow Anglicans, but there was also something more characteristically Elizabethan, an attitude to religion that is not primarily Catholic or Protestant, Puritan or Anglican, but which evades dogma and lives broadly in the spirit. It is common to Shakespeare and to the Queen herself.

The first year of Elizabeth saw a crisis in the social life of every parish. Cranmer's bequest to posterity, the English Prayer Book, was again ordered to be read in place of the Latin Mass. But this change of religion was not accompanied by a corresponding change in the person of the parish priest. Out of some 8000 beneficed clergy not more than 200 were deprived. The parson obeyed the law as a matter of course, and his neighbours, themselves equally obedient, thought none the worse of him for that. If he was a middle-aged man he was well accustomed to altering his religious practice at the behest of the powers that be. In some cases he was an ex-monk or friar who had known a good many 'varieties of religious experience.' In the year when Queen Mary was succeeded by her sister, the average parson was seldom a convinced Protestant; but he had no respect for the authority of the Pope; the idea of consulting his own 'private judgment' was alien to his thought; and if he sincerely wished to obey 'the Church,' where was he to hear her voice? It issued, he had been taught to believe, from the mouth of the Prince, and in 1559 it came to him from no other quarter. To accept religious services and doctrines because they were ordained by Crown, Parliament and Privy Council, seemed to clergy and people not only expedient but positively right.

Such was the Erastian attitude to religion that carried Englishmen through that dangerous century of change. It is repugnant to our modern ideas of denominational and personal freedom, but it was at that time a doctrine sincerely held by the majority of conscientious men. Bishop Jewel, the best exponent of the ideas of the early Elizabethan settlement, declared

'This is our doctrine, that every soul, of what calling soever he be,—be he monk, be he preacher, be he prophet, be he apostle,—ought to be subject to King and magistrates.'

The sphere of King and magistrates covered religion. All were agreed that there could be only one religion in the State, and all except Romanists and very rigorous Puritans were agreed that the State must decide what that religion should be.

This doctrine, equally opposed to mediaeval and modern conceptions, suited Elizabeth's England. It was the political corollary of the social revolt of the laity against the clergy in the time of the Queen's father. The Tudor English were not irreligious, but they were anti-clerical, and therefore they were Erastian. This attitude of mind affected the clergy themselves, who had not been brought up in seminaries as a priestly caste, but were themselves an integral part of English society.

The clergy as a whole were therefore obedient and supine in the first years of Elizabeth. But there was an active and prosely-tizing minority among them of zealous Protestants, who had escaped the Smithfield fires by the accident of Queen Mary's death, or had returned from exile abroad full of Calvinist zeal imbibed at the Genevan fountain-head. Such men were not Erastian at heart. They would have disobeyed a Popish Prince, but they knew that Elizabeth alone stood between England and a Papal restoration, so they accepted her Church compromise, intending to reform it as time and occasion should permit. As against Rome and Spain they were the strongest defence of the new settlement, but from another point of view they were its most dangerous enemies.

The majority of the parish priests of 1559, who were prepared to take their religion ready-made from a Parliamentary Statute, were lacking in any definite tradition that could give enthusiasm and authority to their ministrations. But the extreme Protestants had a living faith that made them for some decades the most influential section of the clergy, at a time when the average parson was deficient both in learning and in zeal.

Since the anti-clerical revolution of King Henry's day, priests were no longer envied or hated, but they were often despised and ill-used. Elizabeth herself continued to filch Church lands and property, and sometimes to keep Bishoprics vacant in order that the Crown should enjoy the rents of the manors. Her Arch-bishops constantly sought the advice of her Secretary, William Cecil, on purely religious matters, while complaining to him unceasingly of the petty oppressions of powerful laymen. 'The Church was treated very much as an arm of the Civil Service, a dignified but pleasantly helpless prey of an impecunious sovereign and a rapacious court.' In the smaller sphere of parish politics, the squire was equally dominant over the parson. The young author of Love's Labour's Lost had seen much of the half kindly, half contemptuous attitude of the laity towards the parish priest, 'a foolish, mild man, an honest man look you and soon dashed. A marvellous good neighbour, faith, and a very good bowler.'

All this betokened that the ground-swell caused by the great anti-clerical earthquake of Henry's reign was subsiding only by degrees. Nevertheless it was subsiding. By the end of the Queen's reign the Anglican clergy were already in a better position, more respected by their neighbours, more sure of themselves and of their message. When the Stuart Kings took the Church by the hand in an honourable partnership, the laity were soon complaining once more 'of the pride of the clergy.' Laud encouraged the parson to look the squire in the face.

It was an important change in social life that the clergy under Elizabeth were again, and this time finally, authorised to take unto themselves wives. Many parsons, who had been ready to accept the restoration of Roman Catholicism in 1553, had been deprived of their livings under Mary, for no reason except that they had been legally married by the laws of Edward VI. Under Elizabeth their connubial liberty was restored. It has been shrewdly suggested that 'as the distribution of monastic property created among certain classes a vested interest in the future of the Reformation, so the removal of restrictions on the marriage of the clergy created what we may call a family interest in its progress among sections of the clergy not sufficiently enlightened to grasp the higher issues, an interest which was not without importance in guaranteeing its ultimate success.' (Miss Hilda Grieve's study of the personal fortunes of the clergy in Essex deprived under Mary. *R.H.S.* 1940.)

Freedom to marry must have been a real comfort to many honest men; and a fine race of children were reared in the parsonages of England, for generations to come, filling all the professions and services with good men and true, and most of all the Church herself. But, in the first instance, clerical marriage involved certain difficulties; priests' wives were looked at askance by Elizabeth and many of her subjects, still under the prejudice of old use and wont. Time was needed before the parson's wife acquired the honourable and important position in parish society that she afterwards filled.

The need to support a wife and children made the parson's poverty yet more acute. Because they were poor, it was not usual for the parish clergy to marry gentlemen's daughters. Clarendon himself, devoted as he was to the Anglican Church, noted as a sign of the social and moral chaos produced by the Great Rebellion, that the daughters of noble and illustrious families bestowed themselves upon divines 'or other low and unequal matches.' The great rise in the economic and social status of the clergy took place only during the Hanoverian epoch. In Jane Austen's novels the squires and parsons form one social group, but that was not the case in Tudor or Stuart times.

Clerical poverty helped to prolong simony and pluralities. Those practices did not cease with the disappearance of Papal jurisdiction, though the holding of English benefices by foreigners living in France and Italy had come to an end for ever.

In the middle of the reign, during the foreign and domestic crisis that culminated in the Armada and the execution of Mary Queen of Scots, English society in town and country was gravely disturbed by the religious differences of neighbours; the Jesuit mission was hard at work in the houses of the unfortunate gentry of the old religion, distraught between the claims of the two rival loyalties. Fear brooded over the land. Men waited, expecting every day to hear of Spanish invasion, Roman Catholic rebellion, the assassination of the Queen. The Jesuits flitted about in disguise, hiding in 'priest holes' in the thickness of manor-house walls, pursued by Justices of the Peace, occasionally caught and executed.

Meanwhile the Puritans, not yet 'dissenters' but parish clergymen and Justices of the Peace on whom the State depended for its existence in this crisis, were working hard to overturn and remodel the Church establishment from within. They denounced the Bishops as 'limbs of anti-Christ.' They held lectures and prayer-meetings forbidden by the authorities. Every merchant of London, Elizabeth complained, 'must have his schoolmaster and nightly conventicles, expounding scriptures and catechizing their servants and maids, insomuch that I have heard how some of their maids have not sticked to control learned preachers, and say that "Such a man taught otherwise in our house." ' In many counties the Puritan clergy held conferences of ministers which were dangerously like Presbyterian Synods, and were intended, with the help of Parliament, soon to wrest authority from the Bishops.

Already the Puritans showed that gift for electioneering and Parliamentary lobbying and agitation which in the next century remodelled the English constitution. In 1584 they flooded Parliament with petitions from clergy, town corporations, Justices of the Peace and the leading gentry of whole counties.

The House of Commons and even the Privy Council were half converted. But Elizabeth stood her ground. It was well that she was firm, for a Puritan Revolution in the Church, effected at that time, would almost certainly have resulted in a religious civil war of Catholic and Protestant from which Spain would not improbably have emerged as victor. In 1640 England was sufficiently strong and sufficiently Protestant to indulge safely in a course of ecclesiastical revolution and counter-revolution which would have been fatal to her half a century before.

Queen Elizabeth and her stiff Archbishop Whitgift weathered the storm, and the Anglican vessel slipped safely on between the clashing rocks of Romanism and Puritanism. By the end of the reign there had been a certain reaction. The Puritans had for a time been reduced to some show of obedience within the Church. Those who were outside the Church, like the 'Brownists,' were few and despised. There had been hard hitting: some of the more extreme Puritans had been hanged and many more imprisoned. And yet the bulk of the Puritan clergy, gentry and merchants were loyal to the Queen. The wonderful woman still 'reigned with their loves.' But a person even more far-seeing and intelligent than Elizabeth—'if ever such wight were'—might have wondered how much longer the State would be able to impose 'one religion' on this divided and obstinate race of Englishmen, where even maid-servants 'sticked not to control learned preachers'! The abomination of Toleration might yet be the ultimate issue, and England become famous for the 'hundred religions,' which so much amused Voltaire on his visit to our island.

But Elizabeth still hoped that all her subjects would accept 'one religion,' that of the middle way, wherein, as Hooker was so eloquently and learnedly explaining, human reason and common sense were to have their place beside scripture and beside Church authority. Certainly there was more chance that such a religion would be acceptable to the English than the scripture-pedantry of the Puritan who must find a text to justify every act of daily life, or the crushing Church authority preached by the Jesuit. Yet the idea of enforcing 'one religion' of any kind on all England was utterly vain, and meant another hundred years of strife and hatred, imprisonments and confiscations, with blood tragically shed on the battlefield and the scaffold. And out of all that misery it was destined that there should be plucked the flower of our civil liberties and our Parliamentary constitution. Truly the ways of man's history are strange and the fate of nations is inscrutable.

As we still use the Prayer Book, it is not very hard to reconstruct in our minds an Elizabethan service. But we must imagine a wooden table in the body of the Church, instead of an altar railed off in the east end. [See § 38, 39.] There was no intoning, either of prayers or psalms. The prayers were said and the psalms were sung. Congregational singing was a great part of the appeal of Protestant worship. But instead of the modern hymns now sung in Church, the psalms appointed for the day were sung in the rhymed, metrical version of Sternhold and Hopkins. That old psalter, so dear to many generations of Englishmen, is now utterly forgotten; only the 'Old Hundredth' psalm is still familiar as a modern hymn:

> All people that on earth do dwell,
> Sing to the Lord with cheerful voice;
> Him serve with fear, His praise forth tell,
> Come ye before Him, and rejoice.

The Elizabethan psalters, containing these rhymed versions of the psalms, often supplied the music of the tunes in four parts, 'Cantus,' 'Altus,' 'Tenor' and 'Bassus,' so that 'the unskilful with small practice may attain to sing that part which is fittest for their voice.' [See § 35, 36.] The music of viols and wind instruments might or might not accompany the psalm-singing of the congregation.[1]

The sermon was the parson's great opportunity, particularly if he were a Puritan. It might be endured or even welcomed for an hour, or haply for two. But the less learned or self-confident of the clergy, especially those of the older generation, confined

---

[1] In Hanoverian times, before organs and harmoniums were common in parish churches, the metrical versions of the psalms was still sung to the accompaniment of various instruments played in the gallery: Hardy in the *Return of the Native*, Chap. V, recalls such homely music:

'One Sunday, I can well mind, a bass-viol day that time and Yeobright had brought his own. Twas the Hundred-and thirty-third [psalm] and [to the tune of] "Lydia"; and when they'd come to *Ran down his beard and o'er his robes its costly moisture shed,* neighbour Yeobright, who had just warmed to his work, drove his bow into them strings that glorious grand that he e'en a'most sawed the bass-viol in two pieces. Every winder in church rattled as if 'twere a thunderstorm.'

themselves to occasional reading of the Homilies provided by the Church. Both sermon and homily, besides making for edification, helped to form religious and therefore political beliefs. [See § 37.]

Weekly attendance at church was a duty enforced by the State. There was a statutory fine on absentees, but it was probably not very regularly exacted, except from a known 'Popish recusant.' We may be sure that in that highly individualistic society not everyone consented to be 'knolled to church' every Sunday of the year.

A Catholic gentleman of Cornwall, John Trevelyan, who used to attend church to avoid the fine, endured the reading of the lesson and the singing of the 'Geneva jig' which was his name for Sternhold and Hopkins' psalms, but always went out before the sermon, calling aloud to the parson in the pulpit 'when thou hast said what thou hast to say, come and dine with me.' He used to frighten Protestant old ladies of his acquaintance by telling them 'they should expect worse days than they suffered in Queen Mary's time, and that faggotts should be dear'! He was a merry old gentleman of whom many stories were told. (*Trevelyan Papers. Camden Soc.*, P. II [1863, pp. 113–118] and Pt. III [1872, p. xxii.])

In the course of Elizabeth's long reign, the younger generation, brought up on Bible and Prayer Book, and sharing the struggle for national existence against Spain, Pope and Jesuits, became for the most part fervent Protestants. Bible reading and family prayer were becoming customs of the English. So early as the first decade of the reign, Roger Ascham wrote in his *Schoolmaster* 'Blessed be Christ, in our city of London, commonly the commandments of God be more diligently taught, and the service of God more reverently used, and that daily in many private men's houses, than they be in Italy once a week in their common churches.' No doubt such family worship was then more general among the London citizens than in the country as a whole, but the custom spread fast and far.

In the year when the Queen succeeded her sister Mary, Puritanism was mainly a foreign doctrine imported from Geneva and the Rhineland; when she died, it was rootedly and characteristically English and had added to itself some peculiarities unknown to continental Calvinism, such as rigid Sabbatarianism, 'the English Sunday' already at war with the idea of 'Merry England.' Anglicanism also had taken root and shape in the Queen's reign. In 1559 Anglicanism had been hardly so much a religion as an ecclesiastical compromise, decreed by a shrewd, learned and moderate young woman, with the consent of Lords and Commons. [See Frontispiece.] But at the end of her reign it had become a real religion; its services were dear to many, after more than forty years of use in the ancient churches of the land; and its philosophy and spirit were being nobly set forth in Hooker's *Ecclesiastical Polity*. George Herbert (1593–1633) is the poet of an Anglican religion that is something better than a convenience of State.

The improvement in the quality of the clergy and in the learning of clergy and laity alike, which marked the end of Elizabeth's reign, was largely due to the grammar schools and Universities. The mass of the people were either quite illiterate, or half taught to read by village dames. But the clever boys of the most various ranks of society received a good Latin education together, sharing the benches and the floggings of the grammar school. Classes were not segregated, as in the schools of later generations.

The Universities, like most other institutions, had gone through a bad time during the religious and economic troubles of 1530–1560. Their numbers and wealth had fallen, with the disappearance of the convents of monks and friars which had composed an important part of mediaeval Oxford and Cambridge. At the same time an Act of Parliament sent back to their parishes the crowds of middle-aged clergymen, who still, as for centuries past, were wont to desert their cures and live in idleness at the University in no too reputable manner. The mediaeval character of the two English seats of learning disappeared during these distressful years of change and impoverishment.

It was a new and more secular Oxford and Cambridge that revived under Elizabeth and flourished exceedingly up to the outbreak of the Civil War. A larger proportion of the undergraduates now looked forward to careers as laymen. The number of great Elizabethans who had been at Oxford or Cambridge is significant of a new attitude to learning in the governing class. A gentleman, especially if he aspired to serve the State, would now finish his education at one of the 'learned Universities,' whence he usually came away with a familiar knowledge of the Latin language and of classical mythology, a smattering of Greek, and a varying measure of mathematical and philosophical acquirements. Sidney and Raleigh, Camden and Hakluyt were at Oxford; the Cecils, the Bacons and Walsingham were at Cambridge, not to mention Spenser and Marlowe. Master Silence, J.P., is at the cost of keeping his son, Will, at Oxford, for some years before he goes on to the Inns of Court; after that double training in the humanities and in law, the young man will be fit to succeed his father as a Gloucestershire landowner and Justice of the Peace. (2 H. IV, III, ii.) [See § 40, 41.]

One reason for this growing connection between the Universities and the governing class, was the improvement in the conditions of academic life. The College system, rapidly replacing the hostelries and lodging-houses of mediaeval times, afforded some guarantee to careful parents. At Oxford and Cambridge, alone of the Universities of Europe, the Colleges were at this time taking over discipline, which the University had grossly neglected, and the function of teaching, which it had fulfilled very indifferently as regards the majority of students. There was as yet no such officer as the College Tutor, but the student or his parents contracted privately with one of the Fellows of the College to act both as teacher and guardian. Each of these private tutors had half a dozen such pupils whom he lectured and coached. Sometimes they slept in his rooms. It was a relationship analogous to that of master and apprentice.

On the whole this system of private tutoring worked well. But there was a tendency for the tutor to neglect those of his pupils who could not pay high fees, and to be too indulgent with those who could. His richer pupils loved to wear 'excessive ruffs, apparel of velvet and silk, swords and rapiers,' contrary to academic rules, and to engage in forbidden pastimes, such as cards and dice in the parlours of inns, fencing, cockfighting and bear-baiting. In 1587 William Cecil, Lord Burleigh, whose paternal eye was turned into every corner of the kingdom over whose welfare he watched, was credibly informed that through

'the great stipends of tutors, not only the poorer sort are not able to maintain their children at the University, but the richer be so corrupt with liberty and remissness that the tutor is afraid to displease his pupil through the desire of great gain.'

Dons, like everyone else in those days, were 'respecters of persons.'
Early in Elizabeth's reign, parson Harrison complained that

'gentlemen or rich men's sons often bring the Universities into much
slander. For, standing upon their reputation and liberty, they ruffle
and roist it out, exceeding in apparel, and riotous company which
draweth them from their books unto another trade. And for excuse,
when they are charged with breach of all good order, think it sufficient
to say they are gentlemen, which greeveth many not a little.'

One may well guess that, without some eye-winking on the
part of the authorities, smart young men accustomed to the outdoor life of the manor-house or the gay life of the Court, would
never have endured the rigid College rules of that day, which
seem indeed more suitable to schoolboys than undergraduates.[1]
In 1571 the Vice-chancellor forbade even the innocent diversion
of swimming in any stream or pool in Cambridgeshire to all
members of the University. Probably the objection was to the
danger of the exercise, like that of climbing the roof of the chapel
in our own more adventurous age. Organized games and ath-
letics did not exist, and sports were either discouraged or forbidden. But since youth must be served somehow, no wonder
there was much breaking of rules. But there were rules to break:
there had been none to speak of in the mediaeval University.

In an age of patronage, nepotism was inevitable, and Fellow-
ships were freely given to the sons or clients of wealthy and
powerful men, or of lawyers who would intrigue and work for the
College. The Colleges were growing rich, while the University
remained poor. During Elizabeth's reign the Great Court of
her father's foundation of Trinity at Cambridge grew up as the
rival of Tom Quad at Christ Church.

A generation later, in the reign of James I, when Simon d'Ewes
studied at St. John's, Cambridge, the chief undergraduate diver-
sions were walking, swimming (in spite of the prohibition !),
bell-pulling, running, pitching the bar, and football, which was
little better than an excuse for a free fight in the backs between
two Colleges.

Most of the students slept four or more in a room. The poorer

---

[1] In Elizabeth's time undergraduates usually came up at sixteen; many were two
or three years younger, but it was becoming increasingly recognized that such boys
were too young for the studies of the place.

were usually destined for the Church, the richer for the world. The Dons who taught them were still compelled to take holy orders, and even to refrain from marriage which was now legalized for other clergymen. To that extent Oxford and Cambridge remained clerical and even quasi-monastic, until the Gladstonian legislation of the late Nineteenth Century. Daily attendance at College Chapel was enforced on all.

A number of the undergraduates, including Kit Marlowe at Corpus, Cambridge, and Philip Sidney at Christ Church, Oxford, [see § 64] were interested in poetry and the drama, which played so great a part in the life of those days. Plays and interludes, some in Latin, were often acted by the students. One elaborate 'rag,' played off on the town by the gown in 1597, was recorded by Fuller in his history of Cambridge University:

'The young scholars, conceiving themselves somewhat wronged by the townsmen, betook them for revenge to their wits. . . They composed a merry but abusive comedy (which they called *Club Law*) in English, as calculated for the capacities of such whom they intended spectators thereof. Clare Hall was the place wherein it was acted, and the Mayor with his brethren and their wives were invited to behold it, or rather themselves abused therein. A convenient place was assigned to the townsfolk riveted in with scholars on all sides where they might see and be seen. Here they did behold themselves in their own clothes (which the scholars had borrowed) so lively personated, their habits, gestures, language, lieger-jests and expressions, that it was hard to decide which was the true townsman, whether he that sat by or he that acted on the stage. Sit still they could not for chafing, go out they could not, for crowding, but impatiently patient were fain to attend till dismissed at the end of the comedy.'

The Corporation, like all Englishmen in Tudor times who felt themselves aggrieved, appealed for remedy to the Privy Council. His Majesty's sage advisers gave indeed 'some slight and private check to the principal actors' but, when the town became importunate for their further punishment, put an end to the matter by merrily proposing to come down in state to Cambridge to see the play acted again and judge it on the spot.

This curious incident illustrates not only the traditional hostility but the personal intimacy that then existed between town and gown. Elizabethan Cambridge was a small community in which all the leading characters were likely to be known to one another and to the double public of townsmen and under-graduates. In 1586 there were 6500 inhabitants of Cambridge, and of whom 1500 belonged to the University.

A large proportion of the tradesmen cultivated a few acres each in the town field beyond the Cam, and there were besides many small farmers ('husbands') in the borough: the shops and farm buildings on the street were timber-framed, of 'mud and stud,' hiding labyrinthine alleys and courtyards, of which relics still survive behind the modern street-fronts of brick. Such was the town in which Hobson the carrier inherited in 1568 a cart and eight horses from his father, and from that slender beginning built up a transport service of riding and wheeled traffic which became famous throughout all East Anglia, enriched our language with the expression 'Hobson's choice,' and the town of Cambridge with Hobson's Conduit, and finally was immortalized by two short poems of indifferent merit by young Mr. Milton of Christ's.

Cambridge was scarcely more famous for its University than for its Fair, held for three weeks in September on the stubble of the town fields, between the Newmarket road and the river. There North and South England exchanged goods, brought by land and water. Streets of booths were erected, where the North bought its hops and sold its wool and cloth. Traders from the Netherlands and the Baltic and great merchants of London did big business there in cloth, wool, salt-fish and corn. In days before the commercial traveller, fairs of this kind were essential to trade, and Stourbridge was the greatest in England: goods of every kind, wholesale and retail, were sold; housewives, thrifty and gay, came from far to furnish their houses or replenish their cupboards and to see 'the fun of the fair.' And there too were many of the farmers and half the bailiffs of East Anglia. The strange thing to our modern notions is that the jurisdiction over this vast annual hive of commerce lay with the University. Stourbridge Fair could not be begun till the Vice-chancellor had come in full academic pomp and proclaimed it open.

The first necessary condition of the recovery and growth of national prosperity under Elizabeth, was an honest coinage. [See § 42.] Her father, as recorded above, had left behind him untold trouble by debasing the currency in the last years of his reign, and so causing under Edward VI and Mary a leap in prices with which neither wages nor fixed rents could keep pace. After the 'settling of religion' in 1559, Elizabeth's next great action was an equally bold grasp of the financial nettle. In September 1560 she called in by proclamation the existing currency of debased coins, to be paid for in new money at a rate somewhat below their nominal value. The skill and success with which this dangerous operation was carried through, bore witness that the new Queen and her Privy Council well understood the economic aspects of government, wherein many otherwise great rulers have gone fatally astray. From that moment forward, prices steadied themselves. They continued to rise gradually throughout the reign, and more rapidly under James and Charles I, because of the increasing effect of new gold and silver from the mines of Spanish America. But wages were now better able to keep pace, and rents were gradually adjusting themselves as leases fell in. The steady, but no longer catastrophic, rise in prices helped trade and industry to prosper, to start new types of manufacture and to find new markets. (See Vol. I, pp. 113–116.)

A great expansion of mining of all sorts—lead, copper, tin, iron and coal—marked the reign of Elizabeth. German miners opened out copper and other diggings in various parts of the remote Lake District. The Mendip hills yielded more and more lead for export by the merchants of Bristol. The innumerable small tin-mines of Cornwall and Devon flourished. Salt pans multiplied. Our iron was recognized as the best in the world. In 1601 an enthusiast told the House of Commons that iron 'appeareth to be a particular blessing of God given only to England, for the defence thereof, for albeit most countries have their iron, yet none of them all have iron of that toughness and validity to make such ordnance of.' And the navy demanded not only cannon but gunpowder, of which the ingredients were still collected at home, till the East India Company in Stuart times brought them back in greater quantities from the East. [See § 43, 44, 45.]

These industrial activities were a drain on the timber of the island, increasingly felt. Iron, lead and the new manufacture of glass, all burnt vast quantities of wood or charcoal. 'As the woods about here decay,' said a native of Worcester late in Elizabeth's reign, 'so the glass houses remove and follow the woods with small charge.' Salt-works, Camden noticed, had recently consumed Feckenham Forest in Worcestershire. Even the forests of the Weald, in Sussex, Surrey and Kent, which had supplied the iron furnaces with charcoal for thousands of years, were running short at last, owing to the drain on the timber made by the increased demand for iron, and by Kent's new agricultural industry which required poles for the hops to climb and charcoal for the oast-houses to burn. [See § 43, 46, 47.]

Household warmth and cooking still depended normally on wood fuel. The yearly increase of shipping, and men's now clear perception that the future of England lay on the sea, made it needful but difficult to maintain growing timber within reach of the docks. Already it was noted that in the lands near the sea, even as far away as Pembrokeshire, 'the woods are consumed and the ground converted to corn and pasture.' No doubt there were trees enough in the island to supply all its furnaces, hearths and shipyards a while longer, if all the timber in the realm could have been used. But it could not. The horse-transport of that day and the soft state of the roads made it economically and even physically impossible to move great masses of timber for any distance, except by water. In many upland districts, therefore, particularly in the West, the 'youthful poet' of *Il Penseroso* could still find untouched primaeval woodlands

> 'Of pine or monumental oak,
> Where the rude axe with heaved stroke
> Was never heard the Nymphs to daunt
> Or fright them from their hallowed haunt,'

while in other districts the disappearance of wood fuel gave the cottager a cold hearth and a bread-and-cheese diet, and sorely restricted the output of the manufacturer. Indeed, works had often to be moved to some place where timber could still be found. Ironworks were destined soon to invade and consume the Forest of Arden.

Under these conditions of increasing wood shortage, coal came more and more into use under Elizabeth, both for household purposes and for manufacture. But the difficulty of carriage limited the supply of coal to regions near the pits or near to navigable water. 'Sea-coal' as it was called from its method of transport, was in general use in London and the Thames valley, and among other coastwise and riverside populations, as along Trent, Severn and Humber. Chimneys and hearths originally constructed for wood fuel had to be remade, and until this was done the 'sulphurous' fumes were a constant nuisance. The great increase of chimneys in Elizabeth's reign was largely due to the increased use of coal. The manufacture of cast-iron fire-backs for coal fires became an important part of the work of the Sussex forges. [See § 46.] An attempt to smelt iron with coal was made at this period, but proved premature. Many other trades already

'A new kind of coal' in 1628

used coal where it could be got cheap. In 1578 it was said that brewers, dyers, hat-makers and others 'have long since altered their furnaces and fiery places, and turned the same to the use and burning of sea-coal.'

Not only London but the Netherlands and other foreign parts were supplied from Tyneside and Durham. Much of the coal went abroad in foreign bottoms, but the still greater trade to London was carried on by fleets of 'colliers' from Tyne. The inadequacy of roads compelled everyone to send heavy goods of all sorts by sea or river as far as possible, and even at the end of the Queen's reign the coastwise trade of England was more than four times as great as the growing export trade.

The two chief nurseries of English seamen were the 'colliers' plying between the Northern ports and London, and the fishermen of Cornwall and Devon, many of whom ventured to the foggy shores of Newfoundland for cod. No less important was the growth in Tudor times of the herring-fleets of the East Coast. Camden noted the size of Yarmouth, the outport of Norwich, now outstripping its rival Lynn, 'for it seems incredible what a great and throng fair is here at Michaelmas, and what quantities of herring and other fish are vended.'

The fishermen were favourites of government, because they so often helped to man the mercantile and royal navies. Laws were passed ordering the observance of 'fish days': none of the Queen's subjects were to eat meat during Lent, or on Fridays— sometimes Wednesdays were added. It was expressly stated that the object was not religious but political—to maintain our sea-faring population, to revive decayed coast towns, and to prevent the too great consumption of beef and mutton which resulted in the conversion of arable into pasture. These fish laws were enforced by actual penalties. In 1563 we read of a London woman being pilloried for having flesh in her tavern during Lent. In 1571 we find the Privy Council busy with returns from Justices of the Peace as to enforcement of this law in various counties. Since people had been accustomed for centuries to observe, more or less, the fasts of the Church, it was relatively easy to prolong the fish-eating habit into a new age for purposes of State. The 'fish days' may not have been always observed in upland districts where it was difficult to get fresh fish from the sea, but no doubt salt fish was sent far inland; even in Northants and Bucks the Justices of 1571 were busy enforcing the law. It helped to prolong the use of the stews and fishponds which had been so common in the mediaeval countryside, and of which the dry beds are still to be observed near many an old manor-house. [See § 48.]

In this and every other way, Secretary Cecil strove to maintain the seafaring population and shipping of the country. He exempted seamen from military service on land; and he enforced Navigation Laws against foreign ships, particularly in the coasting trade. The English marine could not yet carry the whole of English exports, but the Navigation Laws were aiming in that direction.

In the reign of Elizabeth, under the vigorous leadership of Cecil and the Privy Council backed by Parliament, the industrial, commercial and social system of the country was brought under national instead of municipal control.

In the Middle Ages each locality, through its town council or craft gilds, had decided questions of wages and prices; the relations of master, apprentice and journeyman; the right to trade

In a place; and the conditions under which trade should there be carried on. In the Fourteenth Century national control had begun to impinge upon municipal control, when Edward III's foreign policy in France and the Netherlands had affected the whole course of English trade, and when the Statute of Labourers had vainly attempted to fix a maximum wage for the whole country.

Under Elizabeth the national control of wages and prices by the Justices of the Peace was more wisely carried on, without attempting to impose everywhere a fixed maximum wage. At the same time, municipal control of conditions of trade and industry was replaced by State control. The reasons for this great change were various: the decay of many towns and the spread of industry into the country districts where there was no municipal authority; the decline of the craft gilds, which had received their *coup de grâce* in the confiscatory legislation of Edward VI against gild property; the growth of the power of the Crown, working through Privy Council and Parliament; and the joyous sense of nationhood which inspired the Elizabethan English. A man no longer felt his first loyalty owing to his town, his gild, or his 'good lord,' but to his Queen and country.

Under these circumstances the Elizabethan State undertook the control not only of wages and prices, but of apprenticeship, of the right to set up trade and the conditions under which it must be carried on. In these matters the substitution of national policies for the narrower interests of individual towns and gilds gave freer play to the initiative of individuals and to the operations of the capitalist employer and merchant.

The Elizabethan State was more liberal than most towns and gilds in encouraging the settlement of the foreign immigrant: he was usually a Protestant refugee, and he often brought new skill and new processes of manufacture into the land of refuge. Economic nationalism, as interpreted by the Tudors, gave greater liberty to the individual, freeing him from the local jealousies that usually inspired municipal policy.

But this economic liberty was not unconditional *laissez-faire*. The State that gave the individual Englishman or Huguenot the right to manufacture and to trade, laid down rules that he had to obey in the interests of the public. And the craftsman whom he employed was placed under the discipline of a national system of apprenticeship.

The Statute of Artificers (1563) enacted that every craftsman in town or country had for seven years to learn his craft under a master who was responsible for him. The object was quite as much social and educational as it was economic. 'Until a man grow into 23 years,' it was said, 'he for the most part, though not always is wild, without judgment and not of sufficient experience to govern himself.' After the age of 24, having served his apprenticeship, he was at liberty to marry, and either to set up a business of his own, or to become a journeyman for hire.

The good or bad working of apprenticeship varied greatly with the character of the master. There must have been many hard cases, with some of which the Justices of the Peace, who were responsible for the granting of the indentures, were able to interfere, as in the case recorded in the third chapter of *Oliver Twist*. But, on the whole, the relation of master and apprentice—at once domestic, educational and economic—served the purposes of society well. For centuries apprenticeship was the school of Englishmen. It was the very practical answer made by our ancestors to the ever-present problems of technical education and the difficult 'after-school age.' Apprenticeship continued until, in the Nineteenth Century, the Industrial Revolution destroyed it, and substituted, in the first instance, a *laissez-faire* chaos by no means to the advantage of the uncared-for youth of the land. The situation so created has scarcely yet been made good.

But, after all, the greatest social change in Elizabeth's England was the expansion of overseas enterprise. In her reign our merchants found new and more distant markets, some of them on the other side of the globe, in place of that commerce with the Netherlands and France which had from time immemorial furnished the principal vent of English goods. Corresponding to the change of markets was the change of mental outlook. In Court and City, in Parliament and manor-house, in workshop and field-furrow, talk ran upon the ocean and the new lands beyond it, on Drake and Frobisher and Raleigh, on the romance and profit of the explorer's and privateer's life, on sea-power as England's wealth and safety, on the prospect of colonization as a means of personal betterment and national strength. What was the loss of Calais beside all this? Let the dead past bury its dead. [See § 51, 54.]

Englishmen looked forward to new things. The most influential writer in the age of Shakespeare, if it were not Foxe the Martyrologist, was Hakluyt, author of *The Principall Navigations, Voiages and Discoveries of the English Nation*. That book was published in the year after the Armada, and ten years later it was enlarged and brought up to date in three magnificent volumes. Hakluyt, in narrating the deeds of our explorers and seamen, directed across the ocean the thoughts of adventurous youth, of scholars, statesmen and merchants and of all who had money to invest. Even up-country squires and farmers began to dream of boundless expanses of virgin soil, waiting since the dawn of time to be broken by the English plough.

In the lifetime of Elizabeth no colony was successfully planted, though Sir Humphrey Gilbert tried in Newfoundland and Raleigh in Virginia. But the expediency of occupying the temperate regions of North America became a familiar doctrine of State. As early as 1584 Hakluyt had won the Queen's favour and patronage by urging it in his *Discourse of Western Planting*. Meanwhile the actual achievement of the reign in Atlantic sea-power and exploration made ready the path for the folk-wandering of the English people that began in the next generation.

The character of the war with Spain, and the limited and peculiar use to which our victory was turned in the years after the Armada, proved fundamental to the future development of English-speaking lands, and impressed a special character on England herself. The triumph of Elizabeth's subjects over the Spaniards was not a military conquest organized by an Alexander, a Pizarro or a Napoleon. Elizabeth had little in common with those heroes, or with her famous predecessor Henry V: though the tale of Agincourt berattled the common stages and made Englishmen proudly conscious of their past greatness, no one desired to renew such conquests on the continent, or even to find a new field for them in Spanish America. The victory over the Spaniards was merely the establishment of a naval superiority of our ships over theirs, through the co-operation of individual initiative with a thrifty and cautious policy of State. Drake's idea of glory was not Caesar's. He wanted no inch of Spanish soil in the old world or the new. His objects were booty, trade, freedom to sail the seas and to worship God aright, and ultimately to colonize empty lands where the Red Indian nomad would be the only person aggrieved. If Elizabeth's subjects had been less averse to taxation and more in love with the glories of war, the energy that afterwards peopled North America might have been misdirected to the conquest and development of the tropical colonies of Spain. But our sea-victory was not thus abused.

If indeed our triumph over Spain had been won by great armies carried by the fleet, as the Spaniards had intended their victory of the Armada to be achieved; if Spanish colonies had been subjected by force to English rule, then the United States, Canada and Australia that we know to-day might never have come into existence. And in all probability the character of such a military effort would have diverted English society and politics in a martial and monarchial direction.[1]

The Elizabethan sea-war had the opposite influence; it promoted a tendency towards freedom. The possession of a royal navy does not enable the monarch to hold down his subjects, as a royal army may do. In England there was no royal army, and in the Civil War of Charles I, the royal navy actually took the side of Parliament! The other element of the new English sea-power was private enterprise—the action of Drake, Hawkins and their like in American waters, and the merchant companies formed in London to push trade into distant parts of the world: these activities fostered the spirit of self-reliance and self-government.

These novel elements in English society—the new City companies and the fighting seamen—exercised a great influence over the country as a whole. Drake and his rivals and companions became the national heroes. They and the capitalist merchants who backed them were strong Protestants, the more so as their enemies were the Spaniards, and a common result of capture was death by torture in the hands of the Inquisition. Their allies were the French Huguenots from Rochelle and the Dutch Sea-beggars, with many a tale to tell of the tender mercies of Alva and Guise. This rough sea-fellowship, which saved the world from Philip and the *auto-da-fé*, was inspired by a fighting religion of Protestantism which reacted powerfully on English landsmen. The seamen who beat Spain were rough customers, no respecters of

---

[1] It is true that in 1759 French Canada was conquered and annexed, but by that time the free character of the British polity at home and overseas had been fixed. In Elizabethan and Stuart times our political and social constitution was still flexible and might have moved either towards or away from freedom.

persons in Church or State, but faithful to their proved captains, of whom the greatest was the Queen. They took their lives in their hands, and few of them survived many years the chances of battle, shipwreck and sea accident, and the terrible epidemics that raged in the ill-provisioned ships of the period, where food was rotten and the rules of hygiene were unknown.

During the Tudor reigns England changed her national weapon. She laid aside the long-bow and acquired the broadside. The long-bow, that had rendered her soldiers superior to all others in Europe, had lured her into a hundred years of military adventure in France. The broadside—the rows of cannon protruding between the timbers—showed her a better way, along the paths of the ocean to new lands. By the broadside, sea warfare was completely changed. It ceased to be a game of soldiers seeking to grapple their ship to the enemy and fight deck to deck as if on land; it became, instead, a game of sailors, manœuvring their ship so as to fire her cannon with most effect. The ship ceased to be a platform for a storming party and became a moving battery of guns.

This change in the character of warfare at sea was better understood and more quickly exploited by the English than by their enemies. The Spaniards had Mediterranean traditions connected with the oared galley and the grappling of ship to ship. As late as 1571 they fought the great battle against the Turks at Lepanto, by sea tactics the same as those by which the Greeks had defeated the Persians at Salamis. These ancient and honourable traditions hampered Spanish seamanship, even after Philip improvised an ocean-going navy to conquer England in the Atlantic and the channel. His Armada was, in its real spirit, an army embarked; the soldiers outnumbered and bullied the sailors, regarding them as mechanic drudges, whose privilege it was to bring the gallant soldado to grips with his enemies.

But in the English fleet—commanded by Howard, Frobisher, Hawkins, Drake—the Admiral and his Captains were seamen and they were in full command of everyone on board. The soldiers were few and knew their place at sea. Drake, on his voyage round the world (1577–1580) had established the rule that even the gentleman volunteer must haul at the ropes with the mariner. The discipline and equality of the crew at sea was accepted by the Englishman, while the Spaniard could not lay

54

aside his military and aristocratic pride even to save the ship. It was a social difference between the countries, translated into terms of war.[1]

In the twenty years before the coming of the Armada, ocean sailing and the tactics of the broadside had been perfected by English seamen, who learnt their trade in various capacities—in service in the royal ships, as merchants, as explorers, and as privateers. These parts could be easily combined or interchanged. The fighting merchantship, accustomed to defend herself and to force her trade on all the waters of the world, took a large share in the battle against the Armada. But without the Queen's own professional warships the victory could not have been won. [See § 50, 52, 53.]

Henry VIII had founded the royal navy. Under Edward VI and Mary it had been permitted to decay. Under Elizabeth it was revived. Yet during the first twenty years of her reign improvement in the royal dockyards was slow. Elizabeth inherited a bankrupt State, and she dared not lay heavy taxes on her impatient and obstinate subjects. Her proverbial parsimony, though sometimes applied in the wrong place, was as a general rule necessary to the bare survival of her government. Moreover, what money she was able to squeeze out for the navy was much of it grossly ill spent. Cecil and the vigilant Privy Council lacked not the will but the technical knowledge to detect and reform the traditional corruption of the shipyards. Then, in a fortunate hour (1578), Elizabeth put John Hawkins in charge of the building and upkeep of her ships. During the decade before the coming of open war, which the Queen had so long and so wisely postponed, Hawkins did as great a work in the dockyards as Drake on the Pacific and Atlantic coasts.

The Queen's money was at last honestly spent for full value received. But Hawkins did more than stop corruption. This great public servant, who in his trading and privateering days between Africa and Spanish America had had experience second only to Drake's, well understood what kind of ships he ought to build for the new kind of warfare. His critics, clinging to the

[1] Hawkins and a long race of successors carried negro slaves, crimped on the coast of Africa, to the Spanish Colonies of America. But the English seamen as among themselves had the spirit of freedom. They always regarded with horror the use of galley slaves by French and Spaniards. That was not the English idea of the way in which a ship should be manned.

ideas of an older school, clamoured for vessels with a high super-structure, impregnable to assault but difficult to manœuvre, affording houseroom for crowds of soldiers who would consume the stores. Hawkins would have no more of such castles. In spite of protest, he built the Queen's ships low, long in proportion to their beam, easy to handle and heavily gunned. Such a ship was the *Revenge*, destined many years later to justify her designers when she fought the Spanish navy for a day and a night. [See § 65, 66.]

The English merchants, in seeking out more distant markets, were encouraged by the new potentialities of seamanship, and inspired by the adventurous spirit of the age; but they were also compelled along the new course by the closing of old markets nearer home. The loss of Calais, where the wool Staple had functioned for so many generations past, occurred a few months before Elizabeth ascended the throne. It was a blow to English wool-exporters from which they never fully recovered, as the general trend of things was against them and in favour of their rivals, the manufacturers and merchants of cloth. [See § 49.]

After the loss of Calais there still remained the yet more ancient trade centres of Bruges and Antwerp in the Netherlands, as marts of English wool and cloth. But in the next few years that opening also was closed. The quarrel of the young Elizabeth and her Privy Council with Granvelle, then governing the Netherlands for Philip of Spain, arose from a diversity of political, religious and economic motives. English piracy in the channel; English friendship with the Protestants in the cities where they traded, encouraged by the magistrates and people of Antwerp; Spanish intolerance of heretical foreigners, all played their part in the breach. But no less important was the economic clash of the two mercantilist policies of Granvelle and Elizabeth. Each side believed that the other was at its mercy. Granvelle was sure that if the English were forbidden to sell their cloth in the Netherlands they would not be able to sell it anywhere else, and must perforce be content to bring their raw wool to be wrought on the looms of the Netherlands. The English were sure that the Netherlands could not flourish without English trade.

The quarrel came to a head in the first decade of Elizabeth's reign, twenty years before actual war broke out between England and Spain. Excluded from the Netherlands, the English cloth merchants moved in 1567 to Hamburg as their port of entry into Europe, only to be driven thence ten years later by the mercantilist jealousy of the Hanse Towns.[1]

These changes of market caused much distress and periodic unemployment in the cloth manufacture at home, but gradually new markets were found further afield. New trading Companies were formed in London which successfully pushed trade into Russia, Prussia, the Baltic, Turkey and the Levant. Persia was first reached by way of the Russian river system, and finally India by way of the Cape of Good Hope. In 1600 the old Queen granted a charter to the East India Company, destined to an economic and political future surpassing all the tales of romance. These new world-wide adventures rescued the trade of England from the otherwise inevitable consequences of the loss of her old markets on the coast opposite to her own shores. The change-over was rendered possible by the adventurous spirit of the capitalists of the City of London, by the quality of the new school of sailors and sea-captains, and by the enterprise of English explorers by land as well as sea.

Already in 1589, Hakluyt in dedicating to Walsingham the first edition of his *Voyages*, had proudly written:

'Which of the Kings of this land before Her Majesty, had their banners ever seen in the Caspian Sea? Which of them hath ever dealt with the Emperor of Persia as her Majesty hath done, and obtained for her merchants large and loving privileges? Who ever saw, before this regiment, an English Ligier in the stately porch of the Grand Signor at Constantinople? Who ever found English Consuls and Agents at Tripoli in Syria, at Aleppo, at Babylon, at Balsara, and, which is more, who ever heard of Englishmen at Goa before now? What English ship did heretofore ever anchor in the mighty river of Plate? Pass and repass the unpassable (in former opinion) strait of Magellan, range along the coast of Chili, Peru and all the backside of Nova Hispania, further than any Christian ever passed, traverse the mighty breadth of the South Sea, land upon the Luzones, in despite of the enemy, enter into alliance, amity and traffic with the Princes of Moluccas, and the isle of Java, double the famous Cape of Bona Speranza, arrive at the isle of St. Helena, and last of all return home richly laden with the commodities of China, as the subjects of this now flourishing monarch have done?'

[1] E. E. Rich, *The Ordinance Book of the Merchants of the Staple* (1937), chap. IV, tells the story of the loss of the Netherlands market and its consequences.

By the end of Elizabeth's reign not only was English commerce and finance thus reviving and expanding on a modern basis, but her ancient rivals were in rapid decline.

The withdrawal of English trade might not by itself have proved fatal to the prosperity of the Spanish Netherlands, but there followed the appalling religious persecutions and wars of

'The habit of taking tobacco in long clay pipes
was very general by the time the Queen died'

Alva's rule. The complex of these events put an end to the supremacy which Antwerp had long held in the trade and finance of Europe. Amsterdam and the other towns of the rebel Dutch republic rose instead. Ere long the Dutch seamen were to be chief rivals of the English in all the waters of the world; but to the subjects of Elizabeth the Dutch mariners were more important as allies in war than as rivals in trade.

Meanwhile the merchant cities of Italy were being ruined by the increasing difficulties of the overland trade-routes to the

East, and by the rivalry of the Cape route, which they left to the Portuguese, Dutch and English. Italian traders abandoned the big field of world competition. Venetian merchants ceased to visit England in quest of Cotswold wool. In 1587 the last of the argosies sent by Venice to Southampton was wrecked off the Needles; with her sank the mediaeval system of trade and all that it had meant to Italy and to England. Southampton, which had been the Italian depot, declined, and London was further enriched, as the trade with the Mediterranean and the Far East now entered the Thames in English ships.

In the following century, tobacco played a great part in English colonial and commercial expansion and in the trade of Bristol. There were as yet no English colonies, but already in 1597 the new American weed was being smuggled into the creeks of Cornwall on a large scale, by French, Flemish and Cornish ships, in open and armed defiance of the custom-house officers. The habit of taking tobacco in long clay pipes was very general by the time the Queen died.

The expansion of overseas enterprise was closely connected with the growth of merchant capitalism, inimical to the old municipal and gild system.

'The guild system [writes Mr. Fay] was not favourable to capital accumulation. In their technique and the ordering of their life the merchants and craftsmen of the Middle Ages surpassed perhaps the centuries which followed. But the guild outlook was municipal and its structure inelastic, and therefore it gave way to a system which lent itself to expansion and change. This we call merchant capitalism, with its complement domestic industry. The merchant capitalist was a middleman who broke down ancient barriers. He defied corporate towns by giving out work to the country, and evaded the monopolies of privileged companies by interloping. . . He committed excesses, but he was the life-blood of economic growth.' [1]

This movement of merchant capitalism athwart the old municipal and gild system had been apparent in the wool trade as early as the age of Chaucer. In Elizabeth's reign it took another great step forward in the rise of oversea trading Companies of a new type. They were of two kinds. First the 'regulated company,' in which each member traded on his own capital, subject to the common rules of the Corporation; such were the Merchant

[1] C. R. Fay, *Great Britain from Adam Smith to the Present Day*, p. 127.

Adventurers, who had a great past as well as a great future as exporters of cloth; the Eastland or Baltic, the Russia, and the Levant Companies. The other class was joint-stock—the East India Company; the African; and two generations later the Hudson's Bay. In this second class, trade was conducted by the corporation as a whole, and the profits and losses were divided among the shareholders.

To each of these companies, whether regulated or joint-stock, a geographical sphere of operations was assigned by royal charter, and no 'interloper' from England might trade therein. Such monopoly was both just and necessary, because of the expenses in the way of forts, establishments and armaments which the Companies had to maintain; for the royal navy could offer them no protection in distant waters. These Elizabathan companies were in many respects similar in their privileges and functions to the 'Chartered Company' that helped to develop and disturb the interior of Africa late in Victoria's reign. That was, perhaps, an age too late for such political and military powers to be wisely entrusted to a private group of the Queen's subjects—as Jameson's raid showed. But under Elizabeth there was no other way of promoting distant trade, and if the Company mismanaged its policy in distant lands, its members suffered but the English State was not involved in the consequences.

These great London companies, only very slightly dependent on the State, worked under conditions which fostered the spirit of private enterprise, self-government and self-reliance. Supreme as was the ultimate importance of these corporations in the history of India and North America, their influence at home was also very great on the development of the English character and on social and political change, as the history of Stuart and Hanoverian times was to show. A generation after the death of Elizabeth, the traveller Peter Mundy noted as one of the 'seven things wherein England may be said to excel, traffic and discoveries, viz. so many incorporated companies of merchants for foreign trade, who employ their study and means for the increase thereof, by adventuring their goods and sundry fleets and ships into most parts of the known world.' [1] Mediaeval England had been 'traded

[1] Mundy's Travels (Hakluyt Soc. 1924) IV, pp. 47–48. An account of the origin (chiefly Elizabethan) of these companies will be found in vol. II of Lipson's *Economic History of England*.

with' by Italians, French and Germans; Elizabethan England herself traded with remote shores. Commercially we had ceased to be the anvil; we had become the hammer.

To remote posterity the memorable fact about Elizabethan England will be that it produced the plays of Shakespeare. It is not merely that the greatest of mankind happened to be born

A pedlar and ballad-monger

in that age. His work would never have been produced in any other period than those late Elizabethan and early Jacobean times in which it was his luck to live. He could not have written as he did, if the men and women among whom his days were passed had been other than they were, in habits of thought, life and speech, or if the London theatres in the years just after the Armada had not reached a certain stage of development, ready to his shaping hand. [See § 60.]

It was no accident that Shakespeare's plays were more poetry than prose, for the audience he addressed, as indeed the common English in town and country alike, were accustomed to poetry as the vehicle of story-telling, entertainment, history and news of contemporary incidents and sensations. Not newspapers and novels but ballads and songs were hawked about by Autolycus and his comrades to satisfy the common appetite in the city street and on the village green. Ballads were multiplied and sold, many thousand of them, each with a story from the Bible, or classical myths and histories, mediaeval legend or happenings of the day, whether the Armada, the Gunpowder Plot or the latest murder or runaway match. And lyrics and lovesongs, of which the words survive as masterpieces of literature in our modern anthologies, were sung as the common music and sentiment of the people.

Under these conditions, in the twenty years before Shakespeare's first plays were acted, a new drama had suddenly grown up, with a new school of playwrights of whom Marlowe was the chief, and companies of highly-trained actors, taking their profession with a high seriousness. To the mediaeval clown and barn-stormer outheroding Herod had been added men of subtler art, of whom Burbage ere long became the most notable; these men carried the art of interpretative acting to its height, and with them were boy apprentices, strictly trained from childhood to take the women's parts with dignity, gaiety and skill.

In the middle years of Elizabeth a way to wealth and honour had been opened to the actor and the playwright. The travelling companies had the patronage of literary noblemen, whose castles and manors they visited as welcome guests, acting in hall or gallery, like the players who had such princely entertainment at Elsinore. But even better 'both for reputation and profit' were the theatres built in the meadows on the Southwark bank of Thames, to play before the motley and critical audience of the capital; while citizens with their wives, and apprentices with their sweethearts, walked over London Bridge to see the play, men of rank and fashion came over by boat from Whitehall, and sharp young lawyers from the Inns of Court.

The performances were given in the day-time; there was neither curtain nor footlights. The front of the stage was in the open air. The most privileged of the audience sat on 'stools' almost among the actors. The 'groundlings' stood below, gaping up at the spectacle, exposed to rain and sun. The covered galleries, that enclosed the 'wooden O' of the theatre, were also full of folk. Here then were gathered together several classes of society, differing from one another, more or less, in tastes and education. It was Shakespeare's business to please them all. [See § 61, 62, 63.]

When he first knew this exacting audience, they were eager for plot and pageant, noise and knock-about, gross clowning and bouts of courtly and learned wit, and music of the best, for the English had then the finest songs and music in Europe; and they were eager too, as the ordinary modern audience is not, for the rhetoric of poetry as a vehicle for play and passion. All these things Marlowe and his fellow labourers had supplied, creating in a few years the new drama that Shakespeare found ready to his hand. He accepted the tradition, and in twenty more years expanded it into something far greater than the most consummate of public entertainments.

His poetry was of a yet higher strain than Marlowe's 'mighty line,' and he invented a prose dialogue as subtle, as powerful, and sometimes as lovely and harmonious as his verse. He made both forms the vehicles not only of beauty, terror, wit and high philosophy, but of a thing new in the drama, the presentation of individual characters, in place of the types and personified passions that had hitherto held the stage. Even the plot, even the action, became subordinate to the character, as in *Hamlet*, and yet the play pleased. So real were his men and women that we are for ever discussing them as if they had a life of their own off the scene. Indeed, for two hundred years past his plays have lived even more in the study than on the stage. Yet plays they are, even when acted in the theatre of the mind; and only the stage can give them full force, though too often it mars them. It is to the Elizabethan theatre that we owe Shakespeare and all that he created. For that let praise be given to the theatre—and to the Elizabethans.

The social historian of to-day cannot really describe the people of the past; the most he can do is to point out some of the conditions under which they lived. But if he cannot show what our ancestors were like, Shakespeare can. In his pages we can study the men and women of those times. More, for instance, can be found out in his plays about the real relations of the two sexes, the position and character of Elizabethan women, than could possibly be expressed in a social history.

As our study of the English scene emerges from mediaeval into modern times, we obtain in increasing profusion that aid of which Chaucer gave us a foretaste, the literature and fiction that described men and women of the writer's own time, their habits of thought, speech and conduct—contemporary impressions which have by the passage of years become historical documents of priceless value. At the same time, intimate diaries and memoirs become common in the Seventeenth Century, like those of Evelyn, Pepys and, later, Boswell's *Johnson*. These, and the English drama, and the novels of Fielding, Jane Austen, Trollope and a hundred others help social history in just that region where legal and economic documents stop short.

All who crave to know what their ancestors were like, will find an inexhaustible fount of joy and instruction in literature, to which time has added an historical interest not dreamt of by the authors. These are the 'books, the arts, the academes' of the social study of the past, and the greatest of them all is Shakespeare.

### BOOKS FOR FURTHER READING

Besides those mentioned in the text above, Darby, *Historical Geography of England* (1936) Chap. X; Miss Taylor's *Camden's England*; James Williamson, *The Age of Drake* (1938) and J. Corbett's *Drake and the Tudor Navy*; W. Cunningham, *Growth of English Industry and Commerce: Modern Times,* Part I; Lipson, *Ec. Hist. of England,* Vol. II, III, *Age of Mercantilism* (1934); Granville-Barker, *Prefaces to Shakespeare and Henry V to Hamlet* (British Academy Lecture, 1925); *Social England,* Vol. II (ed. H. D. Traill); Blomfield, *Short History of Renaissance Architecture in England*; J. U. Nef, *The Rise of the British Coal Industry.* For Elizabethan ballads see the first Essay in Sir Charles Firth's posthumously published *Essays* (Oxford 1938); Rowse, *Tudor Cornwall,* 1941; Mildred Campell (Professor in Vassar College), *The English Yeoman under Elizabeth and the Early Stuarts* (Yale Press 1942).

§43 'A great expansion of mining of all sorts'

§44 'These industrial activities were a drain upon the timber'

§45 'German miners opened out . . . diggings'

§ 46 Elizabethan cast-iron fire-back

§ 47 Charcoal burning

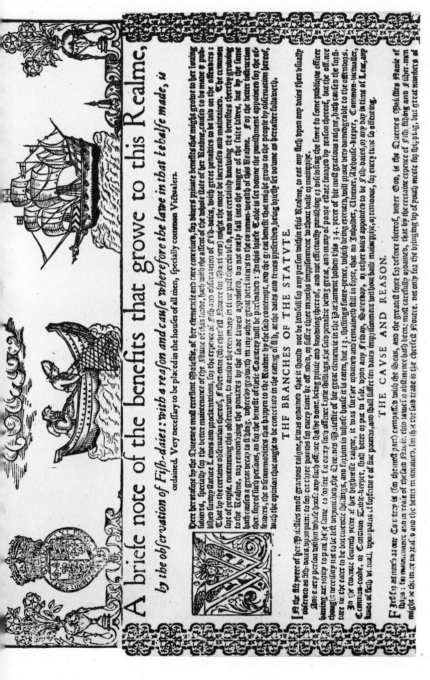

# A briefe note of the benefits that growe to this Realme,

*by the obseruation of Fish-daies: with a reason and cause wherefore the lawe in that behalfe made, is ordained. Very necessary to be placed in the houses of all men, specially common Victualers.*

Heere heretofore by the Queenes most excellent Maiestie, of her elements and care conceiue, for diuers priuate benefits that might growe to her louing subiects, specially for the better maintenance of shipping. Name of this lande, hath with the aduise of the whole state of her Realme, caused to be made & published sundry strait Lawes and proclamations, for the expence of Fish and obseruation of Fish-daies, with great penalties to be laid on the offenders: That by the certaine obseruation thereof, Fisher-men (the chiefest Mariners for Mariters) might the more be increased and maintained. The common sort of people, conteyning this obseruation, to auoide the euen money in time past therein vsed, and not certainly knowing the benefites thereby growing to the Realme, nor remembring the penalties by the saide lawes appointed, do not onely fall into the danger of the saide lawes, but by the same hath caused a great occasion to fishing, whereby growth many other great detriments to the common-wealth of this Realme. For the better instruction therefore of such persons, as for the benefit of their Countrey will be perswaded: In this briefe Table is set downe the punishment appointed for the offenders, the discommodities that happen to the Realme by the said contempt, and the great benefit that might growe to the people by obseruation hereof, with the opinion that ought to be conceiued in the eating of fish, at the daies and times prescribed, being briefly set downe as hereafter followeth.

## THE BRANCHES OF THE STATVTE.

In the fift yeere of her Maiesties most gracious raigne, it was ordained that it should not be lawfull for any person within this Realme, to eat any flesh vpon any daies then vsually obserued as Fish-daies, by paine: to say, of three pounds for euery time: or else of money, or suffer three months imprisonment without baile or mainprise.

And euery person within whose house, any such offence shalbe done, being publique and knowing thereof, and not effectually punishing or publishing the same to some publique officer, (hauing authority to punish by time to consent in euery such offence) shall forfeit fortie shillings. The said penaltie being great, and many of poore estate fauoured by reason thereof, but the offence thought necessary not to be left vnpunished, the Maiors Maiestie of her great reuenue in the Parliament holden this 34 yeere of her most gracious raigne, hath caused the forfeiture to be the entrie to be but twentie shillings, and foysoun in whose house it is eaten, but 13 shillings foure-pence, which being executed, will proue very dammageable to the offendours. In the meane seuenth yeere of her highnesse raigne, it was further enacted and remained still in force, that no Inholder, Taunter, Alehouse-keeper, Common-cooke, or Common Table-keeper, shall bener or put to sale, vpon any Friday, Saterday, or other daies appointed to be Fish-daies, or any day in time of Lent, any kinds of flesh victuall, vpon paine of forfeiture of fiue pounds, and shall suffer ten daies imprisonment without baile mainprise, or moreouer, for euery time so offending.

## THE CAVSE AND REASON.

First for as much as our Countrey is (for the most part) compassed with the Seas, and the greatest force for defence thereof, vnder God, is the Queenes Maiesties Nauie of ships: for maintenance and in vse of the said Nauie, this lande in abstinence hath been most carefully obserued, that by the certaine expence of Fish, fishing and Fisher-men might be thereunto vrged: and the better maintained, for that the said trade is the chiefest Nource, not only for the bringing vp of lusty mariners for shipping, but great numbers of

$\S 48$ Observance of Fish days

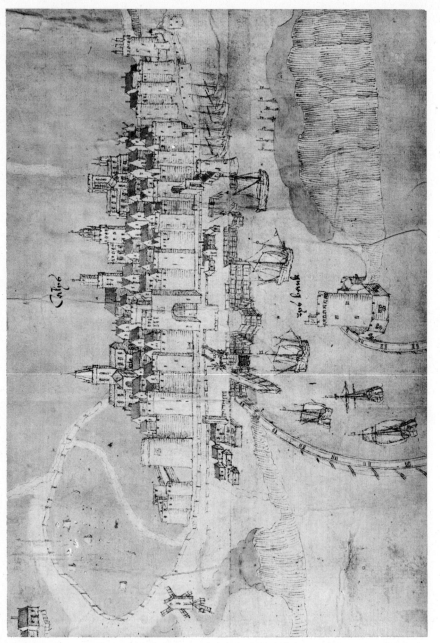

§49 Calais—'where the wool staple had functioned'

§ 50 The *Ark Royal*—flagship against the Armada

§ 51 Sir Walter Raleigh

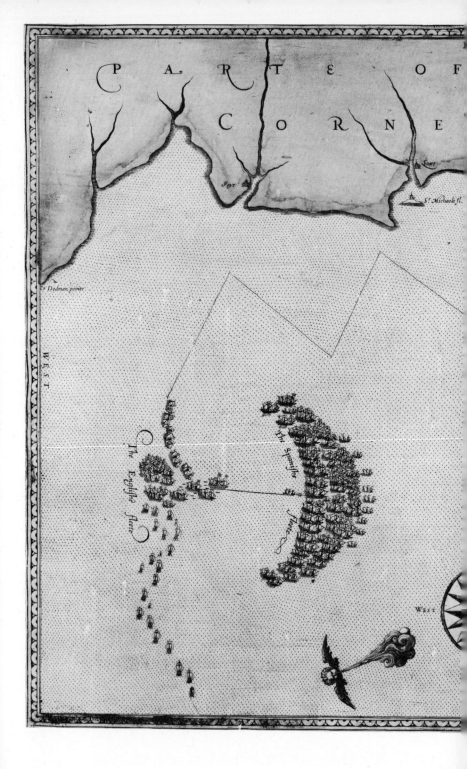

§52 The Armada. The English ships putting out fro[m]

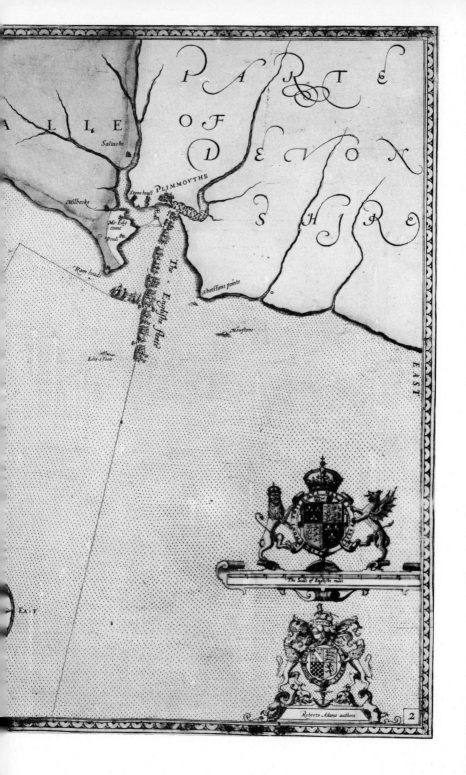

PARTE OF DEVON SHIRE

ALLE

Saltashe

Milbroke

Stonehouse  PLIMMOUTHE

Mo: Edg
come
ba
Penli

Ram head

The
English Fleete

shotssone pointe

Meustone

Edis-sTone

EAST

EAST

The Scale of Englishe miles

Roberto Adams authore

2

ymouth and tacking westward of the Spanish fleet

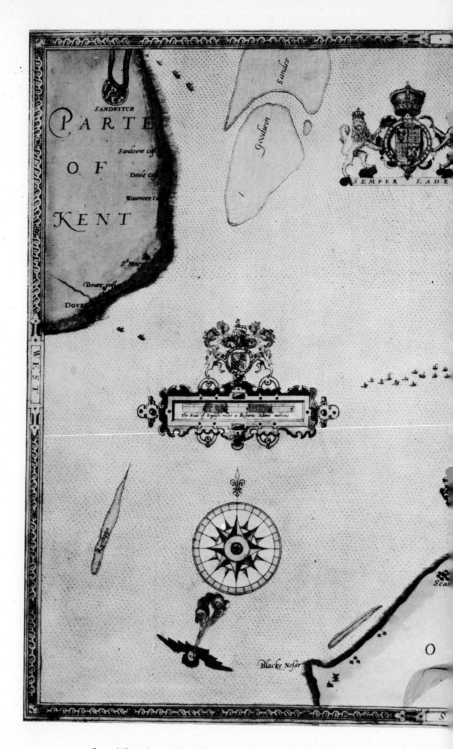

SANDWITCH

PARTE

OF

KENT

Sandowne ca...

Denle ca...

Waumore...

S<sup>t</sup> mar...

Dower casl

DOVER

Goodwin Sandes

SEMPER EADE...

The Estate of English under ye Roberte Adams auth...

WEST

Blacke Nesse

Sca...

O

S

§53 The Armada. The Spanish fleet (having been driven throu

The Spanishe Flote

PARTE OF FLANDERS

GRAVELING

CALAIS

PARTE

PICARDIE

straits) under continual English fire off the Goodwins

Habes Lector candide, fortiss. ac inuictiß. Ducis Draeck ad Uiuum imaginem qui
toto terrarum orbe, duorum annorum, et menßium decem spatio, Zephiris fauen:
tibus eircumducto, Anglium sedes proprias, 4. Cal. Octobr. anno á partu Virgi:
nis 1580. reuisit cum antea portu soluisset sd. Decemꝑ anni 1577.

§ 54 Sir Francis Drake

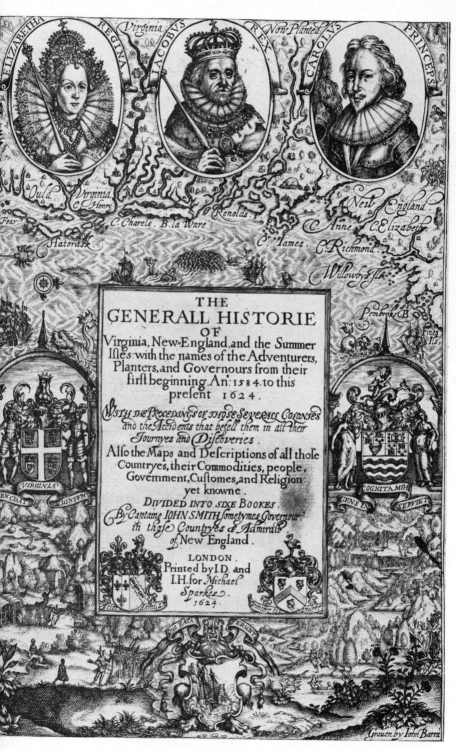

ELIZABETHA REGINA

Virginia

IACOBVS REX Now Planted

CAROLVS PRINCEPS

Ould Virginia C. Henry

Fear

Hatoraſk

C. Charels. B. la Ware

Renolds. I.

Ce. Iames

New England.

C. Anne C.E. Elizabeth

C. Richmond

Wilowbyes Iſle.

Pembroke. C.B.

THE
GENERALL HISTORIE
OF
Virginia, New-England, and the Summer
Iſles: with the names of the Adventurers,
Planters, and Governours from their
firſt beginning An:1584. to this
preſent 1624.

With the Proceedings of thoſe Severall Colonies
and the Accidents that befell them in all their
Journyes and Diſcoveries.

Alſo the Maps and Deſcriptions of all thoſe
Countryes, their Commodities, people,
Government, Cuſtomes, and Religion
yet knowne.

DIVIDED INTO SIXE BOOKES.

By Captaine IOHN SMITH ſometymes Governour
in thoſe Countryes & Admirall
of New England.

LONDON.
Printed by I.D. and
I.H. for Michael
Sparkes.
1624.

VIRGINIA

EN DAT VIRGINIA QVINTVM

COGNITA MIHI

GENS IN SERVIET

Graven by Iohn Barra

§55 Colonization under three reigns

§56 Peace with Spain and the Netherlands.
The Somerset House Conference, 1604

SECOTAN

Dasamonquepnc

Pasquenoke

WEAPEMEOC

Roanoac

Trinety harbor

Hatorask

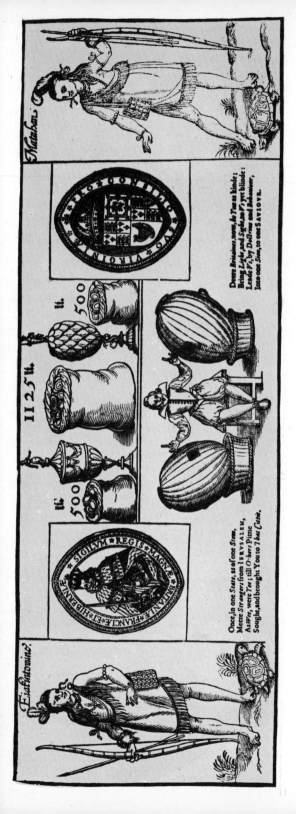

§58 The Lottery for Virginia in 1616

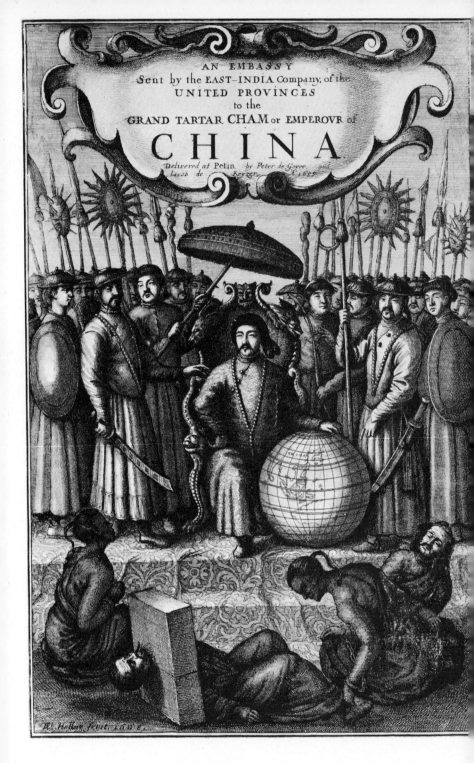

§59 An Embassy to China in 1655

## Chapter Three

## THE ENGLAND OF CHARLES AND CROMWELL

*The beginning of Colonial expansion. East India Company. Fen Draining.
Social conditions and consequences of the Great Rebellion. Household Life.*

(*James I, 1603–1625. Charles I, 1625–1649.
Long Parliament meets, 1640. Outbreak of Civil War, 1642:
Oliver Cromwell, Protector, 1653–1658.*)

IN the realm of social and economic history, the period of the
Stuart Kingship in England up to the outbreak of the Great
Rebellion may be regarded as an uneventful prolongation of the
Elizabethan era, under conditions of peace and safety instead of
domestic danger and foreign war. Agriculture, industry and
commerce all continued very much in the manner described in the
two preceding chapters. A rural society, in which landowner-
ship, opportunity and modest wealth were widely distributed,
gave ample scope and importance to the country gentlemen of
large and of small estates, and to the freehold and leasehold
yeomen. But there were hard times for many, partly owing to
the rise of prices. Industry and commerce moved forward on
the lines laid down in Tudor times. The companies founded in
the reign of Elizabeth for trading to distant parts of the world
grew in wealth and influence, and with them grew London, outstripping other cities more completely than before in population,
wealth, and all the attributes of power. In the country at large,
the apprentice system, the poor law, the regulation of wages and
prices, the economic and administrative functions of the Justices
of the Peace under the control and stimulus of the Privy Council,
were all much the same on the day when the Long Parliament
met as on the day when Queen Elizabeth died. No industrial,
agricultural or social change of importance took place in England
during the forty years when the Parliamentary and Puritan Revolution was germinating beneath the soil of an apparently stable
and settled society.

The slow pace of change in the economic and social life of
England in the first forty years of the new century was but little

accelerated by the union of the English and Scottish Monarchies in the person of Elizabeth's successor. The peoples, Parliaments, laws, Churches and commercial systems of the two Kingdoms remained for another century as separate and as different as before. Nor did any exchange of population result from the union of the Crowns. Scotland was too poor to attract, too jealous to welcome immigrants from England. When James Sixth of Scotland and First of England moved from Holyrood to Whitehall in 1603, he was accompanied or followed by a crowd of courtiers and needy adventurers, the first trickle of the great stream of Scots who have since come across the Border to seek their fortunes. But it was long before that stream swelled to proportions of national significance. Several generations were to pass before Scottish farmers, mechanics, gardeners, administrators, physicians and philosophers came swarming south, bringing with them skill, industry and knowledge sufficient to affect the life and increase the prosperity of England. Throughout the Seventeenth Century it was not to Scotland but to Holland that Englishmen looked for new ideas in religion, politics, agriculture, land-draining, gardening, commerce, navigation, philosophy, science and art.

Nor, under the Stuart Kings, did English thought and practice greatly affect the Scots, whose pride took quick alarm at influences emanating from their too powerful neighbour. Scottish religion had clothed herself in a strongly woven garment of native fabric, and was equally inimical to Anglicanism with its Prayer Book and to English Puritanism with its unorthodox sects. So, too, the peculiar spirit of Scottish society, feudal in the personal loyalty of the vassal to his lord, but equalitarian in the human intercourse between classes, was utterly unintelligible to the English mind until Sir Walter Scott's novels retrospectively afforded the key.

In overseas trade the merchants of the two countries were still rivals, the purse-proud English everywhere bearing the upper hand, and shutting out the Scots from foreign and colonial markets to the best of their power. At home the two peoples glowered at each other across the pacified border. Three hundred years of periodic warfare might be brought to an end by the union of the Crowns, but the long tradition of mutual injury and revenge from Falkirk and Bannockburn to Flodden and Pinkie Cleugh, had left animosities that took long to abate. In the civil and religious troubles of Stuart times, English and Scottish parties, Churches and soldiers often acted together for Parliament or for King, but the more they saw of one another the less they agreed, for the men of the two nations still moved on different planes of thought and feeling.

Slight and gradual as were the changes in England herself during the first forty years of the Seventeenth Century, little as the dynastic union with Scotland affected the social life of the time, these quiet years witnessed the greatest change of all, the beginning of the permanent expansion of the English race overseas. The successful founding of Colonies in Virginia, New England and West Indian Islands like Barbados, and the establishment of the first trading stations on the coast of Hindoostan, were the greatest events of the reign of James I and the early years of King Charles. [See § 55, 57.]

The English race began once more to move outside its island borders, this time in the right direction. The attempt made during the Hundred Years' War to reduce France to an English province had been the first instinctive gesture of an awakening national consciousness and a new-felt power to expand. After it had failed, the English had for a century and a half been confined to England, strengthening themselves there in wealth, intelligence and naval power; now they began once more to expand, by very different methods and under very different leadership from those of the day when

'Our King went forth to Normandy
With grace and might of chivalry.'

This time the 'good yeomen whose limbs were made in England' went forth again, but not with chivalry and not under the King, not with the long-bow to sack and conquer an ancient civilization, but with axe and plough to found a new civilization in the wilderness.

For this enterprise the first requisite was peace. So long as the war with Spain continued, England's limited stock of wealth and energy would run into fighting at sea, in Ireland and in the Netherlands. Under war conditions, the Elizabethan attempt to found Virginia had failed. In the first year of the new reign,

James I had the merit of making peace, on good terms which successful war had won. [See § 56.] In many respects his subsequent foreign policy was feeble and inept; he let down the strength of the navy and cut off Raleigh's head to please Spain. But at any rate his pacifism gave peace to England, and his subjects made use of that breathing space to sow the seed of the British Empire and of the United States. The restoration of an effective navy by Charles I and its maintenance by subsequent rulers enabled the movement to go forward in safety. Government maintained the conditions under which colonization was possible, but private enterprise supplied the initiative, the money and the men.

London Companies like the Virginia Company and the Massachusetts Bay Company financed and organized the emigration, which could never have taken place without such backing. The object of the noblemen, gentry and merchants who found the money, was partly to earn a good percentage on their immediate investments, but even more to create beyond the Atlantic a permanent market for English goods, in exchange for the products of the new world, such as the tobacco that Virginia soon produced in great quantities. Both patriotic and religious motives inspired many of those who supplied the funds, the ships and the equipment for the enterprise. Between 1630 and 1643 £200,000 was spent in conveying 20,000 men, women and children to New England in 200 ships: in the same period 40,000 more emigrants were conveyed to Virginia and other colonies.[1] [See § 57, 58.]

The very efficient 'promoters' of the movement included some of the noblest born and many of the wealthiest of the King's subjects: but the colonists themselves were of the middling and lower orders of town and village. In their minds, also, the motives of colonization were in part self-regarding and economic and in part ideal and religious. The religious motive had little or no weight with the majority of the settlers; but it inspired the leaders in New England, like the Pilgrim Fathers (1620), and after them John Winthrop and his colleagues. Their zeal imposed on the Northern group of colonies a Puritan character which was destined to affect powerfully the social development of the future United States.

[1] Godfrey Davies, *Early Stuarts* (Oxford Hist. Eng.), p. 337.

Those who crossed the Atlantic for religious reasons desired, in the words of Andrew Marvell, to escape from 'prelate's rage.' Under James, Charles and Laud, only one religion was tolerated in England and it was not the Puritan. Some of these religious refugees to New England desired to set up in the wilderness a Kingdom of God on the Geneva model, to be enforced upon all who chose to become citizens of the theocratic republic—for such in effect was early Massachusetts. But another type of Puritan exile, like Roger Williams the founder of Rhode Island, and the various groups of settlers in New Hampshire and Connecticut, not only wished to enjoy religious freedom themselves but were ready to extend it to others. Williams had been driven from Massachusetts because he maintained that the civil power had no authority over the consciences of men. Thus the difference between the two Puritan ideals, the coercive and the liberal, which soon afterwards split the ranks of the victorious Roundheads in the old country, had come to a head in New England as early as 1635. An easy-going attitude towards varieties of religion prevailed in Anglican Virginia, and in Maryland founded by the Roman Catholic Lord Baltimore.

The settlers in Virginia, the West Indian Islands and to a large extent even in New England, had not emigrated for religious motives at all. The ordinary colonist had been drawn oversea by the Englishman's characteristic desire to 'better himself,' which in those days meant to obtain land. Free land, not free religion was the promise held out in the pamphlets issued by the companies promoting the emigration. It was a period of land-hunger in England. Many younger sons of peasants and yeomen could obtain no land at home, and former copyholders often found themselves pushed out of their old secure franchise into the position of lease-holders or tenants at will. Rents were rising and tenants were competing hotly for farms. Unemployed craftsmen, too, could be sure that in the new settlements their skill would be in great demand. Many gentlemen adventurers were attracted not only by the prospect of land, but by the lure of the unknown and the marvellous, and by stories of fabulous riches to be won in America, which in fact only their remote descendants were to realize in ways undreamt. Early New England was not a land of great fortunes or of great contrasts in wealth.

All these classes of emigrants went freely, at the instigation of private enterprise and persuasion. The government only sent out convicts, and later on prisoners of the Civil Wars. These unfortunates, and other youths kidnapped by private enterprise to be sold into servitude in Barbados and Virginia, worked out their freedom if they lived long enough, and often founded prosperous families. For it was soon tacitly agreed that only negroes from Africa ought to be kept in perpetual bondage. The slave-trade, which Hawkins had begun with the Spanish colonies, now supplied Virginia and the English West Indian Islands.

During the Civil Wars of Charles and Cromwell the flow of voluntary emigration diminished. Virginia and Maryland were passively loyal to the King; and even the New England colonies, though sympathizing with the Puritan cause, remained neutral. For already the instinct of 'isolation' from the affairs of Europe was strong in America. Three thousand miles was a very long way, a voyage of several months of misery, during which death took its toll in the ill-found ships. And so, after the first few years, the social history of America ceased for ever to be a part of the social history of England. The new society began to work out its own characteristics, under pioneer conditions of life very different from those that prevailed in the 'garden of England' in the days of Shakespeare and Milton. None the less the Colonies were an offshoot of English Seventeenth Century life, and derived thence ideas and impulses that were to carry them far along new paths of destiny.

England at that period and for two hundred years to come was peculiarly fitted to provide colonists of the right sort. That is why the English language is spoken in North America and Australasia to-day. Until the later Nineteenth Century agricultural life and tradition flourished in England. The ordinary Englishman was not yet a townee, wholly divorced from nature; he was not yet a clerk or a specialized workman of one trade only, unable to adapt himself to pioneering conditions, unwilling to abandon the advantages of a high standard of living at home for a life of hardship and incessant toil in an unknown land. The Englishman of Stuart and Hanoverian times was more adaptable than his descendants and had stronger incentives to emigrate. No standard of life and no pensions for old age were secured to him at home beyond what he could win by his own efforts. The

Blacksmiths

The Cottage Housewife

Haymaking

poor law would keep him from starving, but no more. Moreover, the inhabitant of the Seventeenth Century English town still knew something of agriculture, and the inhabitant of the English village still knew something of craftsmanship. The townsmen tilled their 'town fields.' The village contained not only men to farm its land but men to build its cottages and barns, weave and cut its clothes, make its furniture, farm implements and harness. The cottage wives could bake, milk, cook, help in the harvest, spin, mend or make clothes, as well as rear families of children. A shipload of emigrants drawn from a number of such self-sufficing villages were capable of creating and maintaining a new village in the wilderness, even where there was no shopping town behind it to supply its needs.[1]

The makers of the early American settlements must have been men and women of most admirable versatility, endurance and courage. The greater part of the first colonists—more than three-quarters it is calculated—died prematurely, succumbing to the miseries of the voyage, or to disease, famine, exposure and Indian war. It was only a residue who survived the first years, to people and extend the woodland townships. In many respects it was the story of the Anglo-Saxon settlement of Britain over again—the struggle with virgin forest and marsh, the warfare with the old inhabitants. But the Anglo-Saxon invaders had been barbarians accustomed to savage life; the American settlers were men of civilized intelligence, some of them highly educated. In Massachusetts one of their first acts was to found a University —a Cambridge in the new land. For civilized people to endure hardships incident to primitive life requires fine qualities, which the England of that day was able richly to supply.

The newly founded colonies, whether on the mainland or on the islands, whether under the control of London Companies or more directly under the Crown, at once assumed a large degree of independence. They elected assemblies for the whole colony, and made each township a self-governing unit. In New England the Church congregation strengthened the tie and dominated the policy of the township. The instinct to extrude the authority of the homeland, whether exercised by King or by Company, was

---

[1] In some of the New England townships the first settlers established for a time the system of open village fields and common pasture to which they had been accustomed in England. Gilbert Slater, *English peasantry and the enclosures*, Chap. XVI.

present in the earliest settlements, especially in Massachusetts, though it only assumed continental proportions under George Washington.

The instinct of the first English settlers to manage their own affairs cannot be attributed solely to the great distance from Europe. Spanish, French and Dutch colonies in America and South Africa were no less remote, yet they long remained undemocratic in government and amenable to the authority of the homeland. The self-dependent attitude of the English settlements was partly due to the circumstances of their origin: they had not been founded by an act of State but by private initiative. And many of the colonists had come out with rebellious hearts, seeking to escape from the ecclesiastical government of England. The King of France, on the other hand, would allow no Huguenots in Canada.

Moreover, there were habits of self-government in old English society that were easily transplanted oversea. Thus the squirarchical tradition at home, the local government of the English shire by Justices of the Peace who were the local landowners, gave rise ere long in Virginia to the rule of an outdoor equestrian aristocracy of planters, whose life differed from that of English country gentlemen chiefly in the possession of negro slaves. This aristocratic system grew up naturally with the tobacco plantations that soon became the staple of that Colony's wealth.

In New England a Puritan democracy of farmers and tradesmen arose, which also had its roots in habits brought from the old country. In the early Seventeenth Century, the English shire and village still retained elements of communal self-government, beneath the higher control of the squires and Justices of the Peace. The freeholders had their part in the proceedings of the County Court. The Court Leet of the Manor was still attended by the peasantry who were, nominally and to some extent actually, the judges of the business there transacted. And in every English village there were various humble offices—such as constable, overseer of the poor, headborough, ale-conner, roadrepairer, churchwarden, sidesman and innumerable other small public posts—which the common people filled, either by election or rotation. These habits of local self-government at home helped the creation of the New England Township and Court House.

The emigrants also carried with them the jury system and the English common law, a law of liberty. Last but not least, the right of Parliament, as representing the people, to vote or refuse taxes was a doctrine widely diffused in the England of James and Charles I, especially among the opposition leaders, like Sir Edwyn Sandys, who did so much for the plantation of Virginia, and among the Puritan gentry and yeomen of East Anglia who took so leading a part in the settlement of New England. To such men the immediate establishment of colonial Assemblies seemed a matter of course.

The spirit of independence was further stimulated by the Bible-religion which the Colonists brought with them from home. Even in Massachusetts where the ministers and the godly at first tyrannized over the plain man, there was no sanction for the spiritual and social power they assumed, beyond the temporary acquiescence of their fellow-citizens. The New England ministers could not, like Laud's Anglican clergy, claim authority drawn from the King. Still less could they, like the Catholic priests who directed life in French Canada, exercise a spiritual rule of dateless antiquity derived from Rome. The only foundation for Church power in New England or in Virginia was popular opinion. And so the religion of English-speaking America soon became congregational rather than ecclesiastical, and served further to enhance the democratic spirit of trans-atlantic society.

In this way the American colonies were founded, by private enterprise—financial, commercial, agricultural, and politico-religious. The first application of State policy and military power to promote imperial development was Cromwell's conquest of Jamaica from Spain (1655), followed by Charles II's acquisition from the Dutch of the regions that became New York, New Jersey and Pennsylvania (1667). By that time it was beyond the power of State action to alter the self-dependent character of English colonial society. But the increasing need for the protection of colonial trade by the Royal fleet in the Atlantic, in the face of foreign enemies, rendered possible a policy of State interference with the course of that trade, exercised through the Navigation Laws. From the time of Cromwell onwards these laws were partially at least enforced. They aimed, not without a large measure of success, at enlarging the proportion of English commerce carried in English ships, and in keeping the trade of English colonies mainly for England.[1]

Meanwhile, on the other side of the globe, the ships of another London trading company were beginning another chapter of England's destiny. The East India Company founded by Elizabeth's charter of 1600, held thereby the monopoly among her subjects of trading with the 'East Indies,' the power of legislation and justice among its own servants oversea, and by implication the power of making peace and war beyond the Cape of Good Hope. For generations to come no ship of the Royal Navy rounded the Cape. The Crown made no pretence of being able to take action in the Far East to protect the nation's trade in those parts, as it protected the Atlantic trade with the American colonies. The Company had therefore to defend its factories with sepoys in its own pay; and at sea the great 'East Indiamen' built, equipped and manned at once for commerce and for war, replied with their broadsides to attacks made by Portuguese and Dutch rivals and by the pirates of all nations. But the Company was wisely careful to avoid quarrels with Indian Princes,and had no territorial or political ambition.

The first great Anglo-Indian statesman, Sir Thomas Roe, James I's Ambassador and the Company's agent at the Court of the Mogul Emperor, laid down the policy which guided the action of his countrymen in the East for more than a century to come.

'A war and traffic are incompatible. Let this be received as a rule that if you will profit, seek it at sea, and in quiet trade; for without controversy it is an error to affect garrisons and land-wars in India.'

So long as the Mogul Empire maintained its authority, as it did during the Stuart era, the Company was able to follow Roe's prudent advice. Only when the great Peninsula relapsed into anarchy, the English merchants, in the days of Clive, were unwillingly drawn into war and conquest to save their trade from Indian and French aggression.

Under the early Stuarts the Company established small trading stations at Madras, at Surat north of Bombay,[2] and by 1640 in

---

[1] A high authority on the original Settlements is Charles M. Andrews, *The Colonial Period of American History,* Vol. I, *The Settlements.* (Yale Univ. Press, 1933.)

[2] Later on, Charles II's Portuguese marriage brought Bombay itself as part of the Queen's dowry.

Bengal. The power and privileges they exercised within the walls of the towns and 'factories' assigned them were held by treaty with the native princes. Their enemies were the Portuguese, who soon ceased to be formidable, and the growing power of the Dutch, who drove them by force out of the coveted trade of the Spice Islands farther east (1623), compelling them to develop instead their position on the mainland of the Peninsula. From their factories in Madras and Bombay the English learnt to trade with Canton; ignorance of conditions in the Farther East prevented the London merchants from doing direct trade with China to any purpose, but the Company's servants in India had local knowledge enough to conduct it themselves, and to tap the great resources of Chinese commerce. [See § 59.] The London Company also sent ships direct to the Persian Gulf (first in 1628) to the annoyance of the Levant Company, which endeavoured to trade with the Shah's dominions by the overland route.

The East India trade, implying voyages a year long of ten thousand miles without breaking bulk, did more even than the American trade to develop the art of navigation and the character of ship-building. Already in the reign of James I the East India Company built 'goodly ships of such burthen as never were formerly used in merchandise.' While the ships of the Levant Company ranged from 100 to 350 tons for the Mediterranean traffic, the first voyage to India was made in a vessel of 600 tons, and the sixth voyage (1610) in a vessel of 1100 tons.[1]

The long Indian voyages would not have been possible as a means of regular trade if the crews had been much exposed to the ravages of scurvy. But from the very first (1600) the East India Company supplied its crews with 'lemon water' and oranges. The Royal Navy of Stuart and Hanoverian times was not protected in this manner, and the King's sailors suffered terribly, until Captain Cook, almost as great a sea-doctor as a discoverer of new continents, introduced marked improvements in naval drinks and diet.

In Stuart times the East India Company owned some thirty great vessels for the voyage round the Cape, besides numerous smaller craft that never left the Eastern seas. A considerable

---

[1] Grenville's *Revenge*, one of the large ships of the Elizabethan navy, was 500 tons. The *Mayflower* was only 180 tons; she had previously been engaged in the wine trade between English and Mediterranean ports.

proportion were wrecked, or taken by pirates or by Dutch. But those great ships that survived were so strongly built of the best English oak as to be able to face the high seas for thirty or even for sixty years. Already in James I's reign 'the Company laid out at one time £300,000 in building shipping, which was more than King James had then in the navy.' The Indian trade thus 'filled the nation with great ships and expert mariners.'

Here was a private navy, heavily armed, added to the strength of England. Knowledge of the most difficult parts of navigation, and the habit of distant maritime enterprise became widely spread among the English. London, as the headquarters of the East India Company, drew to itself England's trade with the Orient. Bristol shared in the tobacco and slave trades across the Atlantic, and Liverpool soon followed suit ; but the general effect of the American and Indian trades, and the increase in the size of merchant ships, was to enhance yet further the supremacy of London at the expense of many lesser ports that had sufficed for the small ships and short voyages of earlier times.

The Indian trade increased not only the shipping, but the wealth of England. It proved indeed impossible to sell more than a limited quantity of English cloth in the warm climate of the Far East, and the enemies of the Company always made that a ground of accusation. But Queen Elizabeth had very wisely permitted the Company to export a certain quantity of coin of the realm, on condition that as much gold and silver was returned after each voyage. By 1621, £100,000 exported in bullion, brought back oriental wares worth five times as much, of which only a quarter was consumed at home. The rest was resold abroad at great profit and so, to meet the bullionist criticism, 'the treasure of the realm was increased.'

Before the Civil War, the chief articles conveyed to the Thames in the Company's great ships were saltpetre (for warlike Europe's gunpowder), raw silk, and above all spices, particularly pepper. The scarcity of fresh meat in winter before the era of roots and artificial grasses was a chief reason why our ancestors craved for spices; they were used both to preserve meat, and to season it highly when it had little else to recommend it. After the Restoration, tea and coffee came in, and silks manufactured in the East for the European market, and porcelain of China. By the time of Queen Anne, the East Indian trade had materially altered the drink, the habits of social intercourse, the dress and the artistic taste of the well-to-do classes among her subjects.

These long-distance trading companies, with their great losses and greater profits, became an important part of social and political life under the Stuarts. Their wealth and influence were generally thrown against the Crown in the Civil War, partly for religious reasons and because London was prevalently Roundhead, and partly because the merchants were discontented with the treatment they had received from James and Charles I. Monopolies for the production and sale in England of many articles in common use, had been granted to courtiers and intriguing patentees. This policy, enlarged by Charles I as a means of raising non-Parliamentary revenue by his Prerogative, was frowned on by the common lawyers and Parliament men, and was for very good reasons unpopular with the consumer who found the price of the articles raised, and with the merchant community who saw trade restricted and disturbed.

But the merchants of the East India House felt even more aggrieved because the King, while granting such unneeded monopolies in the home market, infringed their own much needed monopoly of trade in the Far East, though the whole cost of political and military action in that side of the globe fell on the Company and not on the Crown. Charles I had set up a second company for Indian trade—the Courteen Association—which by its rivalry and its mismanagement had nearly ruined all English trade in the Far East, at the time the Long Parliament met. The policy of Pym and Parliament, to suppress Monopolies in England and maintain them for the companies trading oversea, was much better liked in the City. One of the most important results of the victory of the Parliamentary armies in the Civil War was the virtual abolition of monopolies inside the country. Henceforward, though foreign and Indian trade was subject to regulation, industry in England was free, as compared to European countries where mediaeval restrictions still hampered its growth. This was one reason why England in the Eighteenth Century led the world in the race of the Industrial Revolution.

The early Stuart Kings had done nothing effective either in Europe or in Asia to restrain the Dutch from destroying the Company's ships and factories in the East. The 'massacre of

Amboyna' (1623) when the Dutch drove the English traders from the Spice Islands, was a memory that sank deep. More than thirty years later Cromwell exacted compensation for this old injury, by war and diplomacy in Europe. The Protector indeed did much to 'protect' English trade and interests all over the world. But the expense of his military and naval establishment was a burden that before he died was getting too heavy for commerce, and the Restoration, bringing disarmament and lower taxes, came as an economic relief. Cromwell's posthumous reputation as the great 'Imperialist' was in no sense undeserved. By his conquest of Jamaica he set an example to all future governments which Elizabeth had never set, of taking the opportunities afforded by war to seize distant colonies from other European powers.

The rivalry of the Courteen Association followed by the troubles of the Civil Wars in England, had almost destroyed the East India Company and put an end to the English connection with India. But during the Protectorate the old Company, with Cromwell's help, re-established its shaken prosperity and assumed its permanent financial form as a single joint-stock enterprise. Hitherto, money had been raised for each separate voyage (usually indeed on the joint-stock principle). The earliest voyages had often realized 20 or 30 per cent., sometimes 5 per cent., sometimes a dead loss due to battle or wreck. But in 1657 a permanent fund, the 'New General Stock,' was instituted for all future purposes. For thirty years after the Restoration the profit on the original stock averaged first 20 and later 40 per cent. per annum. The market price of £100 stock touched £500 in 1685. There was no need to increase the amount of the original stock, since the Company was in so strong a position that it could borrow short loans at very low interest, sometimes 3 per cent., and reap enormous profits with these temporary borrowings.

The great wealth derived from Eastern trade therefore remained in a few hands, chiefly of very rich men. Under the last Stuart Kings, Sir Josiah Child could set aside great sums of money to bribe the Court before 1688, and Parliament afterwards, in the interest of the Company's monopoly. The general public, having to pay very high prices for the stock if they were allowed to buy it at all, grew every year more indignant that no one except a few fortunate shareholders in a close concern was permitted to trade beyond the Cape. 'Interlopers' from Bristol and elsewhere sent out ships to carry on a 'free trade.' But the Company's monopoly, however unpopular, was legal, and its agents enforced the law with a high hand, in regions a year's sail distant from Westminster, where strange, unreported incidents took place by sea and land between English rivals in high rage with one another.

The struggle between Josiah Child and the Interlopers in the reigns of Charles and James II and William, was only a repetition on a larger scale of the struggle between the Company and its rivals under James and Charles I and Cromwell. All through the Stuart era, there was eager and angry competition, economic and political, for a share in the profits of the Indian trade, all the more because there was no easy, common way of finding investment for money, though savings were rapidly accumulating. There was no regular stock market where a man could make his choice among a number of reasonably hopeful ventures offering shares for sale. The usual way of investing money was to purchase land or mortgages on land. But the amount of land was limited, and it was, moreover, an article which owners were, for reasons other than economic, exceedingly unwilling to sell; the social and the sporting value of landed estate made it hard to buy. And so the question what to do with one's money, other than keep it in a strong-box at home, puzzled many people, from the nobleman to the thrifty yeoman and artisan.

Four-fifths of the population was tilling the land, but a gradually increasing proportion were engaged in trade or industry, more often in the country than in the town. It was a day of small businesses, rapidly increasing in number. A yeoman or craftsman who had saved a little money could not in those days use it to buy Consols or railway or brewery shares. He might spend some of it in a marriage portion to provide his daughter with a husband as an establishment for life. For the rest he would very likely invest his savings in a new venture of his own, employing a few apprentices and journeymen to set up an industry or a shop, or perhaps buying horses, carts and pack-saddles to serve the neighbourhood as a carrier.

The number of such small employers and tradesmen was on the increase, and they, like the East India Company, often wanted to borrow money for their business. So, too, did landowners—not only the squire in distress due to extravagance, but the squire prudently eager to drain, clear and improve his land, and increase the agricultural acreage at the expense of wood and waste. How did these various classes of 'adventurers' borrow money for their enterprises? How were they put in touch with persons wishing to lend and to invest ?

Society had at last, very gradually, in the course of the Tudor reigns, abandoned the mediaeval doctrine that it was wrong to lend money on interest. Lending money on reasonable terms had now been made legal by Act of Parliament, and therefore interest was less exorbitant. Thinkers who led opinion under the early Stuarts, clearly saw the use of a money market. "Tis a vain thing,' Selden told his friends, 'to say money begets not money, for that no doubt it does.' And the very practical mercantile philosopher, Thomas Mun, wrote: 'How many merchants and shopkeepers have begun with little or nothing of their own, and yet are grown very rich by trading with other men's money.'

As yet indeed there were no banks in England. But there were persons who performed some of the functions of modern bankers, receiving deposits and lending out money on interest. Brokers and scriveners, in the way of their ordinary business, had special opportunities to oblige clients by arranging such operations, or by bringing borrower and lender together.

During the Commonwealth and after the Restoration the holding and lending of money passed more and more into the hands of the goldsmiths of London. The merchants of the City had been accustomed to keep their spare cash in the Tower Mint, but after Charles I seized it there, they preferred to trust the goldsmiths. At the outbreak of civil strife, when the wealthy of both sides melted their plate into 'pikes and musketeers,' the goldsmiths' ordinary occupation of selling gold and silver vessels was suspended during the years of war, and they were glad instead to become 'the merchants' cash-keepers, to receive and pay for nothing, few observing or conjecturing the profit they had for their pains.' So great indeed was the profit, that the goldsmiths soon found it worth while to encourage deposits by paying interest—under Charles II they gave six per cent.! For they employed the deposits to great advantage in lending to others.

The principal goldsmiths thus engaged were those in Lombard Street.[1]

The goldsmiths' business as 'proto-bankers' was by no means confined to dealings with city merchants. Many landowners had their rents paid into the goldsmiths' hands; while others, all the country over, came to Lombard Street for loans. The value of these new conveniences can be illustrated by examining the actual method by which a certain noble family managed its extensive affairs in the reign of Charles I.

In 1641, the year of Strafford's execution, died Francis Russell, Fourth Earl of Bedford.[2] There was no bank in which his money could be kept; there were no cheques by which his heir could pay it out. There was, however, a 'great trunk' in Bedford House in the Strand, where his current cash lay guarded by the family servants. The young Earl William, the first time he opened the trunk as its owner, found therein £1557. 14. 1. Out of this he paid all the expenses of his father's funeral and other bills, in money of the realm. But the trunk was speedily replenished: in the next twelve months, immediately preceding the outbreak of the Civil War, the cash poured into it amounted to £8500, a sum worth many times as much in terms of present-day money. It represented rents, and 'fines' for the renewal of leases, while a thousand pounds were accounted for by sales of wood, malt, tallow, sheepskins, hay and other produce of the Russell home farms.

The Earl's principal Steward lived in Bedford House, kept the key of the all-important trunk, and was, in fact, the family treasurer or receiver-general, permanently residing in London. Everything paid to the Earl, or almost everything, came up to the Steward and was by him placed in the trunk and taken out again as required. In 1641 the largest single item came from the great estates in Devon and Cornwall, which sent up £2500 that year. For these western estates—and for them alone—a modern

---

[1] The origin, or one of the origins, of cheques, took the form of notes sent to goldsmiths or others asking them to pay out so much money to such and such a person from the money the writer of the note had lodged with its recipient. The first printed cheques were issued by the Bank of England early in the Eighteenth Century.

[2] For what follows see the excellent book of Miss Scott Thomson, *Life of a Noble Household 1641-1700* (1937), a remarkable contribution to social history in many of its aspects.

and convenient method had already been adopted of transferring the money to London. The estates in East Anglia and other parts sent up hard money guarded from highwaymen by the Earl's mounted servants. But at Exeter there sat a 'Steward of the West.' His office was an old Russell mansion in the western capital, to which the Bailiffs of the various manors in Devon and Cornwall came with hard cash and accounted for the audit at Lady Day and Michaelmas. The Steward of the West, with the moneys thus received by him at Exeter, arranged for a bill of exchange to be drawn upon one of the London goldsmiths, the celebrated Thomas Viner of Lombard Street. When Viner had received the bill, he gave notice to the Steward at Bedford House, who went with bags and porters to fetch away an equivalent sum of coined money from 'Lumber-Street' and deposit it in the trunk.[1]

But the Earls of Bedford, though certainly ' spacious in the possession of dirt,' were by no means mere passive receivers of rent. Francis, the Earl who died in 1641, and his son William the first Duke, who died in 1700, nearly covered the century between them as owners of the Russell property, and as such did a greater work for England than they achieved by their cautious political patronage of 'the good old Cause' in its more moderate aspect. The labour of their lives was given to the improvement of their great and widely scattered properties in London, Bedfordshire, the South-west and in the Fen District. Their very genuine but unobtrusive Puritan religion strengthened and in no wise disturbed their fulfilment of the duties of an English country gentleman upon the national scale.

To these two men, more than to any others, was due the successful initiation of the drainage of Fenland. One of their ancestors while serving Queen Elizabeth in the Low Countries, had observed with wonder how Holland had been built up out of the waters, and brought back with him a Dutch engineer to look at the Russell estate in the Fens, formerly the land and water of the Thorney monks. The project thus engendered in the family mind was given reality forty years later by Earl Francis. In 1630 he promoted the formation of a company of 'adventurers'

[1] The importance of the operations of some of these 'goldsmiths' may be judged from the fact that this Thomas Viner supplied large quantities of bullion and plate both to Cromwell and to the East India Company, and contracted for coining it into money. In 1656 he and Alderman Blackwell bought Spanish prize plate to the value of £60,000.

to drain a large region of South Fenland round Ely Isle. The Earl 'adventured' by far the greatest sum—ultimately at least £100,000. The 'adventurers' were each allotted portions of the land to be drained, answering to the amount of their several investments.

On the advice of Vermuyden, another Dutch engineer, it was decided that it would not suffice to deepen the old winding river-courses; a straight canal, seventy feet wide and twenty-one miles long, was cut from Earith to Denver Sluice. This became known as the Old Bedford River, when twenty years later the New Bedford River was cut in a parallel line to help it at its work. The waters, constantly piling up from the distant catchment area of the Ouse, at last ran freely away down these new channels, instead of spreading over the Fenland as they had done from time immemorial. Arable and pasture were rapidly substituted on the reclaimed lands for fishing, fowling, and reed growing. The change was resented by the fenmen, whose ancestors had for countless generations lived an amphibious life with a fixed economy of its own. (See pp. 9–11 above.) Now, at one blow, their occupation was gone. Whether they received proper compensation for this loss of livelihood we have not the evidence to decide. At any rate they waged a war of midnight raids to cut the dykes as fast as they were built, seriously impeding progress.

During the Civil War the work of drainage was at a standstill, or rather went back, for the destruction of the dykes by their enemies went on apace in the disordered time. But under the Commonwealth, partly through the labour of Scottish and Dutch prisoners of war, the first great stage was completed. Under the Protector, who favoured the enterprise,[1] crops were already growing and cattle feeding over scores of thousands of acres, of late the reedy home of bittern and wild duck. The Earl reaped the reward of his own and his father's 'adventure.' Before 1660 he had paid off the mortgages on all the Russell estates, many of them incurred to drain the fenland which had now made good the investment.

At the Restoration, the draining of the fens, so far as it had yet gone, seemed to be an engineering and an economic success.

---

[1] In 1638 'Mr. Cromwell,' then of local celebrity only, had opposed the injustice of the drainage award in the interest of the Commoners, but he was not opposed to the scheme of reclamation, and in 1649 advocated an Act for its completion.

But before the end of the Century new and grave difficulties had arisen, due to the opposition not of man but of nature. At first the rapid outfall of the new canals had scoured and kept open the estuaries of Ouse and Nene, but as time went on these exits to the sea began to silt up. Moreover, the level of the lands drained by the new system began unexpectedly to fall; the black peaty earth shrank as soon as it was dry, as a sponge shrinks when water is squeezed out of it. The consequence was that the Bedford River and the other canals stood up above the surrounding country, like the similar 'rivers' that drain Holland. Means had therefore to be devised to pump the water up out of the low fields into the high ditches and thence into the still higher canals that were to take it to the sea. Throughout the Eighteenth Century this was the problem, partly solved by the erection of hundreds of windmills to raise the water; they formed a picturesque feature in the flat landscape, but they were not wholly effective. The solution came—so far as it has ever come—in the early Nineteenth Century, when steam-driven pumps were employed instead of windmills. [See § 67, 68, 69.]

Even during the Eighteenth Century, when the drainage difficulty was at its worst, the success of the work of reclamation done in Southern Fenland in the valleys of the Ouse and Nene, was so manifest that similar undertakings were carried out in the Northern Fens, watered by the Welland and the Witham, round Spalding, Boston and Tattershall. Wherever draining took place, the shrinking and attrition of the peat brought the underlying layer of rich clay nearer the surface. In the Eighteenth and Nineteenth Centuries the clay was increasingly dug up to manure the land, or became the land itself by the total disappearance of the peat. To-day the Fenland is one of the best arable soils in England.

Thus, in spite of natural difficulties which are not yet entirely overcome, a great work was accomplished, and a new, rich province, eighty miles long, and ten to thirty miles broad, was added to the farmland of the Kingdom. It had not, like the older fields of England, been won from the waste by the gradual encroachment of innumerable peasants and landowners, diligently working through centuries to increase bit by bit each his own estate. The victory over nature in Fenland was due to the accumulation of capital and its application to an enterprise conceived beforehand on a large scale by men who were ready to risk great sums of money and wait twenty years or more for a return. The draining of the fens is an old-world story, but it is an early example of the working of modern economic methods, and as such worthy of special remark in a social history of England. (H. C. Darby, *Historical Geography of England,* Chap. XII, and his book on *The Draining of the Fens,* 1940; Gladys Scott Thomson, *Life of a Noble Household.*)

Before we return to the early Stuart period, let us follow a little further the economic history of the House of Russell, after the great venture of the fen-draining had turned out so well under the Commonwealth. The family fortunes had been laid long ago in trade with Gascony from Weymouth quay in the days of Chaucer. Three hundred years later, in the days of William III, the Russells went back into overseas trade by a marriage alliance with the governing family of the East India Company. The first Duke of Bedford, who had inherited the Earldom and the family trunk from his father in 1641 and had seen the fens successfully drained, was living at the close of the century in honoured and prosperous old age, but melancholy from the loss of that loved son William who, with less political moderation than his father and grandfather, had given his life for 'the good old cause' by the scaffold and axe in 1683. A dozen years later the old Duke married his grandson and heir to Elizabeth, grand-daughter of Josiah Child and daughter of John Howland of Streatham, the rulers of the East India Company. The bridegroom was 14, the bride 13 years old. It was a marriage of great splendour, with many coaches attendant. Bishop Burnet performed the ceremony. But after the banquet arose a hue and cry. 'The bride and bridegroom were missing. They had slipped away after dinner to play together, and in their play the costly point lace trimming of the young lady's dress had been torn to pieces. She was found hiding in a barn, while her new lord and master was strolling back with seeming innocence to the wedding company.'

And so, by this child marriage, which in the course of years proved happy enough, the Russells got in on the ground floor of the East India Company. They did not come empty handed. As they had formerly put their money into fen drainage, so now they put it into building new docks at Rotherhithe and great vessels for the Cape voyage, which they presented in noble style to the Court of Directors. One ship was called the *Tavistock*. Another called the *Streatham,* built by the old Duke in the year of his death in 1700, survived so many voyages that it carried Clive back to India in 1755.

If the 'great families' had an overlarge share in governing England in the Eighteenth Century, they had done something to earn it. By wise activity in other spheres besides politics and administration they played a great part in the development of the country by land and by sea, they had the interests of trade as much in their minds as the interests of land, and in their veins flowed the blood of merchants and lawyers no less than of soldiers and country gentlemen. The French *noblesse,* with greater privileges, including exemption from taxes, was a close caste with few functions and limited outlook.

But let us return to the generation that followed the death of Queen Elizabeth. The gradual but constant rise of prices, largely due to the flow of silver from the Spanish-American mines into Europe, made it impossible for James and Charles I to 'live on their own revenues,' and their Parliaments were unwilling to make good the deficiency except on religious and political conditions which the Stuart Kings were unwilling to accept. And the same rise of prices, though always injurious to people with fixed incomes and often to wage-earners, tended to enrich the more enterprising of the landowners and yeomen and above all the merchants—precisely the classes who were becoming most opposed to the monarchy on religious and political grounds. These economic causes contributed to bring about the Civil War and to decide its issue.

The financial embarrassments of the Crown had an unfortunate effect on the economic policy of the State. We have already seen how the royal power to control trade, by the grant of 'monopolies' in the manufacture and sale of certain classes of goods, was used not for the public interest but to raise revenue for a distressed monarch, endeavouring to make his Prerogative financially self-supporting. Those expedients were harmful to trade and politically injurious to the popularity of the royal cause.

But in one aspect of economic and social policy—the Poor Law—the continuance and enlargement of the system laid down under Queen Elizabeth was a credit to the Crown, and to the system of Privy Council government with which the names of Strafford and Laud are associated. The historian of the English Poor Law has written [1] that the survival of an effective system of poor relief in England alone of the greater nations of Europe—

was mainly caused by the coexistence in England of a Privy Council active in matters concerning the poor and of a powerful body of county and municipal officers who were willing to obey the Privy Council. Even in the reign of Elizabeth the Privy Council sometimes interfered in enforcing measure of relief, but only as a temporary expedient for relieving the distress caused by years of scarcity. But from 1629 to 1640 they acted continuously in that direction, and by means of the Book of Orders succeeded, as far as children and the impotent poor were concerned, in securing the due execution of the law. The Council also succeeded in inducing the Justices of the Peace to provide work for the able-bodied poor in many of the districts in the eastern counties and in some places in almost every county. This provision of work was provided either in Houses of Correction or in the Parishes. . . The substance of the orders does not appear to have excited opposition. Men of both parties sent in their reports to the Privy Council, and more energetic measures to execute the poor law were taken in the Puritan counties of the east than in any other part of England.

We shall have occasion in later chapters to consider the serious faults of poor law administration in the Eighteenth Century. Some of them resulted from the decline of the control exercised by the Privy Council over local magistrates and parishes, a decay of much-needed central authority which was the heavy price paid for Parliamentary government and constitutional freedom. But the Poor Law had taken such firm root in the days of Royal Prerogative that it survived as custom of the country in Parliamentary times.

The worst horrors of failure, of unemployment and of unprovided old age were not suffered by the poor in England to the same extent as in the continental countries of the *ancien régime*. The regiments of beggars, such as continued to swarm in the streets of Italy, and of France under Louis XIV, were no longer known over here. The scandal and danger of such congregations had alarmed the Tudor and early Stuart governments; the Poor Law was meant to prevent them, and did prevent them by the

---

[1] Miss E. M. Leonard, *Early History of English Poor Relief*, 1900, pp. 293-294. See also Vol. I, p. 107 of the present work, and p. 31 above.

only practical method, the relief of distress and the provision of work.[1] That is one reason why there was never anything like the French Revolution in our country, and why through all our political, religious and social feuds from the Seventeenth to the Nineteenth Centuries the quiet and orderly habits of the people, even in times of distress, continued upon the whole as a national characteristic.

There was no effective system of police until that begun by Sir Robert Peel in 1830. It was a disgraceful condition of things, and had many evil consequences. But the wonder is that society held together at all without the protection of a strong civic force trained to control mob violence and to detect theft and crime. That we dispensed so long with a proper police force is a testimony to the average honesty of our ancestors and to the value of the old Poor Law, in spite of all its defects.

The personal liberty of the poor was not a thing of which much account was taken. The philanthropic action of the State was curtailed by no such consideration. The Poor Law system involved sending the idler (the 'unemployable') to the House of Correction and clapping the drunkard in the stocks. Some, though by no means all, of the Puritans' interference with the lives of their fellow-citizens, that became so intolerable under the Commonwealth, was common form to all religious sects and all shades of political opinion.

The clear modern distinction between offences punishable by the State on the one hand, and 'sins' not cognizable by a court of law upon the other, was not yet so rigid in men's minds as it afterwards became. Mediaeval ideas still survived and the Church Courts still existed to punish 'sin,' though with diminished powers. In Scotland indeed the Presbyterian Church exacted penance for sexual offences more rigidly than the Roman Church had been able to do. In Laud's England the Church Courts attempted something of the same kind, but much more cautiously and even so with disastrous results. The 'libertines' joined the Puritans in the outcry against the Bishops' Courts, though for very different reasons. The 'libertine' objected to standing publicly in a white sheet for adultery or fornication. The Puritan,

[1] In 1631 the Mayor and Recorder of King's Lynn reported that they had 'bought materials to set the able-bodied poor on work, not suffering to our knowledge any poor to straggle and beg up and down the streets of this Burgh.'

on the other hand, thought even more strongly than the Bishop that 'sin' should be punished, but he thought that he and not the Bishop should punish it. The outcome was that the Englishman threw off the yoke first of Bishop and then of Puritan, and the attempt to punish 'sin' judicially lapsed after the Restoration and was never seriously renewed south of the Border.

Under English Puritan rule, it was not the Church Courts but the ordinary lay Courts of the land that were charged with the suppression of sin. In 1650 an Act had been passed punishing adultery with death, and the savage penalty was actually inflicted in two or three cases. After that even Puritan juries refused to convict and the attempt broke down. But during this period, public opinion supported the laws to suppress duelling, which had more success, until the Restoration restored the liberty of the bravo. The employment of soldiers to enter private houses in London to see that the Sabbath was not being profaned, and that the Parliament fasts were being observed—carrying off meat found in the kitchen—aroused the fiercest anger. So, too, in many places did the cutting down of Maypoles and the forbidding of sports on Sunday afternoon. Yet the ban on 'Sabbath' games substantially survived the Restoration. In spite of the Anglican and liberal reaction of 1660, the Puritans left their sad mark on the 'English Sunday' in permanence. [See § 73, 74, 75, 76.]

The horrible mania for persecuting witches, common to Catholic and Protestant lands during the period of the religious wars, was less bad in England than in some countries, but touched its highest point in the first half of the Seventeenth Century. It was caused by a sincere belief in the reality of witchcraft held by all classes, including the most educated, and it only receded as the governing class in the later Seventeenth and early Eighteenth Century gradually reached a point of scepticism on the subject that induced them to stop the witch-hunt, in spite of the continued credulity of the mass of the population. The two worst periods in England were during the first half of the reign of the credulous James I, and during the rule of the Long Parliament (1645–1647) when 200 witches were executed in the eastern counties, chiefly as a result of the crusade of Matthew Hopkins the witch-finder. The government of Charles I and of the Regicide Republic and Protectorate were both honourably marked by a cessation of this foolish atrocity.

In England before the Restoration it would have been difficult to find more than a handful of men who openly avowed a disbelief in the miraculous sanctions of the Christian faith, in one or other of its forms. But there were many Englishmen in whom a dislike of the pretensions of the pious, whether Anglican priests, or Puritan 'saints,' was stronger than positive enthusiasm for any religious doctrine. In this limited, English sense of the word, 'anti-clericalism' has again and again been the decisive makeweight in the balance between religious parties in England. Anti-clericalism had been the chief motive force in the destruction of the mediaeval Church under Henry VIII. In his daughter's long reign it had nerved the national resolution against the Spain of the Inquisition, while at home it had no quarrel with the modest and unprovocative clergy of Elizabeth's tame Church. But when, under Charles I's patronage, Bishops and clergy raised their heads again in social and political life, and even occupied offices of State once more as in the Middle Ages, the jealous laity took alarm. The anti-clerical feeling of great nobles, angry at the presence of clergymen in the Council Chamber and the Royal Closet, and of the London mob howling against Bishops in Palace Yard (1640–1641), joined itself in a blind alliance with Puritanism, then at the apex of its influence, and enabled the Long Parliament to break the Laudian Church.

After the triumph of the Parliamentary armies came the 'rule of the saints,' with their canting piety used as a shibboleth to obtain the favour of the dominant party; their interference with the lives of ordinary people; their closing of the theatres and suppressing of customary sports. Anti-clerical feeling, thus provoked, reacted so violently as to become one of the chief causes of the Restoration of 1660. A generation later it was one of the chief causes of the anti-Romanist Revolution of 1688. For many generations to come, hatred of Puritanism took its place beside hatred of Romanism in the instincts and traditions of the chapel-burning mobs, as well as of the great majority of the upper class. [See § 76.]

The Cromwellian revolution was not social and economic in its causes and motives; it was the result of political and religious thought and aspiration among men who had no desire to recast society or redistribute wealth. No doubt the choice of sides that men made in politics and religion was to some extent and in some cases determined by pre-dispositions due to social and economic circumstance; but of this the men themselves were only half conscious. There were more lords and gentlemen on the side of the King, more yeomen and townsfolk on the side of Parliament. Above all, London was on the side of Parliament. Yet every class in town and country was itself divided. [See § 77.]

The stage of economic and social development which had been reached in the England of 1640 was not the cause, but it was a necessary condition, of the political and religious movements that burst forth into sudden blaze. The astonishing attempt of Pym, Hampden and the other Parliamentary leaders to wrest power from the Monarchy in good earnest, and to govern the State through an elected debating assembly of several hundred members, and the degree of success which that bold innovation actually attained in politics and war, pre-supposed not only an old Parliamentary tradition but the existence of a powerful bourgeoisie, gentry and yeomanry, long liberated from ecclesiastical and feudal control, and long accustomed to share with the monarchy in the work for government. So too the rapid rise to national importance, and for a while to national predominance, of innumerable sects such as Baptists and Congregationalists could not have occurred except in a society where there was much personal and economic independence in the yeomen and artisan classes, and in a country where for nearly a century past the individual study of the Bible had been a great part of religion, and the chief stimulant of popular imagination and intellect. If there had been newspapers, magazines and novels to compete with the Bible in manor-house, farm and cottage, there would have been no Puritan revolution—and John Bunyan would never have written *Pilgrim's Progress.*

Indeed, the Puritan Revolution was itself, in its basic impulse, a 'Pilgrim's Progress.' 'I dreamed [wrote Bunyan], and behold I saw a Man clothed with rags, standing in a certain place, with his face from his own house, a Book in his hand, and a great burden upon his back. I looked, and saw him open the book and read therein; and as he read, he wept and trembled; and not being able longer to contain, he broke out with a lamentable cry, saying *"What shall I do?"* ' [See § 78.]

That lonely figure, with the Bible and the burden of sin, is not only John Bunyan himself. It is the representative Puritan of the English Puritan epoch. When Bunyan was a young man in the years that followed Naseby, Puritanism had come to its moment of greatest force and vigour, in war, in politics, in literature, and in social and individual life. But the inner pulse of the machine that drove all that tremendous energy tearing its way athwart the national life

> 'To cast the Kingdoms old
> Into another mould,'

the prime motive force of it all was just this lonely figure of the first paragraph in *Pilgrim's Progress*—the poor man seeking salvation with tears, with no guide save the Bible in his hand. That man, multiplied, congregated, regimented, was a force of tremendous potency, to make and to destroy. It was the force by which Oliver Cromwell and George Fox and John Wesley wrought their wonders, being men of a like experience themselves.

But it would be a mistake to suppose that this earnestness of personal and family religion was confined to the Puritans and the Roundheads. The Memoirs of the Verney family and many other records of the time show us Cavalier households as religious as the Puritan, though not so wearisomely obtrusive with scripture phrases for every common act of life. Many of the small gentry and yeomen, particularly in the northern and western half of England, felt, like humble and patient Alice Thornton, that the Church of England was that 'excellent, pure and glorious church then established, which for soundness in faith and doctrine, none could parallel since the Apostles' time.' As her biographer has said:

Her account of the religious life of the family must dispel any illusion that to be Church of England, as opposed to the Nonconformists, meant that religion was to be taken any more lightly. The whole family was called to prayers by a little bell at six in the morning, at two in the afternoon and again at nine at night. (Wallace Notestein, *English Folk,* p. 186.)

Many families in all ranks of life who fought and suffered for the Church and the Prayer Book, by those sufferings learnt a love of the Church of England which had not been so consistently felt and expressed before the Civil War as it was after the

Restoration. And that love for the Church as Laud had refashioned it continued, until the Nineteenth Century, to be combined with a family and personal piety and a study of the Bible that was common to all English Protestants who took their religion seriously.

But there are other things in *Pilgrim's Progress* besides the most perfect representation of evangelical religion. The way of the Pilgrims, and of the reader withal, is cheered by the songs, the rural scenery, the tender and humorous human dialogues. It is the England of Izaak Walton's *Angler*. It is still in great measure the England of Shakespeare, though it is the scene of a soul's conflict that afflicted the contemporaries of Shakespeare less often than those of Bunyan. But the human background has little changed. We should feel no incongruity if Autolycus displayed his wares to the Pilgrims on the footpath way, or if Falstaff sent Bardolph to bid them step aside and join him in the tavern.

The country through which the Pilgrims travel and the ways along which they have to pass, are the countryside, the roads and the lanes of the English East Midlands with which Bunyan in his youth was familiar. The sloughs, the robbers, and the other accidents and dangers of the road were real facts of English Seventeenth Century travel. We must indeed except the dragons and giants; but even those Bunyan got from no more alien source than *Sir Bevis of Southampton* and other old English ballads, legends and broadsides that used then to circulate among the common people, instead of the flood of precise newspaper information that has killed the imaginative faculty in modern times.

In those days men were much left alone with nature, with themselves, with God. As Blake has said:

> Great things are done when men and mountains meet,
> These are not done by jostling in the street.

The principle, thus poetically expressed, of the effect of quiet contact with nature upon human achievement and quality, is true not only of the mountains that nursed Wordsworth's genius, but also of the far-stretched horizons of the fenland and of Cambridgeshire, over which the rising and setting sun and the glories of cloudland were often watched by solitary men—Squire Cromwell for instance, and the yeomen farmers who became his Ironsides. In the wide spaces of the East Anglian countryside each of these men had felt himself to be alone with God, before ever they joined to form a regiment. And that same principle is true of the meadows, the lanes and the woodland fens of Bedfordshire, the nurse of Bunyan and all the strivings and visions of his youth.

Fortunately most of the common people who kept the sheep in Shakespeare's countryside, or wandered by Izaak Walton's

May Day

streams, fishing-rod in hand, were untroubled by Bunyan's and Cromwell's visions of heaven and hell; but, saint and sinner, happy fisherman and self-torturing fanatic, all were subject to the wholesome influences of that time and landscape. Their language was the crisp pure English from which the translators of the Bible drew their style, now irrecoverable. As to the songs of the common people, they are well described in a dialogue by Izaak Walton.

PISCATOR: I pray, do us a courtesy that shall stand you and your daughter in nothing, and yet we will think ourselves something in your debt. It is but to sing a song that was sung by your daughter when I last passed over this meadow, about eight or nine days since.
MILK-WOMAN: What song was it, pray? Was it 'Come shepherds, deck your herds?' or 'As at noon Dulcina rested?' or 'Phillida flouts me?' or 'Chevy Chace?' or 'Johnny Armstrong?' or 'Troy Town?'

PISCATOR: No, it is none of those; it is a song that your daughter sung the first part, and you sung the answer to it.

MILK-WOMAN: Come, Maudlin, sing the first part to the gentleman with a merry heart; and I'll sing the second when you have done.

So the song is sung: 'Come, live with me and be my love.' When it is finished, *Venator* says:

Trust me, master, it is a choice song, and sweetly sung by honest Maudlin. I now see it was not without cause that our good Queen Elizabeth did so often wish herself a milkmaid all the month of May.

Such were simple country-folk under the Puritan Commonwealth, most of them little disturbed by its interfering rigours and stern aspirations.

Here is a letter of June 1653 by that charming girl Dorothy Osborne, reporting to her lover what she saw and heard one morning near the 'open field' of a village:

You ask me how I pass my time here. . . The heat of the day is spent in reading or working, and about six or seven o'clock I walk out into a common that lies hard by the house where a great many young wenches keep sheep and cows and sit in the shade singing of ballads. I talk to them and find they want nothing to make them the happiest people in the world, but the knowledge that they are so. Most commonly when we are in the midst of our discourse, one looks about her and spies her cows going into the corn, and then away they all run as if they had wings at their heels.

A Milkmaid

Not all the year round could maids 'sit in the shade singing of ballads,' and Queen Elizabeth only desired to be a milkmaid in the month of May! There was much hardship, poverty and cold in those pleasant villages and farms; but the simplicity and beauty of the life with nature was an historical reality, not merely a poet's dream.

The great generation of men who between them produced the high English tragedy of Roundhead and Cavalier, were not brought up on the Bible and on the influences of the country life alone—though such a limitation would almost be true of Bunyan. The age of Milton, Marvell and Herrick was an age of poetry and learning often in close alliance. Not only were simple and beautiful songs being written and set to music and sung by

**A** Shepherdess

all classes, but in cultivated households more elaborate and scholarly poems circulated in manuscript before they found their way into print or passed into oblivion. When the music of Lawes was married to the immortal verse of Milton's *Comus* for the private theatricals of Lord Bridgewater's family (1634), English domestic culture touched perhaps the highest mark to which it ever attained. And the learning of the time, classical as well as Christian, was very widely spread. [See § 82.]

Political and religious controversy was conducted in books and pamphlets forbiddingly learned to the modern eye, yet in spite of their heavy display of erudition, they caught the eager audience to which they made appeal. Even the famous pamphlet in favour of tyrannicide, entitled *Killing no Murder*, written by a Republican and reissued by the Cavaliers with the very practical object of inducing someone to assassinate Cromwell, is made up of learned citations of classical as well as Biblical authorities. Even under Puritan rule, what the Greeks and Romans had said about tryannicide counted with ordinary readers as much as the views of Hebrew Judges and prophets.

There were in fact a great many students among the upper

and middle classes both of town and country. Every reader had in some sort to be a student, for, apart from poetry and the stage, there was hardly any literature that was not serious. Fiction scarcely existed except in ballads for the common folk, and in the heavy 'tomes' of French romances like *Grand Cyrus,* which seem to us as dull as sermons, but in those days pleased cultivated young ladies like Dorothy Osborne.

Professor Notestein has in our day unearthed the diaries of a Yorkshire yeoman named Adam Eyre, who at one time served in the Parliament's army, but by 1647 had come home to his farm in the Dales. No doubt he read and thought more than the majority of his class, but the range and character of his reading throws light on the intellectual habits of the time and shows why yeomen were quite capable of choosing a side for themselves, in politics and religion, often different from that of the neighbouring gentry.

Adam had a carpenter in to furnish his study with shelves and his friends (yeomen like himself) were always borrowing from those shelves. Rarely did he return from a visit to one of the larger towns without bringing home a book; sometimes he had a whole package sent to him, and he went through them with care. 'This day I rested at home, and spent most of the day reading,' such is a typical entry. He began to make a table of a book called *The State of Europe.* He read *A Discourse of the Council of Basel,* 'wherein as in all the actions of men is little save corruption,' a comment that gives us an inkling of Adam's philosophy of history. He read Lilly's queer books of prophecy, and Walter Raleigh's *History of the World,* a best seller of the century; he dipped into Erasmus' *Praise of Folly* and James Howell's *Dendrologia* (a political allegory of events from 1603–40). He owned Dalton's Country Justice, a practical manual concerning the duties of Justices of the Peace and other local officials.

A larger part of his reading was in religious books, pleas for presbytery, arguments for independency or congregationalism, volumes of sermons by this or that famous preacher. The number of religious books he covered is astonishing. 'This day I rested at home all day and had various thoughts by reason of the variety of men's opinions I find in reading.' Surely it was the beginning of wisdom to reflect upon the variety of opinions. Adam was not a deeply spiritual man; he read these books because religion was in the air. It filled the newsletters and pamphlets [1] of the day, as strikes and sports items crowd our

---

[1] There was a spate of printed pamphlets between 1640 and 1660, but few printed newspapers. News was conveyed by news-letters written in London, and sent

dailies. Religion was involved with village squabbles in the West Riding as with factions at Westminster. (W. Notestein, *English Folk*, pp. 250–251.)

Such was the reading of this Cromwellian yeoman. In the manor-houses of the gentry a larger proportion of poetry and of classical learning circulated, or settled down on the library shelves, besides the sermons and pamphlets. No doubt most yeomen, most squires, and most merchants read very little, but many of them read a great deal. The Civil War was a war of ideas, and the ideas had been spread in print and in manuscript, as well as by the voice of the preacher and the talk of men.

The Civil Wars of Charles and Cromwell were not, like the Wars of the Roses, a struggle for power between two groups of aristocratic families, watched with disgusted indifference by the majority of the population, particularly by the townsfolk. In 1642 town and country alike rushed to arms. Yet it was not a war of town against country, though to some extent it became a struggle for London and its appendages against the rural North and West. Least of all was it a war between rich and poor. It was a war of ideas in Church and State. [See § 79, 80.]

Men chose their sides largely from disinterested motives and under no compulsion. They made their choice on account of their own religious and political opinions, and most of them were in such an economic and social position as to be able to exercise that choice with freedom. In the rural districts, feudal dependence was mainly a thing of the past, and the great consolidated estates were mainly a thing of the future. It was the golden age of the small squire and the yeoman, who prided themselves on their political independence, whereas the tenant farmers on the large estates a hundred and two hundred years later were proud to follow their landlords to the poll, in the interest of Whig or Tory. But in 1642 many yeomen drew sword against the neighbouring squires.

In the towns also it was an age of independence and individualism. Corporate life had decayed; a man's municipal loyalty to his town was already less important than this national loyalty to a party or a sect which he chose for himself. Personal opinions were strongly held in a society composed chiefly of small masters

down in manuscript to subscribers in the country who circulated them among their neighbours. This continued to be the chief way of spreading news till after the end of the century.

and their apprentices, so the inhabitants of the towns took free and intelligent interest in the land's debate.

But on the outbreak of the Civil War it was easier for the majority to seize power and muzzle the minority in a town, than in a large country district. Thus the Roundheads were able to suppress the Cavaliers at once in London, the seaports and the manufacturing cities. But in many shires of England a local civil war dragged on spasmodically for several years together, distinct from the campaigns of the main armies, though they too sometimes became involved in these regional struggles.

Where the local wars were conducted under the command of gentlemen who had known each other as neighbours and often as friends, though now differing in politics, there was little bitterness and much personal courtesy, especially in the first year or two. But some local wars had a fiercer character, where two sharply contrasted systems of society were at each other's throats. For example, in Lancashire the squires were many of them Roman Catholics, representing the old half-feudal world of the Pilgrimage of Grace; a deep gulf of misunderstanding and hatred was fixed between them and their Puritan neighbours in the towns that had recently sprung up with new industries of woollens, fustian, cotton and linen.

But in the great majority of the counties of England the Royalists were Anglicans, decisively Protestant; many of them had been opposed to Laud. Such a one was grand old Sir Edmund Verney, the King's standard-bearer, who died for his master at Edgehill but declared, 'I have no reverence for Bishops for whom this quarrel subsists.'

To speak in general terms, Royalism was strongest where the economic and social changes of the previous hundred years had been least felt. The King and the Church were best loved in rural regions and market towns furthest from the capital, and least connected with overseas commerce. Parliamentary and Puritan sympathy was strongest where recent economic change had gone furthest, as in London under the influence of the great Elizabethan trading companies; in the seaports (including the King's own ships and dockyards): and in the newer type of manufacturing town or district like Taunton, Birmingham and the clothing Dales on both sides of the Pennines. The squires who had most business connection with London, or with trade and industry anywhere, tended most to the Roundhead side in politics and religion. The London area, including Kent, Surrey and Essex, was at once seized for Parliament, and the Royalist minority there was never able to raise its head. The same happened in the counties of East Anglia, organized in the 'Eastern Association' and held in the firm grip of Colonel Oliver Cromwell—the region whence in the previous generation the majority of the Puritan emigrants to New England had been drawn, and where the first Ironsides were now enlisted among the Bible-reading yeomen.

Cromwell himself was a man of good family, related to several of the most important people in the House of Commons. He was a gentleman farmer, owning a small estate near Huntingdon which he worked himself until, in 1631, he sold his land to buy leases of rich river pastures near St. Ives. This sale of his patrimony shows that he regarded land as a means of making a livelihood, rather than as an hereditary possession and a matter of social and family pride. He preferred to be a hard-working farmer and business man, mixing on equal terms with common folk, whose champion he became, in various local quarrels, rather than to be a mere squire. This point of view is characteristic of the kind of business agriculturist who was likely to be a Puritan and a Roundhead, while the old-fashioned, west country squires, who took a more feudal attitude to life and society, were the typical Cavaliers. Even the great landed magnates of the Puritan party, like the Earls of Bedford and Manchester, were deeply interested in increasing their fortunes and estates by modern capitalistic methods. The Puritan, high or low, was taught by his religion to idealize business, enterprise and hard work. The Cavalier was usually of a more easy-going and enjoying nature.

The Civil War was not therefore a social war, but a struggle in which parties divided on political and religious issues, along a line of cleavage that answered, roughly and with many personal exceptions, to certain divisions of social type. In the events that followed the War, during the Roundhead Commonwealth (1649–1660), the class cleavage became more marked. The gentry as a whole became more and more alienated from the Roundhead cause and its leaders. Meanwhile democratic ideas of the equality of men irrespective of their rank and wealth affected the political happenings of the period. But these 'levelling' ideas were more political than social. The theorists in the ranks of the New Model Army advocated manhood suffrage for Parliament, but not a socialist redistribution of property. Only the small sect of 'Diggers,' under Winstanley, claimed that the land of England belonged to the people of England and had been stolen by the squires. They were quickly suppressed by the army chiefs. When the Diggers warned the Regicide Government that the political revolution would not stand its ground unless it was based on a social revolution, they spoke the truth, as the Restoration shortly afterwards showed.

Even the idea of political democracy was almost confined to the Radicals of the triumphant army. There was no movement in that direction among the mass of the people, and if a general election had been held on a wide franchise it would have resulted in a Cavalier Restoration.

But although there was no breaking up of estates into smaller units of land on a democratic basis, a certain amount of land passed for a short time from Cavalier to Roundhead ownership. This consisted chiefly of the Church and Crown lands sold to meet the needs of the Revolutionary government, as the monastic lands had been sold a century before. The purchasers were for the most part men of the advanced Republican party. But all these lands went back to Church and King at the Restoration, so that no 'new aristocracy' was founded out of them. And indeed the soldiers and merchants who held them for a decade on this insecure tenure had made little attempt to set up as country gentlemen in their new estates, which they had bought chiefly as commercial speculations.

Otherwise the amount of land that changed hands was remarkably small. The Cavalier squire had the government of the county taken out of his hands, and had to pay heavy fines for 'malignancy.' But severe as these fines were, they were paid by cutting of woods, borrowing, economy and various arrangements with family and friends.[1] For the squires were ready to make

---

[1] One of Charles I's wealthiest and most loyal supporters, the last Earl of Southampton (owner of Bloomsbury property that went to the Russells by the marriage of his daughter Rachel) was fined £6,466 for the part he had taken in the Civil War, a sum reckoned to be a tenth of all his landed property. He paid it, retired to his country estates for awhile, and emerged as a very wealthy nobleman at the Restoration. This is very far from rooting out a class, or forcing property to change hands by fines. Miss Scott Thomson, *The Russells in Bloomsbury*, Chap. II.

great sacrifices to avoid parting with their lands. Recent detailed research into ownership land-holding in several Midland counties in the Seventeenth Century, shows how little private land changed hands under the Commonwealth. Indeed, small estates were more freely sold after the Restoration, from economic causes which then became prevalent; but it is indeed possible that the Parliamentary fines may have permanently embarrassed some small estates and helped to compel their sale in a later generation.

In any case it does not appear to be true that, as has sometimes been conjectured, the 'Whigs' of Charles II's reign were a new type of landowner who had risen in the country during the Commonwealth period. The older squirearchy suffered much indignity and distress and was put to many mean shifts, but it was not uprooted. When in the autumn of 1654 the Cavalier diarist, John Evelyn, made a sporting tour among his friends' country houses in the Midlands, from the 'pleasant shire of Nottingham, full of gentry,' to Cambridge and Audley End, he noted many 'noble seats' and says nothing of the ruin or absence of their proprietors, or of any changes of ownership. [See § 83.]

The nobility were even more in eclipse than the squirearchy, for hardly any of the House of Peers followed the fortunes of the Roundhead party in the regicide period. Under the rule of Saints and Soldiers, Lords ceased to count for much in England. Dorothy Osborne, ever sensible and ever gay, remarked on the folly of her cousin in choosing a wife because she was an Earl's daughter, 'which methought was the prettiest fancy and had the least sense in it, considering that it made no addition to her person, and how little it is esteemed in this age, if it be anything in a better.' The 'better age' of the Restoration brought back, sure enough, a respect for Earls and a more general desire to marry their daughters.

On the other hand, many important results of the victory of the Parliamentary armies survived the Restoration. One of these was the increased power of London and of the merchant community in high politics. Another was the triumph of the English Common Law over its rivals. [See § 81.]

In Tudor times, to strengthen the Royal Prerogative and meet the real needs of that age, there had been a great increase in the number and the power of independent Courts each administering its own legal system with little regard to the procedure and principles of the Common Law. But the Parliaments that opposed James and Charles I, instructed by Edward Coke, the greatest of English lawyers, endeavoured to uphold the supremacy of the Common Law, and in 1641 were able to enforce it by legislation; the Star Chamber, the Ecclesiastical Court of High Commission and the jurisdiction of the Councils of Wales and of the North were then abolished. The Admiralty Court had already been compelled to accept the control of the Common Law in the development of the important commercial law of England.

Thus the English judicial system escaped the fate of being broken into fragments. The only dualism left was the independence of the Court of Chancery; but even that ceased to be a weapon of Royal Prerogative, and became a complementary system of Judge-made law, ingeniously dovetailed into the principles enforced in the ordinary Courts.

The victory of the Common Law involved the abolition of torture in England long before other countries, and paved the way for a fairer treatment of political enemies of government when brought to trial. Above all, the victory of the Common Law over the Prerogative Courts preserved the mediaeval conception of the supremacy of law, as a thing that could not be brushed aside for the convenience of government, and could only be altered in full Parliament, not by the King alone. This great principle, that law is above the executive, was indeed violated during the revolutionary period of the Commonwealth and Protectorate. But it re-emerged at the Restoration, and was confirmed at the Revolution of 1688, which was effected against James II precisely to establish the principle that law was above the King. That mediaeval idea of the supremacy of law as something separate from and independent of the will of the Executive, disappeared in continental countries. But in England it became the palladium of our liberties and had a profound effect on English society and habits of thought.

Under the Commonwealth and Protectorate, constitutional law was trodden underfoot in the exigencies of Revolution, but even during that period the common law and the lawyers were very strong, strong enough unfortunately to prevent the fulfilment of a loud popular demand for law reform, a crying social need which Cromwell vainly endeavoured to supply. The

lawyers were too many for him. Even he was not wholly a dic-
tator: the soldiers on one side, the lawyers on the other, at once
supported him and held him in check. When at the Restoration
the army was disbanded, the lawyers were left victorious.

It may well be imagined that there was scant building of
manor-houses between 1640 and 1660. But the peaceful generation that preceded the Civil War had been, on the whole, a
prosperous period for the gentry, great and small, who had continued the work of the Elizabethan age in filling the English
countryside with more and yet more lovely and commodious
dwellings. [See § 70, 71, 72.]

Certain changes were taking place in the structure of the houses
newly built. The lofty, raftered hall, the essential feature of the
country house from Saxon to Elizabethan times, went out of
fashion. 'Dining-rooms' and 'drawing-rooms' were now built
of one storey's height, as the various purposes of the old 'hall'
were divided up among a number of different chambers of ordinary size. The courtyard in the centre of the older type of manor-
house, where so much of the life of the establishment used to go
on, also shrank or disappeared in the plans of the Jacobean
mansion; the yard was placed no longer in the middle of the
house but behind it. [See § 84, 85.]

Cornices and pilasters decorated the exterior in classical style.
Inside, the staircase and its landings were broad, and the baluster
elaborately carved. On the walls, Jacobean panelling more and
more displaced tapestry, hangings and wall paintings, for common use, though much fine tapestry was still manufactured and
highly valued. Framed pictures and marble sculpture were becoming common, after the example set by the art-loving Charles I
and his great subject the Earl of Arundel. Rubens, Van Dyck
and the homelier Dutch painters did much work for English
patrons. [See § 86, 87 and Plate III.]

The plaster-work of the ceilings was elaborately decorative.
On the floors, rushes were giving place to carpets and matting;
that meant fewer fleas and diminished the chance of the flea-
borne Plague. Good carpets were now made in England, or
imported from Turkey and from Persia. But in 1645 the Verneys
at Claydon had 'leather carpets for dininge and drawinge rooms,'
'greene wrought velvet furniture' and 'stooles with nailes guilt':

most of the company still sat on stools, chairs being reserved for the elder or more honourable. The trestle table was giving place to solid tables with ornamental legs. Many magnificently carved beds and cupboards of the period still survive in their grandeur of polished and time-blackened oak.

Out-of-doors, it was a great age for gardens in England, as indeed it has been ever since. Bacon, after saying that 'God Almighty first planted a garden,' declared that without one 'building and palace are but gross handiworks.' The period of late Elizabeth and the early Stuarts saw the development of the flower garden as distinct from the garden of useful vegetables (to which the potato from America had now been added). Then, too, there was the well-loved orchard with its green walks, and the 'pleached bower' into which Beatrice stole

> Where honeysuckle ripened by the sun
> Forbids the sun to enter.

The flower-garden proper was arranged in rectangles and squares, divided by broad walks, set in full view of the house. Box and lavender were trimmed into hedges and ornamental shapes. [See § 88, 89, 90, 91.]

Many trees, plants and flowers were introduced into England at this period, among many others the crown imperial, the tulip, the laburnum, the nasturtium, the everlasting, love-in-a-mist, honesty, the tulip tree, the red maple. The love of gardening and of flowers that now became so characteristic of the English, was in part taught them by Huguenot refugees from the low countries, settled in Norwich and in London. The Huguenot weavers of Spitalfields started the first gardening societies in England. In the reign of Charles I, English books, such as *Paradisus,* praising and describing flowers, taught and popularized the fashion of gardening. (Eleanor Rohde, *Story of the Garden,* 1932.)

Besides the flowers of this period that are still with us, our ancestors had then a passion for herbs, which has not survived to the same extent. Herbs were much used for medicinal and for culinary purposes. Mazes and dials were laid out by plantations of herbs and flowers. These verses of Andrew Marvell, the lesser of Cromwell's two poet secretaries, tell of a side of life that was not destroyed by the wars of Roundhead and Cavalier:

III.  The Painted Room at Old Wilsley, Kent (c. 1680)

Here at the fountain's sliding foot,
Or at some fruit-tree's mossy root,
Casting the body's vest aside,
My soul into the boughs does glide;
There, like a bird, it sits and sings,
Then whets and combs its silver wings,
And, till prepared for longer flight,
Waves in its plumes the various light.

How well the skilful gardener drew
Of flowers, and herbs, this dial new;
Where, from above, the milder sun
Does through a fragrant zodiac run,
And, as it works, the industrious bee
Computes its time as well as we!
How could such sweet and wholesome hours
Be reckoned but with herbs and flowers!

The ideal family life of the period that ended in such tragic political division, has been recorded once for all in the *Memoirs of the Verney Family*. Their household at Claydon, Bucks, represented all that was best in the Puritan and Cavalier way of life, practised in unison by Sir Edmund Verney and by his son Ralph, till the obstinacy of the King and the violence of his enemies, forced even those two men of moderation to take opposite sides in civil war, without less love for one another and without any weakening of their common interest to maintain the family house and estate intact in evil times.

The picture we get of the Verneys at Claydon in the reign of Charles I shows the English country house as a centre not only of estate management but of domestic industry, in which the members of the family, as well as their army of servants and dependants of both sexes, have essential parts to play.

'A great house provisioned itself with little help,' writes the historian of the Verneys.

'The inhabitants brewed and baked, they churned and ground their meal, they bred up, fed and slew their beeves and sheep, and brought up their pigeons and poultry at their own doors. Their horses were shod at home, their planks were sawn, their rough ironwork was forged and mended. Accordingly the mill-house, the slaughter-house, the blacksmith's, carpenter's and painter's shops, the malting and brewhouse, the woodyard full of large and small timber, the sawpit, the out-houses full of all sorts of odds and ends of stone, iron and woodwork and logs cut for burning—the riding house, the laundry, the dairy with a large churn turned by a horse, the stalls and styes for all manner of cattle and pigs, the apple and root chambers, show how complete was the idea of self-supply.'

The dovecots and the stew-ponds full of fish, and the decoy for water fowl were not less important. And game brought down by the hawk or the 'long gun' was the more valued in winter because otherwise the only meat was that which had been salted at the autumn slaughtering. Skin diseases were a frequent result of the salt diet, at Claydon and in all other households high or low. For winter vegetables were scarce; potatoes and salads were only beginning to come into use.

'The work with the needle and the wheel was a very necessary part of a lady's education, and as some of the poorer relations of the family resided in great houses as "lady helps" (the equivalents of the pages of the other sex) they were useful and welcome in carrying out these important household labours. There are letters from five or six of these ladies, connected with the Verneys, well born, well bred, and as well educated as their neighbours, who seem to have been treated with great consideration.'

Among the employments of the female part of the household at Claydon were spinning at wool and flax, fine and coarse needlework, embroidery, fine cooking, curing, preserving, distillery, preparing medicines from herbs at the prescription of the doctor or by family tradition, and last but not least the making of fruit syrups and home-made wines from currant, cowslip and elder, which played a great part in life before tea and coffee began to come in at the Restoration.

Ten of Lady Verney's children grew up. This large and affectionate family, in which no hand was idle, found time for long correspondence with absent members. In the Verney archives four hundred letters survive from a single year. Frequent journeys were taken by Sir Edmund and his children, on the King's or the Parliament's business, or on family and personal affairs. They were made on horseback at a good pace along the soft roads. In 1639 Sir Edmund rode 260 miles in four days with the King from Berwick to London. Much slower was the walking pace of the family 'coch—a sort of cart without springs,

with leathern curtains against the weather, which most un-
luxurious luxury was used only by infirm persons or delicate
women who could not ride.' [See § 92, 104, 105.]

Public conveyances were becoming common in the period of
the Commonwealth, but were still expensive and slow.  In 1658

A hackney coach

'stage coaches' set out from the George Inn, Aldersgate, London,
to various cities on the following terms:

To Salisbury in two days for 20 shillings.
To Exeter in four days for 40 shillings.
To Plymouth for 50 shillings.
    and to Durham for 55 shillings (no time of arrival guaranteed)
    and every Friday to Wakefield in four days for 40 shillings.

The breeding and purchase of horses of every kind and for
every purpose was an essential part of the Verneys' way of life at
Claydon.  In that part of England horses were gradually replacing
oxen in cart and plough.  Sir Edmund Verney's cart-horses were
sent periodically to an estate he had in the fens to 'gather flesh at
an easy charge.'

When we compare the life and letters of the Verneys in the
reign of Charles I to the life and letters of the Pastons under
Henry VI, we are aware of the general resemblance, but we are
aware also of higher moral instincts and traditions, of greater

kindliness and less hard outlook on family relationships and on duty to neighbours. Long generations of peace and order in the countryside, and possibly other changes as well, had made life more gentle and more just. Sir Tobie Matthew, a courtier of Charles I who knew several foreign lands almost as well as he knew his own, and being a Roman Catholic convert was able to take an outside and critical view of his countrymen, writes in the preface to his Letters that the English had a monopoly of 'a certain thing called Good Nature,' and that 'England is the only Indies where this bottomless mine of pure gold is to be found.' 'No man is more remote than an Englishman from the doggedness of long-lasting and indelible revenge.' These good qualities were put to an exacting test when civil war came to every man's gate, a war more ubiquitous in its scope and area than the Wars of the Roses, but fought from less selfish and material motives.

### Books for Further Reading

*Memoirs of the Verney Family in the Civil War* (1892); Dorothy Osborne's *Letters*; Mrs. Hutchinson's *Memoirs of Colonel Hutchinson*; Lipson, *Ec. Hist. Eng.*; Darby, *Hist. Geog. Eng.*, chap. xi; Margaret James, *Social Problems and Policy during the Puritan Revolution*, 1930; Godfrey Davies, *The Early Stuarts* (Oxford Hist. Eng.), chap. xi.

## Chapter Four

## RESTORATION ENGLAND

*Charles II, 1660–1685. James II, 1685–1688.*
*(The Revolution, 1688–1689.) William III, 1689–1702.*

POLITICALLY, the Restoration of 1660 restored King, Parliament and Law in place of the 'forced power' of military dictatorship. Ecclesiastically it restored the Bishops and Prayer Book and the Anglican attitude to religion, in place of Puritanism. But socially—and its social aspect concerns us most in this work—the Restoration restored the nobles and the gentry to their hereditary place as the acknowledged leaders of local and national life. The Englishman's proverbial 'love of a lord,' his respectful and admiring interest in ' the squire and his relations,' again had full play. Indeed, as events were to prove, the social importance of the peer and the squire, of the gentleman and his lady, was much more completely 'restored' than the power of the King. The Englishman was, at bottom, something of a snob but very little of a courtier.

Under the Commonwealth, with its democratic ideals and its military realities, the majority of the hereditary 'upper class,' being Cavaliers, had suffered an eclipse without parallel in our social history. They had not been destroyed as a class, but had been put into cold storage. They had not lost their lands or more than a certain proportion of their wealth by fines. But their place in national and local government and in social importance had for awhile been usurped by successful soldiers, or by politicians who could adapt themselves to the rapid changes of a revolutionary era. Some of these, Algernon Sidney and Ashley Cooper, had been men of good family; others, like Colonels Pride and Birch, had been such 'plain russet-coated captains' as Cromwell loved, whom he had raised up with him to rule the land. At the Restoration many of the Roundhead leaders disappeared into obscurity or exile; but others, like Monk, Ashley Cooper, Colonel Birch and Andrew Marvell, retained their status in the Parliamentary or Governmental ranks. Once the Regicides had been disposed of, there was no proscription of former Round-heads, except only of such as obstinately continued to attend 'conventicles,' as the places of Puritan worship were now called.

Throughout the reign of Charles II, religious nonconformists suffered severe though intermittent persecution, under the laws of the 'Clarendon Code.' The victims were members of the middle and lower classes, chiefly residing in the towns. Many of them were wealthy merchants, more were industrious artisans; and statesmen were soon complaining that religious persecution interfered seriously with trade. Very few of those who suffered belonged to the landowning gentry: among the squires, the Roundhead spirit suffered change into the Whig, which refused to hamper its worldly ambitions by too scrupulous an adherence to the proscribed Puritan religion. A common Whig type was that of the sceptical Shaftesbury or the blasphemous Wharton, although these attitudes were no less fashionable among Cavalier courtiers and Tory leaders of Parliament. There were, however, plenty of Whigs who were good Christians, though never High Churchmen; the Russells and other Whig families attended the Anglican worship with sincere piety, while they engaged silenced Puritan clergymen as private chaplains and tutors for their children. The distinction between the two Protestant religions was by no means absolute for all men.

After the Restoration, the members of the landowning class who attended conventicles and suffered persecution as Noncon-formists were a mere handful. Anglicanism became distinctively the upper-class religion, far more completely than it had been in the days of Elizabeth or of Laud. There were indeed still a certain number of Roman Catholic country gentlemen, especially in Lancashire and Northumberland; they were shut out from all participation in local and national government by laws which the King was occasionally able to break for their benefit. Other-wise the upper class, the gentlemen of England, were socially united by common conformity to the Anglican worship. Hence-forth the services of the parish Church were under the special patronage of the ladies and gentlemen in the family pew; the great body of the congregation were their dependants, the farmers and labourers of the village. Addison's Sir Roger de Coverley in church affords a pleasant example of the social side of rural worship as it remained for many generations to come:

## To the Reader.

This Figure, that thou here seest put,
  It was for gentle Shakespeare cut;
Wherein the Grauer had a strife
  with Nature, to out-doo the life:
O, could he but haue drawne his wit
  As well in brasse, as he hath hit
Hisface; the Print would then surpasse
  All, that was euer writ in brasse.
But, since he cannot, Reader, looke
  Not on his Picture, but his Booke.

                        B. I.

§ 60 William Shakespeare—the engraving for the 'First Folio' (1623)

§61 An inn yard with galleries—The New Inn, Gloucester, fifteenth century

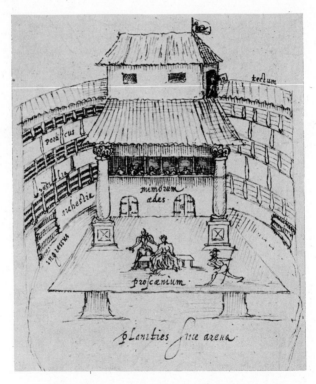

§62 Interior of the Swan Theatre in 1596

Ye Temple Stayres

Temple

Black freyars

The Globe

Beere bayting h

§63 The Bankside showing the theatres in 1647 (*see notes*)

§64 Sir Philip Sydney

§65 Sir Richard Grenville

§66 The last fight of the *Revenge*

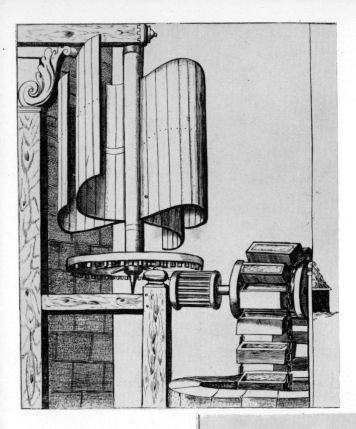

§67 & 68 Windmills

Both.
*The Mills made open that the whole Engins may appeare*

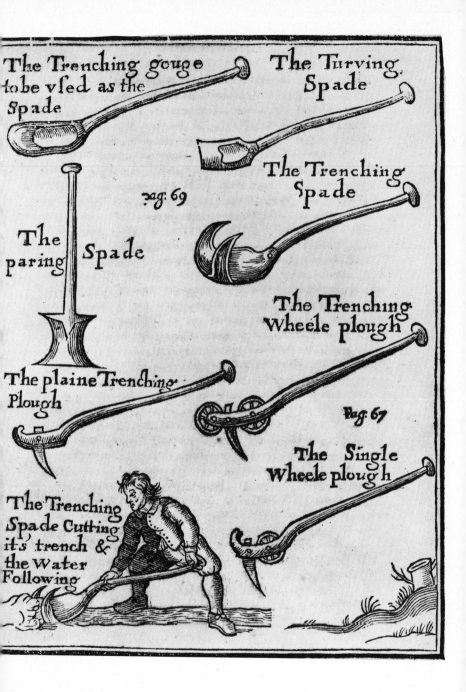

The Trenching gouge to be vſed as the Spade

The Turving Spade

The Trenching Spade

pag: 69

The paring Spade

The Trenching Wheele plough

The plaine Trenching Plough

Pag: 69

The Single Wheele plough

The Trenching Spade Cutting it's trench & the Water Following

§69 Trenching tools

§70 Inigo Jones

§71 Air view of the Queen's House, Greenwich

§72 The Double Cube Room at Wilton House

# THE
# LAMENTABLE
## COMPLAINTS
### OF
### NICK FROTH the Tapſter, and
### RVLEROST the Cooke.

*Concerning the reſtraint lately ſet forth,*
*againſt drinking, potting, and piping on the Sab-*
*bath day, and againſt ſelling meate.*

Printed in the yeare, 1641.

§73 Sunday observance
in 1641

§74 Abuses of the Spiritual
Courts

# THE
# PROCTOR
## AND
## PARATOR
### their Mourning:
#### OR,
The lamentation of the Doctors Commons
for their Downfall.
*Being a true Dialogue,*
Relating the fearfull abuſes and exorbitancies of thoſe
ſpirituall Courts, under the names of *Sponge*
the Proctor, and *Hunter* the Parator.

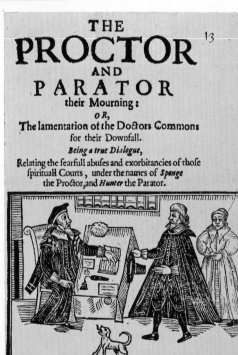

Printed in the yeare 1641.

§75 The Maypole

The Orthodox true Minister,

the Seducer and false Prophet.

§76 'The rule of the Saints'

§77 'An elected debating Assembly'
—the House of Commons in 1651

§78 John Bunyan—'The lonely figure with its Bible
and the burden of sin . . . is the representative Puritan
of the English Puritan epoch'

§79 The Battle of Naseby

(for description see notes)

§ 80 'A War of ideas in Church and State'
(*for explanation see note*)

My friend Sir Roger, being a good Church-man, has beautified the inside of his Church with several texts of his own choosing. He has likewise given a handsome pulpit cloth and railed in the communion table at his own expense. He has often told me that at his coming to his estate he found the Parishioners very irregular; and in order to make them kneel and join in the responses, he gave every one of them a hassock and a Common-Prayer book; and at the same time employed an itinerant singing-master, who goes about the country for that purpose, to instruct them rightly in the tunes of the Psalms. As Sir Roger is landlord to the whole congregation, he keeps them in very good order, and suffers no body to sleep in it besides himself; for if by chance he has been surprised into a short nap at sermon, upon recovering out of it he stands up and looks about him, and if he sees anybody else nodding, either wakes them himself or sends his servants to them.

The dissenting congregations, on the other hand, alike in times of persecution and toleration, were made up of men who prided themselves on their independence, and who liked to feel that the chapel and its minister belonged to themselves. Socially at least they were 'at ease in Zion,' safe from the inquisitorial eye of the squire and his lady. Until the Wesleyan movement, dissenting congregations and meetings were almost confined to cities, market towns and industrial districts, though many villages had isolated families of Quakers and Baptists. Some of the Dissenters were poor artisans like John Bunyan; others, especially in London and Bristol, were wealthy merchants who could have bought up the squires who persecuted them. And often such merchants did in fact buy out needy gentlemen, after accumulating mortgages on their land. In the next generation the dissenting merchant's son would be a squire and a churchman. Yet another generation, and the ladies of the family would be talking with contempt of all who attended meeting-houses or engaged in trade !

Thus the social character of English religious divisions was stereotyped at the Restoration and continued with little change until the Victorian era.

Though the upper class was now substantially one in the form of its religious observance, it was divided politically into Whigs and Tories. The Tories, who were far the most numerous, sought to extirpate religious Dissent and to make the Anglican

Church coextensive with the nation. But the Whig Peers and gentry, an able and wealthy minority, advocated the new doctrine of Toleration, at least for all Protestants. They derived their political power from alliance with the Puritans of the industrial and commercial regions, who were able to control the municipal and Parliamentary elections in many boroughs. The Tories, like the Cavaliers before them, were the section of the society that stood most whole-heartedly in the old ways of rural England. The Whigs, like their Roundhead fathers, were usually those members of the landowning class who were in close touch with commercial men and commercial interests. And therefore Whig rather than Tory policies stood to gain in the long run by the continuous process of economic change, as it moved with gradually accelerating momentum towards an agricultural and industrial revolution which would leave only too little of the ancient ways.

The Restoration world had turned back from that pre-occupation with matters ecclesiastical which had characterized Cromwellian England. The popular reaction that overthrew the Puritans had been less religious than secular. *Hudibras* is not a work of Anglican piety. Indeed, the principal reason why the English witnessed the return of the old Church establishment with relief, was because it made less constant and obtrusive demands for professions of religious zeal upon the common occasions of life. The Puritans had made men 'eat religion with their bread,' till the taste of it sickened them.

For a generation after 1660 the Puritans were often bitterly persecuted, but more for political and social reasons than from genuinely religious motives. The object of the 'Clarendon Code' was to prevent the revival of the Roundhead party, and to avenge the wrongs suffered by Anglicans and Cavaliers. But the spirit of the persecution was not ecclesiastical; it was not a heresy hunt. The hard-drinking fox-hunters of the manor-house hated the Presbyterians of the neighbouring Town not because they held the doctrines of Calvin, but because they talked through their noses, quoted scripture instead of swearing honest oaths, and voted Whig instead of Tory.

In 1677 the Writ *De haeretico comburendo* was abolished, and all 'punishment by death in pursuance of any Ecclesiastical Censures' was abolished by law; but in fact no heretic had been put to death in England since the Unitarians who had been burnt in the lifetime of Shakespeare. Puritanism in the day of its power had not made for orthodoxy; Cromwell's England had abounded in strange doctrines and attenuated creeds, and had left to the restored Kings an island of 'a hundred religions.' Where religions are many and various, irreligion is less likely to be persecuted. But in Presbyterian Scotland, where sects had little hold and where the spirit of orthodoxy in doctrine was popular with the masses, a lad of eighteen was hanged for denying the authority of the Scriptures as late as the year 1697; whereas in England, any time after the Civil War, a reputation for 'atheism,' though it might be socially disadvantageous, no longer endangered a man's life or freedom. By the end of the Century, Unitarian doctrines, for which men were burnt a hundred years before, were not uncommon among English Presbyterian congregations of the highest bourgeois respectability, while many of the leading statesmen, not to mention King Charles himself in his merrier moods, were sceptics in the sense of being scoffers.

It was of graver import that experimental science was spreading fast in England. Under the Commonwealth there had been a group of remarkable scientists resident at the Universities and in London, whose work came into the limelight of fashion and favour at the Court of the Restoration. The Royal Society was founded under the patronage of King Charles and of his cousin Prince Rupert, himself a conductor of chemical experiments.

The uses to which science might be turned, in agriculture, industry, navigation, medicine and engineering, appealed to the practical English mind. Another hundred years were to pass before the Industrial Revolution gathered full force, largely as a result of the application of science to manufacture, but already in the reign of Charles II many subjects of daily importance were being studied in a scientific spirit, and this new spirit already had a great influence on educated thought in England. Robert Boyle, Isaac Newton and the early members of the Royal Society were religious men, who repudiated the sceptical doctrines of Hobbes. But they familiarized the minds of their countrymen with the idea of law in the Universe and with scientific methods of inquiry to discover truth. It was believed that these methods would never lead to any conclusion inconsistent with Biblical history and miraculous religion; Newton lived and died in that faith. But his law of universal gravitation and his calculus supplied methods of approaching truth that had no relation to theology. The spread of scientific inquiry affected the character of religious belief, though not as yet its content. The age of latitudinarian piety that followed the Revolution of 1688 was being prepared by these intellectual movements of the Restoration. [See § 96, 97.]

Early in the reign of Charles II, the first 'History of the Royal Society,' its character and aims, was written by Sprat, some years later Bishop of Rochester, a man highly characteristic of the new age both in the versatility of his mind and the politic flexibility of his opinions. This High Church divine commends the 'learned and inquisitive age' in which he lives, praises the practical objects of the Fellows of the Royal Society, 'to increase the powers of all mankind and to free them from the bondage of errors,' and claims for these new philosophers the widest range of inquiry—'these two subjects, God and the Soul, being only forborne: in all the rest, they wander at their pleasure.' God was to be praised by studying the plan of His creation, but no further attempt was to be made to fit the findings of science into the scheme of theology, as the schoolmen of old had striven so long and so painfully to do. 'God and the Soul' were taken for granted—and left aside. It was an orthodox position no doubt, but not essentially religious. God was no longer all in all. In a world governed by such studies, superstition would be exposed, and poetry would yield pride of place to prose; would even religion be quite the same again?

Sprat was one of the excellent writers who formed the lucid prose of the Restoration era, but he was not an original thinker, and his book on the Royal Society (1667) is on that account all the more symptomatic of the mind of the new age. Like Locke and Newton a few years later, the Bishop concedes to 'the ancient miracles' of Bible times a passport as privileged phenomena, unusual interferences of God with His creation. But modern miracles were no longer to be expected in the Protestant, Anglican climate. 'The course of things,' Sprat declares, 'goes quietly along, in its own true channel of natural causes and effects.' It is no longer even Shakespeare's world: 'King Oberon and his invisible army of fairies' are 'false chimeeres' to this philosopher Bishop. When the Englishmen of the Revolution epoch laughed at 'Popish miracles,' it was not only because they were Popish but because they were miracles. Sprat even warns his too credulous countrymen 'not to be hasty in assigning the causes of plagues, or fires or inundations' to the judgments of God for sin. Finally, 'the new philosophy' of the physical sciences is to be the mother of inventions useful to man, enriching and comforting his life. 'While the old philosophy could only bestow on us some barren terms and notions, the new shall impart to us the uses of all the creatures and shall enrich us with all the benefits of fruitfulness and plenty.'

While the episcopal blessing was thus enthusiastically given to the questioning spirit of science, it is not surprising that in the later years of the Century, the reaction of educated minds to charges of witchcraft was very different from what it had been a short time before. Evidence of these 'odd stories' was now critically and sometimes contemptuously examined by magistrates. Popular superstition on this subject was almost as gross as ever, but the gentry were now predisposed to be sceptical. The accused witches had two advantages; England was a country where the common Law did not permit the use of torture to extract confession; and the judges had almost as much control as the juries over the course and outcome of trials. More generally speaking, it was lucky for the witches that England was still aristocratically governed. In many rural parts the populace, if it had not been restrained by the gentry, would have continued to drown or burn witches down to the Nineteenth Century. But in 1736, greatly to the indignation of many simple folk, Parliament repealed the already obsolete law that condemned a witch to die.

We can trace this gradual change of opinion, affecting in the first instance the educated classes, in Sir John Reresby's account of a witch trial that he attended at the York Assizes in 1687:

A poor old woman had the hard fate to be condemned for a witch. *Some, that were more apt to believe those things than me,* thought the evidence strong against her, the boy that said he was bewitched falling into fits before the bench when he see her. But in all this it was observed that the boy had no distortion, no foaming at the mouth, nor did his fits leave him gradually, but all of a sudden; *so that the judge thought fit to reprieve her.*

However, it is just to relate this odd story. One of my soldiers, being upon the guard at eleven o'clock at night at Clifford Tower Gate the night the witch was arraigned, hearing a great noise at the Castle, came to the porch, and being there see a scroll of paper creep from under the door, which, *as he imagined by moonshine,* turned first into the shape of a monkey, then a turkey cock, which moved to and fro by him. Where upon he went to the gaol and called the under-gaoler, who came and see the scroll dance up and down and creep under the door, where there was scarce the room of the thickness of half a crown. *This I had from the mouth both of the soldier and gaoler.*

It will be observed that Sir John Reresby and the Judge, the men of education, were more sceptical than the Jury, the soldier and the turnkey.

For their patronage of science, Charles II and his courtiers deserve all praise. Their patronage of the theatre, struggling to revive after its suppression by the foolish bigotry of the Puritans, was also a well-timed service to the nation, but the manner of it was less deserving of unqualified eulogy.

The revived theatres differed in several important respects from those in which Shakespeare had first been played. The whole playhouse was now roofed in, and the stage artificially lighted with candles: there were 'footlights,' a drop curtain and painted scenery. Moreover, the women's parts were no longer, as before the Civil War, taken by well-trained boys, but by women actresses. Men came to see the actress as much as the play. Nell Gwynne's personal vigour and charm counted for more perhaps than her professional skill. It was to a large extent a new theatre and a new dramatic art, with new possibilities, and new dangers.

For many years there was one theatre open in London, the Theatre Royal, at Drury Lane, and sometimes one or two more. But there were no fixed theatres in the provinces and the touring companies were few and bad. Acting was not, as music then was in the age of Purcell, a national pastime and an art widely practised at home by many small groups of connoisseurs. The drama was localized in London, and even there it appealed not to the citizens but to the Court and the fashionables of the Town. It was for their vitiated taste that the drama of the early years of the Restoration catered. [See § 93, 94.]

At that time a hard-hearted and cynical frivolity prevailed in Whitehall and Westminster much more than in England as a whole. The men who haunted Charles II's Court, the first leaders of the Whig and Tory parties in the time of the Popish Plot and the Exclusion Bill, laughed at all forms of virtue as hypocrisy, and believed that every man had his price.

> What makes all doctrines plain and clear?
> *About two hundred pounds a year.*
> And that which was proved true before
> Prove false again? *Two hundred more.*
>
> (*Hudibras.*)

So they thought, being themselves for sale. Yet two thousand Puritan Ministers had just given up their livings and gone out to endure persecution for conscience' sake (1662), following the example of their enemies the Anglican clergy, who had suffered like things for twenty years past rather than desert the Church in her extremity. The Puritan and Anglican clergy who refused to save their livelihoods by recantation were nearly ten times as numerous as the Catholic and Protestant clergy who had similarly stood out during the frequent Tudor changes of religion. Conscience meant more, not less, than of old. England was sound enough. But her courtiers and politicians were rotten. For the King himself and the younger generation of the aristocracy had been demoralized by the break-up of their education and family life, by exile and confiscation leading to the mean shifts of sudden poverty, by the endurance of injustice done to them in the name of religion, by the constant spectacle of oaths and covenants lightly taken and lightly broken, and all the base underside of revolution and counter-revolution of which they had been the victims.

For these reasons a hard disbelief in virtue of any kind was characteristic of the restored leaders of politics and fashion, and was reflected in the early Restoration drama which depended on their patronage. One of the most successful pieces was Wycherley's *Country Wife*; the hero, by pretending to be a eunuch, secures admission to privacies which enable him to seduce women; one is expected to admire his character and proceedings. In no other age, before or after, would such a plot-motive have appealed to any English audience.

However, the theatre had been restored, and much of its work was good. It revived plays by Shakespeare and Ben Jonson. It was adorned by the poetic genius of Dryden's dramas and the musical genius of Purcell's incidental tunes and operatic pieces.

And in the following generation Wycherley's brutalities went clean out of fashion. They were succeeded by the new English comedy of Congreve and Farquhar. Those great writers are usually lumped with Wycherley as 'Restoration Dramatists,' but in fact it would be more chronologically correct to call Congreve and Farquhar 'Revolution Dramatists,' for they wrote in the reigns of William and Anne.

So the Wycherley period of the English stage did not last long, but it had done permanent harm, because it had confirmed many pious and decent-minded families, High Church as well as Low, in a hostile attitude to the drama, which had in Shakespeare's time been peculiar to rigid Puritans. Till late in the Nineteenth Century, not a few well-brought-up young people were never allowed to visit the theatre. And if such stringency was the exception rather than the rule, it is at least true to say that the serious part of the nation would never take the theatre seriously. This misfortune was not a little due to Puritan bigotry and to its outcome in the licentiousness of the early Restoration drama. These unhappy conditions were peculiar to England: the age of Wycherley over here was the age of Molière, Corneille and Racine in France. There the drama, comic as well as tragic, was decent and was serious, and the French have ever since taken their drama seriously, as the Elizabethan English took theirs, regarding it as a civilizing influence and a criticism of life.

The age which produced Newton's *Principia,* Milton's *Paradise Lost,* Dryden's *Absalom and Achitophel,* Purcell's Music and Wren's Churches, and all the varied interests and curiosities of the daily life recorded by Evelyn and Pepys, such an age was one of the greatest for English genius and civilization. It could not have been what it was without the printing press, yet it is remarkable what a small amount of printing served its turn.

In the first place there was a rigid censorship. No book, pamphlet or news-sheet could be legally printed without licence obtained from the authorities. Enemies of the existing establishment in Church or State, could only print their views in secret presses, operated in London garrets by desperate men, who were spied upon by informers in the pay of Roger Lestrange, and savagely punished if caught.

But the censorship that thus stifled debate no longer derived its sanction from the Royal Prerogative, as of old, but from an Act of Parliament. The first Licensing Act, passed in 1663 by the Cavalier Parliament, aimed at preventing the publication of seditious and heretical works—meaning in the first instance Roundhead and Puritan writings. The Act was periodically renewed, except during the period of the Whig Houses of Commons and the years without a Parliament that followed (1679–1685). Revived by the Parliament of James II, the Licensing Act was finally allowed to expire in the more liberal age ushered in by the Revolution. After 1696 an Englishman was permitted to print and publish whatever he chose, without consulting any authority in Church or State; only he could be called to account for it on a charge of libel or sedition before a jury of his countrymen. Thus Milton's dream of 'liberty of unlicensed printing' was realized in England, a generation after his death.

Under the restrictions of the Censorship while it still existed, men of letters and science had been able to make a freer use of the press than politicians. The ecclesiastical licensers,[1] while refusing their sanction to the specific doctrines of Dissent, were not so obscurantist as to prevent the publication of *Paradise Lost* or *Pilgrim's Progress*. Newton's *Principia* bears the *imprimatur* of Samuel Pepys as President of the Royal Society in 1686.

Yet the aggregate of books and pamphlets published was not large. By the provisions of the Licensing Act the number of master-printers in the Kingdom was reduced to twenty and the number of presses they might each use was rigidly limited. Except for the two University Presses, all the master-printers congregated in London, to the detriment of intellectual life in the country at large. In the following century, when the Licensing Act was no more, printing became widely diffused, to the great benefit of the literary and scientific life of the Provinces. But in Stuart times, London and the two Universities monopolized printing and publishing. When William of Orange occupied Exeter on his famous march from Torbay, the Capital of the West was unable to furnish a single printer or machine to strike off copies of his manifesto.

[1] By the Licensing Act of 1663 Political treatises were to be licensed by the Secretary of State, Law books by the Lord Chancellor, books of Heraldry by the Earl Marshal or Kings of Arms, and all other publications by the Archbishop of Canterbury and the Bishop of London. These authorities appointed Licensers to read the books.

Except during the few years in Charles II's reign when the Censorship was in abeyance, there were practically no newspapers, for the meagre official *Gazette* could not be so called. News circulated in 'newsletters' written by hand in London and sent down to correspondents in distant towns and villages: the recipients, if they wished, could read or lend them to their neighbours. It was largely by this means that the Whig and Tory parties were formed and held together in the constituencies. And news of all sorts—sporting, literary and general, went round in the same way. The composition and multiplication of these newsletters employed an army of scribes in London, answering to the journalists and the printers of newspapers of later times.

Private libraries were growing more common, varying in size and character from the noble collections of Samuel Pepys and of the Cotton family, to the modest bookshelf in the yeoman's farm. That a fine country house ought to have a fine library was an idea already becoming fashionable, but it was not yet put in practice so generally as in Hanoverian times. [See § 98.]

On the other hand, since public libraries were extremely rare outside Oxford and Cambridge, it was difficult for readers of slender means to obtain the use of books. In 1684 a public library in London was established by Tenison, then Rector of St. Martin's in the Fields, afterwards Archbishop of Canterbury; Evelyn writes in his diary:

Dr. Tenison communicated to me his intention of erecting a library in St. Martin's Parish, for the public use, and desired my assistance, with Sir Christopher Wren, about the placing and structure thereof, a worthy and laudable design. He told me there were thirty or forty young men in orders in his parish, either governors to young gentlemen or chaplains to noblemen,[1] who being reproved by him on occasion for frequenting taverns and coffee-houses, told him they would study or employ their time better, if they had books. This put the pious Doctor on this design; and indeed a great reproach it is that so great a city as London should not have a public library becoming it.

Tenison built a large house in the ground of St. Martin's churchyard, and used the upper part for the library, the ground floor as a workroom for the poor. (Strype's *Stow's London*, 1720, Ch. VI, p. 68.)

---

[1] Viz., the class of clergymen most likely to rise to Bishoprics and Deaneries in that age of patronage.

Ten years before, Wren had been engaged by his friend, Isaac Barrow, Master of Trinity, Cambridge, to design the noblest of all College Library buildings; and the bookcases were adorned by the wood-carving of Grinling Gibbons. If books were still somewhat rare, they were held in all the more honour and were housed like Princes. [See § 99.]

A fair proportion of the people, even in remote villages, could read and write. Accounts were made up; letters of business, gossip and affection were exchanged; diaries, as we know, were kept both in short and long hand. But though it was an age of reading and writing in the conduct of the ordinary affairs of life, very little printed matter came in the way of the less educated. This gave all the greater importance to the sermon, which dealt as freely with political as with religious doctrines. In the Puritan era gone by,

> The pulpit, drum ecclesiastic
> Was beat with fist instead of a stick.
>
> (*Hudibras.*)

Now the jack-boot was on the other leg; it was said that the country parsons of the restored Church preached more often about King Charles the Martyr than about Jesus Christ. A fierce political tone was no doubt too common, but much also was taught and preached by the rural clergy that was better than politics. Moreover, there existed, chiefly in London, an influential minority of the Anglican priesthood, whose sermons, broadly human, learned and eloquent—raised the reputation of the Church and its pulpit deservedly high with all men. Such were Tenison, Stillingfleet and Isaac Barrow, and above all Tillotson.

Moreover, the Church of the Restoration and Revolution made great contributions to learning. The ecclesiastico-political controversies of the time, in which all sides appealed to the practice of the past, set a premium on historical research, and helped to produce in England the first great age of mediaeval scholarship. It inspired the researches of clergymen and religious laymen like Sir William Dugdale of the *Monasticon,* Anthony Wood and Hearne of Oxford, Jeremy Collier, Nicholson, Burnet, the first serious historian of the Reformation, Wharton of *Anglia Sacra,* Rymer of the *Foedera* and Wake and Wilkins of the *Concilia.*

The publication of mediaeval texts, and the study of Anglo-Saxon and mediaeval antiquities by these men between 1660 and 1730 were astonishing alike in quality and volume. After that, interest in mediaeval history died away under the influence of encyclopaedic 'enlightenment' in the age of Voltaire, which was in turn succeeded by the sentimental romantic antiquarianism of the epoch of *Ivanhoe*. But when, in the middle and later years of the Nineteenth Century, the two Maitlands and Stubbs and a host of other scholars unearthed the realities of mediaeval life and thought, the work of these moderns was based upon that of the scholars of the later Stuart period, whose exact and monumental studies had been inspired by the desire to defend the Church of England against Rome and Geneva, or by zeal to espouse one side or the other in the Nonjuror and Convocation controversies. (See *English Scholars*, Prof. David Douglas, 1929.)

In classical scholarship, Richard Bentley, Professor of Divinity and Master of Trinity, Cambridge, shone supreme among the English scholars not only of his own day but of all time. The publication of his *Phalaris* in 1699 made a new epoch in Greek studies, as Newton's *Principia* had done in physical science only a dozen years before. The fact that Bentley and his opponents published their lucubrations on *Phalaris* in English, not in Latin, betokened the increasing number of the general public who could take an intelligent interest in a learned controversy. But even Bentley still published the notes of his editions of the classics in Latin, just as Newton published his *Principia*, for scholarship and science still regarded themselves as cosmopolitan first and national afterwards.

Meanwhile the Quaker community was spreading its influence among the people faster than any other of the persecuted sects. Founded by George Fox in the period when the sword of Cromwell guarded the 'liberty of prophesying' against presbyter and priest, the strange religion was able to take root, but the unusual proceedings and manners of the first Friends subjected them to much ill-usage even in that era of sectarian liberty. And when the Restoration brought back the avowed persecution of Dissent, the Quakers suffered most severely of all the sects exposed to the severity of the Clarendon Code. Averse from institutional religion, regardless of sacraments, without priesthood or dogma, the Quakers, if they had come into existence half a century before they did, would have been burnt in batches. But the kind of persecution they had now to undergo, of stripes and imprisonment, enabled them to win proselytes by the display of patience and meekness under suffering.

With the meekness went a strain of mild obstinacy exquisitely calculated to infuriate the self-important bumbledom of that time, as when the Friends refused to remove their hats before the Court that was to try them. Their protest against snobbery and man-worship of the age was invaluable, but sometimes it took very foolish forms.

The nature of early Quakerism in the lifetime of its founder (Fox died in 1691) was a popular revivalism, profuse in its shrill utterance, making converts by thousands among the common folk. In the reigns of William and Anne, the Friends had become numerically one of the most powerful of the English sects. They settled down in the Eighteenth Century as a highly respectable and rather exclusive 'connection,' not seeking to proselytize any more, but possessing their own souls and guiding their own lives by a light that was indeed partly the 'inner light' in each man and woman, but was also a tradition and a set of spiritual rules of extraordinary potency, handed on from father to son and mother to daughter in the families of the Friends.

The finer essence of George Fox's queer teaching, common to the excited revivalists who were his first disciples, and to the 'quiet' Friends of later times, was surely this—that Christian qualities matter much more than Christian dogmas. No Church or sect had ever made that its living rule before. To maintain the Christian quality in the world of business and of domestic life, and to maintain it without pretension or hypocrisy, was the great achievement of these extraordinary people. England may well be proud of having produced and perpetuated them. The Puritan pot had boiled over, with much heat and fury; when it had cooled and been poured away, this precious sediment was left at the bottom.

The autobiography of Sir John Reresby, Baronet, of Thrybergh in the West Riding of Yorkshire, supplies a typical instance of the changing fortunes of a Cavalier landed family. Sir John's father died in 1646, the year after Naseby, leaving the estate in debt for £12,000, 'not through ill husbandry but through reason of the war.' He had been taken prisoner by the Roundheads two years before his death, 'confined to his own house,' and forced by fines to sell 'a large wood, all of it great timber, that stood in the Park.' His son, Sir John, aged twelve at the time of his succession to the encumbered estate, managed, under the careful conduct of his mother, to pull things round. In the next twenty years the debts were gradually paid off, and in 1668 Sir John was in a position to begin a series of improvements in his country house.

He rebuilt the exterior of the manor-house with stone in place of rough-cast; he put 'a new wainscot in several of the rooms'; he enlarged the deer park by taking in some arable fields, and 'encompassed it with a stone wall'; to replace the timber sold during the troubles, he planted ashes and sycamores, chosen as more suitable to the soil than 'trees of better kinds'; he brought the garden up to date, making a '*jett d'eau* or fountain, in the middle of the parterre, and the grotto in the summerhouse and brought the water in lead pipes,' and he raised the height of the garden wall. These operations were frugally spread over a number of years. Finally, just before the Revolution, he was 'at some charge to repair and beautify the Church and the windows and to give a new bell to the steeple.'

So far from being an 'illiterate squire,' Sir John was a fair Latin scholar and had a smattering of Greek; he talked Italian fluently and French like a Frenchman. In his youth he had spent some time in Padua University and in Venice, learning music and mathematics. At home he was an active Justice of the Peace; his clerk, he tells us, made '£40 a year out of the place'—more than many clergymen received from their livings. Sir John sat for the rotten borough of Aldborough (Yorks), where there were only nine electors, privileged owners of 'burgage houses.' A moderate and cautious Tory, Sir John became a House of Commons man, a courtier, sometimes a paid servant of the Crown. But he never ceased to be, first and foremost, a country gentleman.

Landowners of this type, with estates of the middling size and with outside connections and sources of profit, could more than hold their own in the Restoration world. But the small squire who lived on the proceeds of farming his own land but had little or no rents or other property, a man of meagre education and no knowledge of the world outside his own country, was beginning to lose ground in the latter part of the Seventeenth Century. The economic situation was gradually turning against him, for capital was needed to keep up with the new methods of land improvement. The fines and losses of the Civil War period might be a weight round the neck of a small estate for many years after the Restoration. And henceforth, more than ever, the great landowners and the men who had acquired new wealth by law, politics or commerce, were on the look-out for land, and ready to buy up the needy small owner with tempting offers. In this way the Dukes of Bedford added acre to acre, and manor to manor, till it seemed as if all Bedfordshire were theirs.

This process of increasing the great estates by extinguishing the small, culminated in the reign of George III, but it had already begun in the reign of Charles II. It accounts for much of the bitterness of Tory feeling immediately after the Revolution of 1688 against the moneyed men and the great Whig Lords. The small squire was usually a Tory and he specially detested the burden laid on his vanishing patrimony by the land tax, raised to pay for the wars of William and Marlborough, the more so as he believed that the proceeds of the tax went into the pockets of low-born army contractors, and of rich Dissenters, Londoners and Dutchmen who lent money to government. Though less fatal to the whole race of landowners than our modern Income Tax and Death Duties, the Land Tax was a sore burden to many small estates.

War and taxation certainly hastened the change, but at bottom the creation of great estates out of small was a natural economic process, analogous to the absorption of small businesses by large in the industrial world of our own day. If once agriculture came to be regarded as a means of producing national wealth, and no longer as a means of maintaining a given state of society, the change was inevitable. The capital in the hands of the great acquisitive landowners, and their devotion to the business and profit of landowning, were necessary conditions of that 'agricultural revolution' which in the Eighteenth Century so greatly increased the productivity of the English soil by wholesale enclosure and by the general application of new agricultural methods.

In the reign of Charles II these changes were still in the experimental stage. Agricultural writers were advocating, and a few more enlightened landlords and farmers were practising the improvements which became general in the following century—scientific rotation of crops, proper feeding of stock in winter, roots and clovers, the field cultivation of turnips and potatoes, oil-cake, silos, the storage of water. In the Restoration period all these things were known, but their general adoption was retarded by the open-field system with its half-communal agriculture, and by the want of capital and knowledge among the small squires and yeomen freeholders to whom so much of the land still belonged. And even the big landowners, in the generation immediately following the disturbance of the Civil Wars, had not enough confidence in the future, not enough capital or credit, nor enough personal interest in agriculture to take the lead in land improvement on a large scale, like their descendants in the days of 'Turnip Townshend,' Coke of Norfolk and Arthur Young.

After the Restoration rents were rising, but the landlords put too little of them back into the land and failed to encourage good farmers.

> He that havocs may sit:
> He that improves must flit

was a Berkshire saying of this time: 'Our gentry are grown ignorant in everything of good husbandry,' wrote Pepys. For lack of leadership and capital the age of change was postponed.

So, under merry King Charles, the old rural world still survived, with its wide diffusion of rights in the soil, its comparative economic equality, its open fields and its small productivity. But the movement towards great estates, enclosed fields, and improvement of agricultural methods was already on the way. [See § 95.]

For one thing, national policy was already promoting increased production for the domestic and foreign markets. Acts of Parliament restricted the import of cattle from Ireland and of corn from abroad, and offered the English farmer bounties for export. This policy, introduced step by step from Charles II to Anne, was partly meant as a set-off to the heavy incidence of the land tax and was, of course, popular with the small squires and freehold yeomen. Yet, if it helped them at the expense of the home consumer, it helped still more the larger landlords, and the men with

§81 The Lord Mayor and the Court of Aldermen

§82 John Milton

Gal. Faithorne ad Vivum.    Delin. et sculpsit.

Joannis Miltoni Effigies Ætat: 62.
1670.

§83 John Evelyn

Meliora Retinete.

§84 Ham House, Surrey. The Jacobean north front (1610) with alterations of 1672

§85 Coleshill House, Berkshire (1650–64)

§86 The Staircase at Tythrop House, Oxfordshire (*c.* 1680)

§87 The Grinling Gibbons carved room at Petworth House, Sussex

§88 An Elizabethan formal garden with pleached bower (1568)

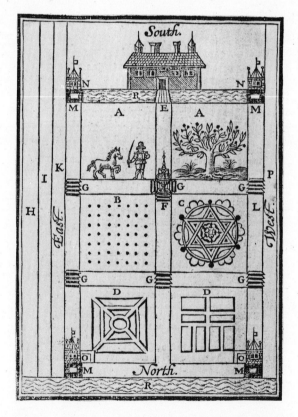

§89 A new orchard and garden (1618) (*for key see notes*)

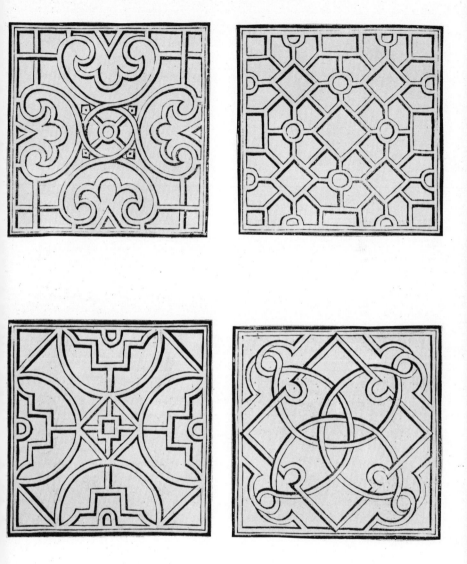

§90 Mazes and dials for the country housewife's garden (1618)

§91 Design for the garden at Wilton House (1645)

The Road from
LONDON TO BARWICK
Tottenham high Cross
MIDDLESEX

BARWICK

NORTHUMBER LAND

YORKE

LANCA SHIRE

DERBY SH.

LINCOLN SHIRE

BRITANNIA
VOL. I
or an
Illustration
of ye Kingdom of
ENGLAND
and Dominion of WALES
By a
Geographical & Historicall
Description
of the Principal
ROADS.

§92 The Seventeenth-century Road

§93 Travelling players

§94 The Stage of the Red Bull
(*Note the candelabra and footlight*

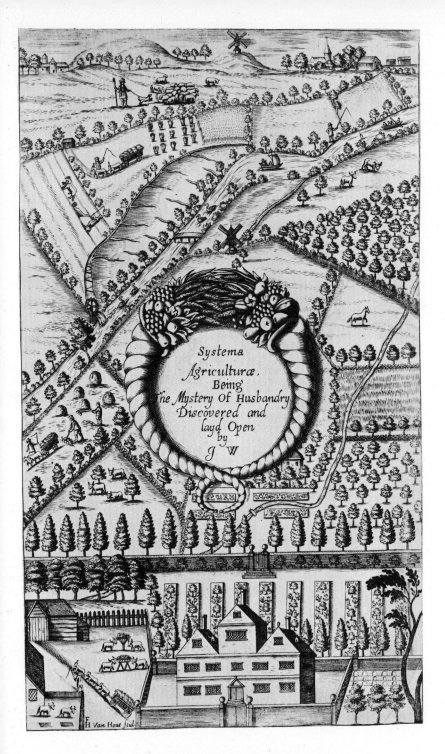

Systema
Agriculturæ,
Being
The Mystery Of Husbandry
Discovered and
layd Open
by
J W

H Van Hout fcul.

§95 The improvement of agricultural methods
(*for explanatory dedication see notes*)

§96 Isaac Newton

§97 Robert Boyle

§98 Pepys' library, in his original bookcases, at Magdalen College, Cambridge

§99 Grinling Gibbons carving on the bookcases in the Library of Trinity College, Cambridge

§ 100 Water transport—coal barges and 'tilt' boats

§ 101 A stage wagon

§ 102 Packhorses

§ 103 Coach and dray

& Metrop. &c. Theatri hujus Funda-
tori Munificentissimo
D.D.C.Q. Dav. Loggan.

Dav. Loggan Delin: et Sculp. cum Privil. S.R.M.

§ 104 A coach and four

§ 105 A travelling coach

John Dunstall fe.

capital and enterprise to increase production for the market, the men who were gradually buying up the small estates.[1]

These protective corn laws and bounties did not have their full effect until Hanoverian times, but their adoption under the later Stuarts is significant of the social forces that were moulding our national policy, the more so as export bounties on corn were not a system in general use in other countries. Its singular adoption in England was due to the control of economic policy which Parliament had won from the Crown as a result of the Civil War. The power of the House of Commons over the business affairs of the country was confirmed at the Restoration and further enlarged at the Revolution. And the House of Commons was very much alive to the interests of the landowners, to which class nine-tenths of its members belonged. The voters in the Parliamentary boroughs, most of them small country towns, preferred to be represented by neighbouring gentry rather than by real 'burgesses' from their own ranks. By this arrangement, so characteristic of the advantages of English snobbery, the interests of the townsfolk received more attention at Westminster and at the same time the political and social power of the House of Commons was increased. If, for example, Aldborough, instead of electing Sir John Reresby, had sent up one of its small shopkeepers to Parliament, neither King, Lords nor Ministers would have cared what such a man said or thought. Only London and a few other great cities chose their own merchant princes to speak for them on the floor of the national Senate: for what they said carried weight.

But although the House of Commons was becoming, to an ever increasing degree, a House of landlords, whose personal interest was mainly agricultural, it did not follow that trade and industry were neglected. After all, more than four hundred of the five hundred members sat for boroughs; such a Chamber consisting mainly of squires whose constituents were townsfolk,

---

[1] The actual working of the bounty of five shillings a quarter on wheat exported, may be seen in the following letter from Falmouth in 1675:

'Much corn is buying up in those parts for the Canaries and Holland, so that the price is raised since harvest three shillings on twenty gallons and is like to be dearer, for the encouragement the merchant has at five shillings per quarter paid them at the custom house very much encourages them to buy, so that the Act, which is good for the farmers, is not beneficial to the town and tradesmen.' (*State Papers, Dom.* 1675, p. 403.)

was more likely than any other assembly to give due consideration both to the agricultural and to the trading needs of the nation. Moreover, a large proportion of the landlords in both Houses of Parliament, particularly the richer and more powerful among them, were personally interested in industrial or commercial affairs. It is therefore no surprise to find that in this same period Parliament protected cloth manufacture as assiduously as corn growing; forbade the import of foreign cloth and the export of raw wool, killed the Irish cloth trade for the benefit of the English clothiers, and ordained that everyone who died should be buried in English cloth.[1]

The Navigation Act, which aimed at keeping the trade of the country for English instead of Dutch shipping, had been passed in the Long Parliament in 1651, at a time when State policy was much under the influence of the merchant community of London. The Restoration made no change in this respect. Court and Parliament were at one on the policy of the Navigation Laws, to keep the trade of England and her Colonies in English bottoms, and on the concomitant policy of hostility to our Dutch commercial rivals.

The Princes and Ministers of the Court of Charles II, as well as their critics in Parliament, were in close personal contact with the City magnates who conducted the great adventures of foreign commerce. The highest persons in the land held shares in the joint-stock companies trading in Indian, African and American waters. James, Duke of York, Lord High Admiral and heir to the throne, was Governor of the Royal African Company and shareholder in East Indian stock; he succeeded Prince Rupert as the Governor of the Hudson's Bay Company and was in turn succeeded by Marlborough.

In this way the magnates who controlled English diplomatic, naval and military policy were in the closest possible touch with the mercantile community and personally shared its interests and its outlook. The wars with Holland in the reign of Charles II, and with France in the reigns of William and Anne were to a large extent mercantile and colonial wars, on the necessity and profit of which Court, Parliament and City were agreed.

'Odious! in woollen! 'twoold a saint provoke,'
Were the last words that poor Narcissa spoke.
(Pope, *Moral Essays*, I.)

The pacificist and 'little England' feeling of the squires with small rent rolls and rustic outlook played its part in Tory election-eering, but had not much influence on the action of statesmen at Westminster and Whitehall. A series of wars of commercial and colonial expansion, first against Dutch, then against French, increased the English territories in America and pushed English commerce into the markets of Europe and the world. These wars were paid for largely by the land tax. It cannot, therefore, be said that English policy from Charles II to Anne neglected the mercantile or the national interest from a prejudice in favour of the land, or from undue attention paid to the opinions of the majority of the landowners.

Old rural England, on the eve of the wholesale enclosures and the industrial revolution, is often presented to the mind's eye of posterity in one or other of two rival pictures. On the one hand we are asked to contemplate a land of independent and self-respecting peasants, most of them attached to the soil by small personal rights therein, contented with the country quiet and felicity which have been since destroyed, and celebrating their rural happiness in ale-house songs about 'Harvesthome,' which we have since promoted to the drawing-room; and the same land, we are reminded, was also the land of craftsmen in village and market town, not divorced from rural pleasures because they pursued industry, using tools instead of watching machines, and therefore enjoying in their daily work the delight of the individual artist, for which a poor substitute is found in the feverish excite-ment of our modern amusements, organized *en masse* as a counter-poise to the dullness of mechanical and clerical toil. On the other hand we are shown the opposing picture: we are asked to remember the harsh, backbreaking labour of the pre-mechanical ages, continued for thirteen or more hours in the day; child-labour instead of primary schools; disease and early death uncontrolled by medical science or hospital provision; and absence of cleanliness and comforts which we now regard as necessities; neglectful and unimaginative harshness not only to criminals and debtors but too often to women, children and the poor at large; and, finally, a population of five and a half millions in England and Wales, with less material comfort than the present population (1939) of more than seven times that number.

Confirmation of both these pictures emerges from a study of

the period. But which picture contains the greater and more important body of truth it is hazardous to pronounce, partly because the dispute is about intangible values—we cannot put ourselves back into the minds of our ancestors, and if we could we should still be puzzled; partly also because, even where statistics would help, statistics are not to be had.

It is true that about the time of the Revolution, the able publicist Gregory King made a calculation from the hearth tax and other data of the probable numbers in various classes of the community. The figures he gave represent a shrewd guess, but no more. They will indeed serve negatively as a check on the enthusiasm of the *Laudator temporis acti,* by recalling the fact that, even before the great enclosure and the industrial revolution, the number of farmers and yeomen was relatively small and the numbers of the agricultural proletariat large.

The two largest classes by far in King's analysis of the nation are the 'cottagers and paupers' and the 'labouring people and outservants.' The former represent, we may suppose, those who attempted to be independent of wages and, according to King, made a very poor business of the attempt. Yet such persons, who picked up a living off the common whereon they had squatted, or off the small field they owned behind the hovel, may have been happier than King knew, even if they were poorer than is realized by modern idealizers of the past. King's second large class, the 'labouring people and outservants,' are the wage-earners. But many of them had also some rights on the common, some garden or tiny holding which added to the interest and dignity of life, without entitling the owner to the proud rank of English yeoman. Even the servants of industry had many of them small gardens or plots of land to till in their off hours, especially the woollen weavers in all parts of the island. On the stony heights around Halifax each clothworker had a 'cow or two' in a field walled off on the steep hillside whereon his cottage stood.

On the other hand, there were very large numbers of employees both in agriculture and industry who had no rights in land and no means of subsistence but their wages.

The wages in agriculture and in industry were supposed to be regulated by schedules issued for each county by the Justices of the Peace, who also occasionally set a limit to the price at which certain goods might be sold. These schedules did not pretend to fix either wages or prices exactly, but only to set a maximum which was not to be surpassed. Variations were therefore permissible inside every county, as well as differences between one shire and the next. Moreover, the maximum announced was very often transgressed in practice.[1]

Judging by negative evidence, we may conclude that concerted strikes and combinations to raise wages were not common; we hear much more about strikes in the reign of Edward III than in the reign of Charles II.

The Elizabethan Statute of Artificers, that was still partially in force, penalized the leaving of work unfinished, as well as the giving or taking of wages above the maximum fixed by the Justices of the Peace. But the maximum was often exceeded when excess payment was to the interest of both employer and employed. If there was little trade-unionism, there was much individual bargaining about wages.

Even when the low prices are taken into account, some of the wages paid seem low by modern standards. But they were high in comparison with the Europe of that day. The national characteristic of Englishmen, then as now, was not thrift but insistence on a high standard of life. Defoe, writing as an employer, declared that:

Good husbandry is no English virtue. English labouring people eat and drink, especially the latter, three times as much in value as any sort of foreigners of the same dimensions in the world.

The staple diet was bread, or rather bread, beer and usually meat. Vegetables and fruit played a small, and meat a very large part in the English meal of that date. Among the middle and upper classes, breakfast was often a 'morning draft' of ale with a little bread and butter; that sufficed till the noonday dinner, a tremendous meal of various fish and meats. As to the poorer

---

[1] Wages differed from one estate to another; in 1701 a Yorkshire squire wrote: 'The wages of a good husbandman in the parts about Barnsley and Wortley I find to be no more than £3 a year, and Sir Godfrey gives his keeper but £3 14s., and his bailiff £4, so that we are worse served for high wages. About Wortley all the husbandmen are up every morning with their beasts at three o'clock and in our house they lie abed till near seven. But above all Warne's £20 vexes me.' I expect both food and lodging were given, as well as the wages mentioned. That year wheat stood as low as 34s. a quarter and other grain in proportion, and chickens could be bought in the West Riding at twopence apiece.

households, Gregory King reckoned that half the population ate meat daily, and that of the other half the greater number ate meat at least twice a week. The million who 'received alms,' 'eat not flesh above once a week.'

Reliable statistics of the population of England, and of the classes into which it was divided cannot be obtained before the first Census of 1801, but the calculations—or shall we call them guesses?—that Gregory King made with the help of the hearth tax and other data at the time of the Revolution (1688) are well worthy of examination. At least they represent the map of society as it presented itself to the thought of a well-informed contemporary. The reader would do well to study the figures, knowing indeed that they cannot be exact, but not knowing in what direction the errors lie.

To interpret this table, several points should be borne in mind. The 'heads per family' are the persons living under one roof: the 'family' includes the servants in the house as well as the children. The poor, therefore, are put down as having much smaller 'families' than the rich, although the average number of children still alive and still at home might be the same in all classes. The 'families and incomes' given are, of course, guesses at the *average* figure: in each class, some householders would have larger 'families' and incomes than the figure set down, while others in the same class lived on a smaller scale. The 'Freeholders' include, not only owners of their own farms, but also copy-holders and tenants for life. Finally, it must be remembered that 'Labouring people and out-servants,' and 'Cottagers and paupers,' the two largest classes in the community, include many who had small rights in land of one kind or another.

According to Gregory King over one million persons, nearly a fifth of the whole nation, were in occasional receipt of alms, mostly in the form of public relief paid by the parish. The poor-rate was a charge of nearly £800,000 a year on the country and rose to a million in the reign of Anne. There was seldom any shame felt in receiving outdoor relief, and it was said to be given with a mischievous profusion. Richard Dunning declared that in 1698 the parish dole was often three times as much as a common labourer, having to maintain a wife and three children, could afford to expend upon himself; and that persons once receiving outdoor relief refuse ever to work, and 'seldom drink other than

| Number of Families | Ranks, Degrees, Titles and Qualifications. | Heads per Family | Number of Persons | Yearly Income per Family |
|---|---|---|---|---|
| 160 | Temporal lords . . . . | 40 | 6,400 | £3,200 |
| 26 | Spiritual lords . . . . | 20 | 520 | 1,300 |
| 800 | Baronets . . . . . | 16 | 12,800 | 880 |
| 600 | Knights . . . . . | 13 | 7,800 | 650 |
| 3,000 | Esquires . . . . . | 10 | 30,000 | 450 |
| 12,000 | Gentlemen . . . . . | 8 | 96,000 | 280 |
| 5,000 | Persons in greater offices and places . | 8 | 40,000 | 240 |
| 5,000 | Persons in lesser offices and places . | 6 | 30,000 | 120 |
| 2,000 | Eminent merchants and traders by sea | 8 | 16,000 | 400 |
| 8,000 | Lesser merchants and traders by sea . | 6 | 48,000 | 198 |
| 10,000 | Persons in the law . . . . | 7 | 70,000 | 154 |
| 2,000 | Eminent clergymen . . . | 6 | 12,000 | 72 |
| 8,000 | Lesser clergymen . . . . | 5 | 40,000 | 50 |
| 40,000 | Freeholders of the better sort . | 7 | 280,000 | 91 |
| 120,000 | Freeholders of the lesser sort . . | 5½ | 660,000 | 55 |
| 150,000 | Farmers . . . . . | 5 | 750,000 | 42 10s. |
| 15,000 | Persons in liberal arts and sciences . | 5 | 75,000 | 60 |
| 50,000 | Shopkeepers and tradesmen . . | 4½ | 225,000 | 45 |
| 60,000 | Artisans and handicrafts . . . | 4 | 240,000 | 38 |
| 5,000 | Naval officers . . . . | 4 | 20,000 | 80 |
| 4,000 | Military officers . . . | 4 | 16,000 | 60 |
| 50,000 | Common seamen . . . . | 3 | 150,000 | 20 |
| 364,000 | Labouring people and out-servants . | 3½ | 1,275,000 | 15 |
| 400,000 | Cottagers and paupers . . . | 3¼ | 1,300,000 | 6 10s. |
| 35,000 | Common soldiers . . . . | 2 | 70,000 | 14 |
|  | Vagrants, as gipsies, thieves, beggars, etc. . . . . . . |  | 30,000 |  |
|  | **Total** . . . . |  | 5,500,520 |  |

(Printed in Charles Davenant's Works (1771), Vol. II, p. 184, with further figures.)

the strongest ale-house beer, or eat any bread save what is made of the finest wheat flour.' The statement must be received with caution, but such was the nature of the complaint of some rate-payers and employers about the poor-law.

These problems of outdoor relief have a family likeness in all ages. But one peculiarity of the English Poor Law in the Restoration era and the Eighteenth Century was the Act of Settlement, passed by Charles II's Cavalier Parliament. By this Act every Parish in which a man tried to settle could send him back to the parish of which he was native, for fear that if he stayed in his new abode he might at some future date become chargeable on the rates. Nine-tenths of the people of England, all in fact who did not belong to a small class of landowners, were liable to be expelled from any parish save their own, with every circumstance of arrest and ignominy, however good their character and even if they had secured remunerative work. The panic fear of some parish authorities lest newcomers should some day fall on the rates, caused them to exercise this unjust power in quite unnecessary cases. The Act placed a check upon the fluidity of labour and was as much an outrage as the Press-gang itself on the boasted freedom of Englishmen. Yet it was seldom denounced, until many years later Adam Smith dealt with it in scathing terms. It is hard to ascertain the exact degree to which it operated, and Adam Smith appears to have exaggerated the harm done and the number of cases in which cruel wrong was inflicted. But at best it was a great evil; it is the reverse side of that creditable effort of Stuart England to provide for the maintenance of the poor through the local public authorities. That effort, on the whole, was not unsuccessful, and largely accounts for the peaceable character of English society.

Nothing marked more clearly the growing power of squire-archy in the House of Commons and in the State than the Game Laws of the Restoration period. By the Forest Laws of Norman and Plantagenet times, the interests of all classes of subjects had been sacrificed in order that the King should have abundance of red deer to hunt; but now the interests of the yeomen and farmers were sacrificed in order that the squire should have plenty of partridges to shoot. Even more than politics, partridges caused neighbours to look at one another askance: for the

yeoman freeholder killed, upon his own little farm, the game that
wandered over it from the surrounding estates of game preservers.
And so in 1671 the Cavalier Parliament passed a law which prevented all freeholders of under a hundred pounds a year—that is
to say the very great majority of the class—from killing game,
even on their own land. Thus many poor families were robbed
of many good meals that were theirs by right; and even those
few yeoman whose wealth raised them above the reach of this
remarkable law, were for that reason regarded with suspicion.
The best that even the good-hearted Sir Roger de Coverley can
bring himself to say of the 'yeoman of about a hundred pounds
a year,' 'who is just within the Game Act,' is that 'he would make
a good neighbour if he did not destroy so many partridges'—
that is to say upon his own land.

For many generations to come, grave social consequences were
to flow from the excessive eagerness of the country gentlemen
about the preservation of game. Their anxieties on that score
had grown with the adoption of the shot-gun. During the Stuart
epoch shooting gradually superseded hawking, with the result
that birds were more rapidly destroyed, and the supply no longer
seemed inexhaustible. In Charles II's reign it was already not
unusual to 'shoot flying.' But it was regarded as a difficult art,
the more so as it was sometimes practised from horseback. But
the 'perching' of pheasants by stalking and shooting them as they
sat on the boughs, was still customary among gentleman. [See
§ 106, 107, 108.]

The netting of birds on the ground was a fashionable sport,
often carried on over dogs who pointed the game concealed in
the grass. [See § 109.] It is written that Sir Roger 'in his youthful
days had *taken* forty coveys of partridges in a season' probably
by this means. To lure wild duck, by the score and the hundred,
into a decoy upon the water's edge was a trade in the fens and a
sport on the decoy-pond of the manor-house. Liming by twigs,
snaring and trapping birds of all kinds, not only pheasants and
wild duck but thrushes and fieldfares, had still a prominent place
in manuals of *The Gentleman's Recreation*. But the shot-gun was
clearly in the ascendant, and with it the tendency to confine sport
more and more to the pursuit of certain birds specifically listed
as *game*. In that sacred category a place had recently been granted
by Statute to grouse and blackcock; already the heather and

bracken where they lurked were protected from being burnt except at certain times of the year, and the shepherd transgressing the law was liable to be whipped. Addison's Tory squire declared the new Game Law to be the only good law passed since the Revolution.[1]

Fox-hunting, under the later Stuarts, was beginning to assume features recognizably modern. In Tudor times the fox had been dug out of its earth, bagged, and baited like a badger, or had been massacred as vermin by the peasantry. For in those days the stag was still the beast of the chase *par excellence*. But the disorders of the Civil War had broken open deer-parks and destroyed deer to such an extent that at the Restoration the fox was perforce substituted in many districts. As yet there were no county or regional packs supported by public subscription, but private gentlemen kept their own packs and invited their nearer neighbours to follow. The idea that gentlemen should hunt 'the stag and the fox with their own hounds and among their own woods,' was gradually yielding to the chase across the country at large, irrespective of its ownership.

In some countries earths were stopped and the endeavour was made with frequent success to run the fox down in the open. Under these conditions runs of ten or even twenty miles were not unknown. But in Lancashire and probably elsewhere 'the hunters ran the fox to earth and then dug him out; if he refused to go to earth he generally got away. It is possible that there had not yet been developed as tireless a breed of hounds as to-day.'[2]

The chase of the deer, with all the time-honoured ritual of venery, still continued as the acknowledged king of sports, but it was steadily on the decline, as the claims of agriculture for more land reduced the number of forests and set a limit to the size of the deer-park that a gentleman was likely to keep enclosed round his manor-house. [See § 111.]

More widely popular than the hunting of deer or fox was the pursuit of the hare, with a 'tunable chiding' of hounds, the

[1] The two leading Game Laws are those of 22-23 Charles II, cap. 25, and 4 W. and M. cap., 23.

[2] Thus Thomas Tyldesley writes in his diary—'went early to Sullom a fox hunting to meet brothers Dalton and Frost, found two foxes, but could get neither of them into the earth.' (Notestein, *English Folk*, p. 172.) Compare the account of fox-hunting in Bloome's *Gentleman's Recreation*, 1686, II, pp. 137-139.

gentlemen on horseback, and the common folk running, headed by the huntsman with his pole. This scene partook of the nature of a popular village sport, led indeed by the gentry but shared with all their neighbours, high and low. [See § 110.]

Other popular sports were wrestling, with different rules and traditions in different parts of the country; various rough kinds of football and 'hurling,' often amounting to a good-natured free-fight between the whole male population of two villages. Single-stick, boxing and sword-fighting, bull and bear baiting, were watched with delight by a race that had not yet learnt to dislike the sight of pain inflicted. Indeed the less sporting events of hanging and whipping were spectacles much relished. But cockfighting was the most popular sport of all, on which all classes staked their money even more than upon horse-racing. But the turf was beginning to take a greater place in the national consciousness owing to the patronage of Newmarket by Charles II and the improvement in the breed of riding-horses by the introduction of Arab and Barb blood. [See § 112.]

Under the late Stuart kings, Spas were much frequented for purposes of fashion and of health. The waters of Bath were beginning to attract the great, for the first time since Roman days, but the fine town of Beau Nash and Jane Austen had not yet been built. [See § 114.] Buxton and Harrogate were much attended by northern gentry and their families. But the Court and the world of London fashion were found oftenest and in greatest number among the rustic cottages round the Tunbridge Wells, where in 1685 the courtiers built a church for their own use, dedicated to King Charles the Martyr. [See § 123.]

As yet the seaside had no votaries: doctors had not yet discovered the health-giving qualities of its air; no one wanted to bathe in the waters of the ocean or to rhapsodize over its appearance from the shore. The sea was 'the Englishman's common,' his way to market, his fishpond, his battleground, his heritage. But as yet no one sought either the seaside or the mountains for the refreshment they could give to the spirit of man.

During the century of Stuart rule, frequent assessments of the counties of England were made for fiscal purposes; the returns indicate roughly the geographical distribution of wealth. The richest county was Middlesex, as it included so much of London;

the poorest was Cumberland. Surrey, owing to the expansion of London and its market, rose from the eighteenth place in 1636 to the second in 1693. Next in order of wealth came Berks and the group of agricultural counties north of the Thames—Herts, Beds, Bucks, Oxfordshire and Northants. Their wealth is remarkable, considering that they possessed no great towns, industrial districts or coal-mines and that their agriculture was chiefly open-field; but it was not far from the London market. Thus the central counties were on the average the richest. Next came the southern, including Kent and Sussex, with lands of old enclosure and fruit gardens, and with downland sheep-runs; next East Anglia, enjoying the farmer's blessing of a low rainfall, and with Essex abutting on London; next in order of wealth came the West, distant from the capital, and suffering from a damper climate. And last of all, the lately turbulent and still impoverished North. The seven poorest counties in England were Cheshire, Derybshire, Yorkshire, Lancashire, Northumberland, Durham and Cumberland. The poverty of the Northern shires is the more remarkable because they all had coal-mines, and Yorks and Lancs had textiles as well. But the wealth produced by these industries had not yet been applied on a large scale to the improvement of agriculture in these backward northern parts. That was done in the following century, when the wealth of the Tyneside mines was poured out into the soil, to fertilize the moorland farms of the neighbouring counties.

If a line be drawn from Gloucester to Boston, the area of England without Wales is divided about equally into a North-Western half and a South-Eastern half: to-day the majority of the population live North-West of the line, owing to the development of heavy industries, though a return drift towards the South has recently begun. But in Charles II's reign it is probable that only a quarter of the population lived North-West of the line. The land tax returns indicate that the wealth of the North-Western half was only 5 : 14, while the Excise returns make it 1 : 4. (Ogg, *England in the reign of C. II*, p. 51.)

In the course of the Seventeenth Century, changes had taken place in Warwickshire significant of industrial progress and of its reactions on agriculture. In Elizabeth's reign Camden had noted in his *Britannia* that Warwickshire was divided by the Avon into two parts, the Feldon or rich arable district of open field to the

South-East of the river, and the Woodland (the Forest of Arden) to the North-West. In the reign of William III, Gibson, afterwards the famous Bishop of London, brought out a new edition of the *Britannia*, adding notes of changes that had taken place since Camden's day: the Forest of Arden had disappeared, and had become a rich arable district:

For the ironworks in the counties round [viz. in Birmingham and the Black Country] destroyed such prodigious quantities of wood that they quickly lay the country a little open, and by degrees made room for the plough. Whereupon the inhabitants, partly by their own industry, and partly by the assistance of marl have turned so much of wood and heath-land into tillage and pasture that they produce corn, cattle, cheese and butter enough not only for their own use but also to furnish other counties.

Meanwhile, on the other side of Avon, the Feldon, once the great arable region supplying Bristol with corn, had been largely laid down to grass, and the population of many villages had been reduced, according to Gibson, to a few shepherds; the reason for the change to pasture in the Feldon is, he thinks, the superior arable quality of the old forest lands on the other side of Avon recently brought under plough. Here, then, in both parts of Warwickshire, we have a great increase of enclosed fields—to the North-West enclosure of old forest and heath, to South-East hedging of former open fields. All this occurred in the Stuart era, with very little said, for the feeling against enclosure, so vocal in Tudor times, seems to have died away.[1]

In Stuart times, in spite of the rapid growth of iron trades in Birmingham and the Black Country to the west of it, coal or coke fires were not yet applied to iron. Coal, however, was used in many other processes of manufacture; and it had become the regular domestic fuel in London, and in all regions to which it could easily be carried by water. Under these conditions the Stuart era saw an increase in the coal trade, hardly less astonishing, in the circumstances of that earlier time, than the second great

---

[1] In his 'Additions to Warwickshire' since Camden's day, Gibson also notes in the 1695 edition of the *Britannia* (pp. 510–512) that in Stratford church 'in the chancel lies William Shakespeare, a native of this place, who has given proof of his genius and great abilities in the 48 plays he has left behind him.' There are only 37 in the present canon ! But the passage at least shows the considerable place Shakespeare already held in his countrymen's estimation.

increase in the early Nineteenth Century, the age of 'coal and iron.'[1]

ESTIMATED ANNUAL PRODUCTION IN TONS

|  | 1551-60 | 1681-90 | 1781-90 | 1901-10 |
|---|---|---|---|---|
| Durham and Northumberland | 65,000 | 1,225,000 | 3,000,000 | 50,000,000 |
| Scotland | 40,000 | 475,000 | 1,600,000 | 37,000,000 |
| Wales | 20,000 | 200,000 | 800,000 | 50,000,000 |
| Midlands | 65,000 | 850,000 | 4,000,000 | 100,180,000 |
| Cumberland | 6,000 | 100,000 | 500,000 | 2,120,000 |
| Kingswood Chase and Somerset | 10,000 | 100,000 | 140,000 | 1,100,000 |
| Forest of Dean | 3,000 | 25,000 | 90,000 | 1,310,000 |
| Devon and Ireland | 1,000 | 7,000 | 25,000 | 200,000 |
|  | 210,000 | 2,982,000 | 10,155,000 | 241,910,000 |

*Approximate increase :*     14 *fold*     3 *fold*     23 *fold*

The Midland coal area included mines in Yorks, Lancs, Cheshire, Derbyshire, Shropshire, Staffs, Notts, Warwickshire, Leicestershire and Worcestershire.

Throughout the Seventeenth Century coal played a great part in developing, not only the national wealth and therewith the well-being of many classes of the community above ground, but also the less pleasant characteristics of the Industrial Revolution in the life of the miners themselves. Their 'capitalist' employers saw little and cared less about their conditions of life and labour. As the pits grew deeper, the miners spent more time far away underground, and were more and more segregated from the rest of humanity; explosions due to fire-damp became more frequent and more terrible, and women and children were more often employed underground as bearers. In Durham and Northumberland great combinations of thousands of miners and keelmen in the Tyne coal-barges, strove with indifferent success to better their conditions of life. In Scotland the miners were reduced to the condition of 'bondmen' bound to the service of the mine. In England this could not be done, but the condition of the miners and their families were in many respects worse than that of any other large class of the community.

Mr. Nef, who has collected a great body of facts relating to mining conditions in Stuart and early Hanoverian times, writes:

Coal created a new gulf between classes. The mediaeval peasants and artisans, whatever their disabilities and trials may have been, were not

---

[1] The following figures given by Mr. Nef in his *Rise of the British Coal Industry*, pp. 19-20, [Routledge], show how rapid was the advance in coal production between the reigns of Elizabeth and William III, and show also the geographic distribution of the coalfields, much the same as at the present day.

segregated from their neighbours to anything like the same extent as were the coal miners of the seventeenth century in most colliery districts.

Moreover, within the coal-mining industry itself, there was now a complete barrier between the capitalist employer and the manual worker, similar to that which became general in so many other trades in later times. Indeed, under the later Stuart Kings many new industries which sprang up as a result of the supply of coal for furnaces, tended to be of the same large-scale and capitalistic character. (Nef, *Rise of the British Coal Industry*, Vol. II, chap. IV.)

But there were many districts which could not obtain coal either by sea or by river. Some of these regions, owing to the decrease of timber, went short of fuel for the elementary needs of warmth and cooking, and remained in that condition until the improved roads, the canals and finally the railways of later times brought coal to every door. Thus, in the reign of William III, the adventurous Miss Celia Fiennes,[1] on a riding tour in the South-West, found her supper at Penzance 'boiling on a fire always supplied with a bush of furze, and that to be the only fuel to dress a joint of meat and broth'; for the Cornish forests had disappeared, and the French privateers in time of war prevented the delivery of Welsh coal in the south Cornish ports. In Leicestershire, cowdung, that ought to have enriched the fields, was gathered and dried for fuel.

So, too, in 1695, Gibson, in his edition of Camden's *Britannia*, comments on the description given by the Elizabethan antiquary of the Oxfordshire hills 'clad with woods'; 'this is so much altered,' writes Gibson, 'by the late civil wars that few places except the Chiltern country can answer that character at present. For fuel is in those parts so scarce that 'tis commonly sold by weight, not only in Oxford, but other towns in the northern part of the shire.' Oxford town and gown could, however, warm their parlours and cook their food with coal conveyed by the Thames barges, whereas the 'towns in the northern part of the shire' found the storage of wood fuel a more serious matter.

---

[1] *The Journey of Celia Fiennes,* edited by Christopher Morris (1947). This delightful and important record was composed on tours made partly in the reign of William III, partly in that of Anne. Miss Fiennes was a lady of means and a dissenter. She was sister of the Third Viscount Saye and Sele. She rode through England on tours of pleasure and curiosity.

The bread-and-cheese diet to which many English working-class families were increasingly limited in the following century, was largely the result of this lack of kitchen fuel; and in winter time their poor cottages must have been terribly cold. In those parts of the country where there was a time-gap between the timber age and the coal age, there was much suffering for the poor and some inconvenience for the rich.

But even before the days of hard roads, coal could at a cost be carried far inland, at a great distance from the mines, wherever the service was well organized. Thus Miss Fiennes describes the barges with 'sea-coal' from Bristol coming up by river through Bridgwater to a place within three miles of Taunton, 'where the boats unload the coal, the packhorses come and take it in sacks, and so carry it to places all about. The horses carry two bushell at a time, which at the place of disembarkation cost eighteen pence, and when it's brought to Taunton cost two shillings. The roads were full of these carriers going and returning.' [See § 100, 101, 102, 103.]

The growth of London, more and more outdistancing all other cities, continued after the Restoration without a check. By the year 1700 the capital contained well over a tenth of the five and a half million inhabitants of England.[1] Bristol and Norwich, the cities next in size, numbered about 30,000 each. And London trade was proportionately great. In 1680 the Custom House administration of the Port of London cost £20,000 a year, of Bristol £2000, of Newcastle, Plymouth and Hull £900 each; the rest were nowhere. The port of Newcastle lived on the export of coal, three-quarters of it to London; Hull flourished on the whaling and fishing industries, and on its importance as the chief garrison town of Northern England; Plymouth, like great Bristol and rising Liverpool, benefited by the growing trade with the transatlantic colonies, and on its own importance as the western base of the Royal Navy.

Whitby, Yarmouth and Harwich had flourishing shipbuilding

---

[1] It has been estimated from the registers of baptisms that in 1700 when England and Wales contained rather more than five and a half million inhabitants, the Metropolitan Area contained 674,350. Of these the 'City' proper contained about 200,000. (Mrs. George, *London Life*, etc., pp. 24-25, 328-330.) On the figures of population for England and Wales see Talbot-Griffith, *Royal Statistical Society Journal*, 1929, Vol XCII, Pt. II, pp. 256-263.

§ 106 Partridge hawking

§ 107 Perching the pheasant

§ 108 Shooting flying

The Setting Dogg & Partridge

§ 109 Netting birds on the ground

HUNTING y HARE
with deep mouthed hounds

Ia: Collins Sculp

§ 110 Hunting the hare

UNHARBOVRING Ỹ STAGG

§ 111 Unharbouring the stag

August 1684
The last Horse-Race
Run before
CHARLES the Second of
Blessed Memory
By Dorsett Ferry
near
Windsor Castle.

Drawn from the Race and Design'd
by Francis Barlow
1687

Rome, with her Olimpick Game,
did achive so great a Fame,
the Circus the bright Chariots whirld,
with delight the Gazing world,
compaires to Englands nobler Chase,
as lightning or the winged Race

noreos Beast out-strips y mind,
eaves the wondering Croud behind.

In this Debate Monarchs their Umpirage boast,
And even an Empires wealth is won & lost;
The noble Brutes with Emulation fir'd,
Scorning by Managers to be inspird,
As if they understood their Betters will,
They shew w th pride their eager forces & skill,

And without aid of spur, or reins,
They cutt y air, & scoure y plaine.

To future times may these Illustrious Sports
Be only the divertisements of Courts,
Since the best man best Iudge, & best of Kings,
Whose President the best Example brings,
When ere his God-like mind unbent from care
To all his pleasure, this he would preferr:

So Gods of old did not disdaine
The rural pastimes of the plaine.

And Dorsett ever celebra
For this last honour which a
Blest for thy Prospect all aug
Blest for the memory of this
The last great Race the Roya
O Dorsett to thy much lov'd p

For this alone a lasting
Records thee in the Boo

Sold by P. Tempest over ag.st Somerset, house Water gate in the Strand. and T. Baker at the White Horse in Fleet Stre

§112 The last horse-race run before Charles II
at Dorsett (=Datchet) Ferry 1684

§ 113 Flying from the plague in 1630

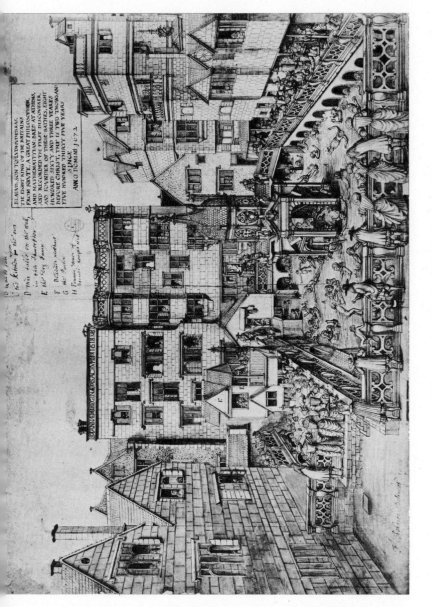

§ 114 Bathing in 1675 in the King's Bath at Bath

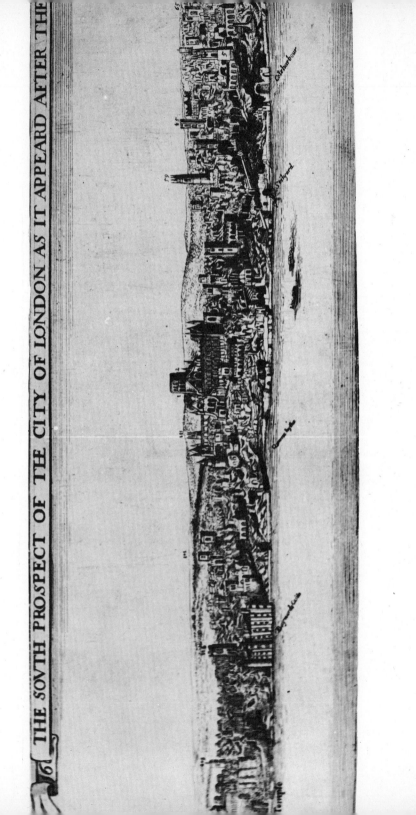

THE SOVTH PROSPECT OF THE CITY OF LONDON AS IT APPEARD AFTER THE

the Tower

Cuſtomehouſe

Billingſgate

75

OLD Swan

The Bridge

§ 115 & 116 London after the Great Fire

§117 John Lofting's Fire Engine of 1690

§118 Portland stone quarries in 1790

§119 Transporting Portland stone in 1790

§120 Air view of St. Paul's

§ 121 St. Bride's, Fleet Street

§ 122 St. Magnus the Martyr
(interior)

§ 123 The Church of K
Charles the Martyr, T
bridge Wells (c. 1685)

§ 124 The Chapel, Petwo
House, Sussex
Thirteenth-century ch:
redecorated c. 1690

yards. But many other ports, such as King's Lynn and the smaller harbours of East Anglia, were declining as trade increasingly sought the mouth of the Thames, or shifted to the West to catch the American trade. The effect of the Navigation Laws was to foster England's colonial trade across the Atlantic, and diminish her foreign trade with Scandinavia and the Baltic, to the disadvantage of the east coast ports, all save London. And even in the West, smaller ports like Fowey and Bideford suffered from the large size of ships necessitated by the long oceanic voyages. Moreover, London merchants and London capital controlled the trade of other cities.

The vital and recuperative force of London, perpetually fed by the inflow of immigrants and of wealth from outside, was heavily tested by the Plague and the Fire (1665–1666), disasters of the first magnitude, which however seemed scarcely to affect the onward movement of the power, opulence and population of the capital.

The famous 'Plague of London' was merely the last, and not perhaps the worst, of a series of outbreaks covering three centuries. Between the campaigns of Crécy and Poitiers, the Black Death had first swept over Europe from some unknown source in the Far East, with the ubiquity and violence usual to the incoming of a new disease. The obscurest hamlet had little chance of escape. It is thought probable that a third, and possibly that one half of the fellow-countrymen of Boccaccio, of Froissart and of Chaucer, perished within three years. The Black Death remained in the soil of England, and became known as 'The Plague.' It never again swept the whole country at one time, but it perpetually broke out in different localities, particularly in the towns and ports and the riversides, where the ship-borne, flea-bearing rat multiplied. In London under the Lancastrian and Tudor Kings the plague was for long periods together endemic and nearly continual; under the Stuarts it came in rare but violent outbursts. The rejoicing in London for the accession of James I had been cut short by an outbreak of the Plague that carried off 30,000 persons; the accession of Charles I was the signal for another, no less destructive. [See § 113.] In 1636 a slighter attack occurred. Then followed thirty years of comparative immunity for London, during which other events took place calculated to make men forget in their talk the Plague horrors that their fathers and grandfathers had endured. So when the last outbreak came in 1665, although it did not destroy a much larger proportion of the Londoners than some of its predecessors had done, it struck the imagination more, for it came in an age of greater civilization, comfort and security, when such calamities were less remembered and less expected, and it was followed close, as though at the Divine command, by another catastrophe to which there was no parallel in the most ancient records of London.[1]

The Great Fire (1666) raged for five days and destroyed the whole City proper between the Tower and the Temple; yet it probably did not unroof half the population of the capital. The 'Liberties' beyond the walls were only touched, and these contained by far the greater part of the inhabitants. London had been increasing with immense rapidity in the last sixty years. It was just short of half a million. In all other cities of England the townsfolk still lived within breath of the country, under conditions of what we should now call country-town life. In London alone the conditions of great-city life were growing up, in many respects in a peculiarly odious form. The poor were crowded out of the City into the slum districts of the 'Liberties' beyond— St. Giles's, Cripplegate, Whitechapel, Stepney, Westminster, Lambeth—where they multiplied exceedingly in spite of an enormous death-rate among infants.

The fire and rebuilding made little improvement in the sanitary and moral condition of the slum populations. For the seat and origin of the Plague had always been in the 'Liberties' outside the City, where the poorest dwelt. Now as these districts were not burnt down they were not rebuilt, and in 1722 Defoe declared that 'they were still in the same condition as they were before.' It is therefore evident that the 'rebuilding of London' due to the Fire was not the main reason why the Plague disappeared from England after its last great effort.

---

[1] During the Civil War (1642–1646) the Plague raged in other parts of the island, particularly the South and West; in some towns, such as Chester, a quarter of the inhabitants died of it. The 'Plague of London' (1665) was not quite confined to the capital. East Anglia suffered very severely, but the Plague did not extend far west or north. In Langdale, Westmorland, tradition still points to the ruins of an isolated farmhouse where all the inhabitants died of the Plague, owing to the infected clothes of a soldier being sent there; but the rest of the valley and district remained immune. The soldier's clothes presumably carried the flea that bore the Plague.

IV.  Sir Christopher Wren

The portion of London that was changed by the Fire was the residential and business quarter in the heart of the City itself, the great commercial houses where the merchants with their orderly and well-fed households worked and slept. These abodes of wealth, commerce and hospitality dating from the Middle Ages, with their gardens behind and courtyards within, still presented lath and plaster walls to the narrow and crooked streets; the gables sometimes protruded so far over the shop fronts that the prentices in their garrets could shake hands over the way. When the Fire came racing before the wind, these old and flimsy structures were tinder to the flame. Only in the few places where the Fire met brick walls was it forced to linger and fight. The merchants took the opportunity to rebuild their houses of brick, and in a more wholesome if less picturesque relation to the street. Sanitation in the City itself was improved by the enforced rebuilding of so many very ancient dwellings. [See § 115, 116, 117.]

The fact that the Plague did not again recur in England is due in part to the increase of brick building, and the substitution of carpets and panelling for straw and cloth hangings, since the infected fleas and the rats that carried them were thus deprived of harbourage. But it is probable that the chief cause of the disappearance of the Plague was due to no human agency at all, but to an obscure revolution in the animal world; about this period the modern brown rat extirpated and replaced the mediaeval black rat, and the brown rat was not a carrier of the plague-flea to nearly the same extent as its predecessor. (Saltmarsh's article in *Cambridge Hist. Journal*, 1941.)

The reconstruction of the City of London was accomplished at a pace that astonished the world.

'The dreadful effects of the fire [wrote Sir John Reresby] were not so strange as the rebuilding of this great city, which by reason of the King's and Parliament's care, and the great wealth and opulency of the city itself, was rebuilded most stately with brick (the greatest part being before nothing but lath and lime) in four or five years' time.'

And London, which had lost a fifth of its population by the Plague made good that loss also without seeming to notice it at all, so continual was the flow of immigrants from all the shires of England and half the countries of Europe.

The Mediaeval and Tudor City had disappeared in the flames; only the ground plan of its rabbit-warren of streets and alleys was retained. The layout of the greatest city in the world continued to be the worst; and mortal eye has never yet had a view of Wren's St. Paul's.[1]

Eighty-nine churches, including the old Gothic Cathedral, had been burnt. If they were doomed to perish, no happier date could have been chosen for the holocaust since Christopher Wren, just arrived at the height of his powers, was beginning to be known in Court and City. His genius was stamped on the ecclesiastical architecture of the new London. His churches, which survived general rebuildings of the streets in which they stand, still (1939) testify to the spacious classical dignity of the age and of the man who put them in place of their mediaeval predecessors. [See § 121, 122, and contrast § 124.]

The rebuilding of St. Paul's was a communal effort worthy of a great nation. A tax on the coal entering the port of London was voted by Parliament for the purpose. The great work went steadily forward year by year, undeterred by all the excitements of the Popish Plot, the Revolution and the Marlborough Wars. It was completed in the height of Queen Anne's glory, a dozen years before the death of its architect. [See Plate IV and § 120.]

The new St. Paul's was built of the white stone of Portland, fetched by sea direct from the quarries of that strange peninsula. Though the quarries had long been known, it was only in Stuart times that Portland stone began to be extensively used. The needs of Wren's colossal work gave a new life to the 'Isle of Portland' and its inhabitants. Vast quarries were opened and roads and piers built. Great sums were spent on

'salaries to agents and wharfingers and repairing ways, piers and cranes, with the expenses of several persons sent from London to view and direct the same, to regulate the working of the quarries and to adjust matters with the Islanders.' (*Ec. Hist. Rev.*, Nov. 1938.)

Henceforth the white Portland Stone plays an important part in architectural history of England, and seems specially associated with the cold majesty of the monumental work of Wren and Gibbs, just as the warm red brick suits the comfortable

[1] This sentence was written before the Blitz !

domesticity of the common dwellings of the same period. [See § 118, 119, 120.]

## Books for Further Reading

Besides the books mentioned in the notes to this chapter, see Pepys' and Evelyn's *Diaries*, and Arthur Bryant's *Life of Pepys*; David Ogg, *England in the Reign of Charles II* (1934), Chaps. II and III; Basil Willey, *The Seventeenth Century Background* (1934).

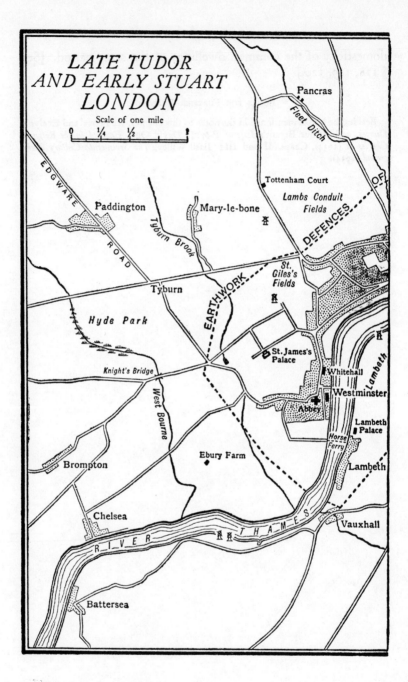

LATE TUDOR
AND EARLY STUART
LONDON

Scale of one mile

0    ¼    ½

Pancras

Fleet Ditch

OF

EDGWARE ROAD

Paddington

Mary-le-bone

Tottenham Court

Lambs Conduit
Fields

DEFENCES

Tyburn Brook

St.
Giles's
Fields

Tyburn

EARTHWORK

Hyde Park

St. James's
Palace

Knight's Bridge

West Bourne

Whitehall

Westminster

Lambeth

Abbey

Lambeth
Palace

Horse
Ferry

Brompton

Ebury Farm

Lambeth

Chelsea

Vauxhall

RIVER          THAMES

Battersea

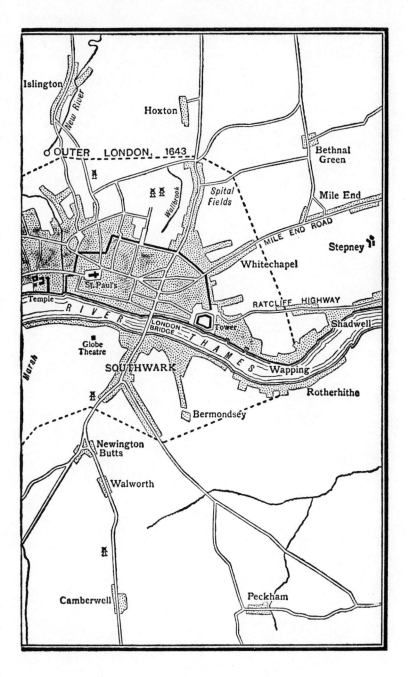

# DESCRIPTIVE NOTES
## TO THE ILLUSTRATIONS

These are grouped into three categories: 1. Colour Plates; 2. Gravure Plates (marked §); 3. Illustrations in the text

Colour Plate I *Frontispiece* (cf. text p. 41)

Queen Elizabeth. Crayon drawing by Federico Zuccaro (1575). Dept. of Prints and Drawings, British Museum.

Federico Zuccaro (1542/3–1609), a native of Tuscany, who had worked on decorative schemes in the Vatican and at Florence, came to England for four years, from 1574 to 1578, after which he returned to Italy, where he founded the Accademia di San Luca at Rome.

The delicacy and realistic simplicity of this crayon drawing form a welcome contrast to the many elaborate portraits of Elizabeth, in which interest is so often centred in her jewels and dress, the face suggesting stereotyped representation rather than portraiture.

Colour Plate II (cf. text p. 20)

Miniature of a young man by Nicholas Hilliard (*c.* 1588). Salting Bequest, Victoria and Albert Museum.

Nicholas Hilliard (1547–1619) was appointed goldsmith and limner to Queen Elizabeth and enjoyed her continued patronage; he executed miniatures (or 'portraits in little') of the Queen herself and many of her courtiers. As the Queen's goldsmith he executed her second Great Seal.

Interest in the miniature is thought to have derived in part from the Elizabethan love of jewellery and of precious stones in intricate settings. This portrait of an unknown young man of about 1588 is one of Hilliard's most exquisite studies. It portrays a youth leaning against a tree, enshrined in roses; he wears a large lacy ruff, a padded doublet and short velvet cloak, while long silk hose clothe his elegant legs. The miniature is inscribed *Dat poenas laudata fides* ([My] praised faith causes [my] pain).

Colour Plate III (cf. text p. 105)

Painted room at Old Wilsley, near Cranbrook, Kent (*c.* 1680). Photographed by kind permission of the owner, Mrs. Herbert Alexander.

This XVth century house was built for a family of Kentish clothiers. At the end of the XVIIth century a certain John Weston (also a clothier) was living there, and it was at this time that the paintings shown in this illustration were carried out. Biblical scenes in the upper panels of the decoration are combined with sporting subjects in the lower ones, where harriers are shown pursuing a hare. This is an interesting example of the fashion of painted walls in a more modest house, where one would expect at this date to find plain panelling, in contrast to the sumptuous decoration of such great houses as Wilton and Petworth (cf. § 72 and 87).

Colour Plate IV (cf. text p. 148)
Sir Christopher Wren by Sir Godfrey Kneller (1687). From the portrait in the possession of the Royal Society.
Kneller, born at Lubeck in 1646, came to England in 1675. Besides royal portraits he painted nearly all his important contemporaries before his death in 1723. This painting of Wren shows the architect against a prospect of his new St. Paul's. Christopher Wren was born in 1632; at twenty-five he was Professor of Astronomy at Gresham College, London. One of the foundation members of the Royal Society, he became its president in 1680. Besides his studies in medicine and anatomy, he grew increasingly interested in architecture, becoming surveyor-general to the King's works in 1669. After the Great Fire he prepared his plan for rebuilding the city and was appointed its principal architect. From 1668 he was engaged on the rebuilding of St. Paul's, the first plan of which he completed in 1673, but later modified to that of the one we know to-day, superintending the work of construction until 1710 (cf. § 120). In addition to this he built fifty-two churches in London (cf. § 121 and 122), as well as numerous buildings outside London, including the Sheldonian at Oxford and Trinity College library at Cambridge. He died in 1723.

§ 1 (cf. text p. 7)
The Noble Arte of Venerie or Hunting, by George Turberville (1611 edition). From the copy in the Dept. of Printed Books, British Museum.
George Turberville (?1540-?1610), like so many Elizabethans, combined the activities of poet, scholar and diplomat. His Booke of Faulconrie and The Noble Arte of Venerie or Hunting, first produced in 1575, were useful compendiums of all matters dealing with hunting and hawking, ranging from the care of falcons and hounds to such difficult problems as 'the place where and how an assembly should be made, in the presence of a Prince or some honourable person,' and this our present illustration from the 1611 edition shows. It is exactly the same illustration as that in the 1575 edition, except for the substitution of the figure of James I for that of Elizabeth; the feasting courtiers are regaling themselves on the same flagons of wine or ale and are being handed the same baskets of fat roast capons.

§ 2 (cf. text p. 4)

*Civitates Orbis Terrarum*, by G. Braun and F. Hohenberg (Cologne, 1577–88 edition). From the copy in the Cambridge University Library.

This book gives maps and views of many of the chief cities of Europe as well as of such far-flung places as Constantinople and Cuzco, Jerusalem and Calicut.

Although engraved by foreigners and published abroad, this map of Norwich (like those of London and Bristol reproduced in § 3 and 4) seems to have been faithfully copied from some English original.

The map will repay close examination with a magnifying glass, when the cathedral and castle can be easily discerned, and the mediaeval walls with their gates, while in the left-hand corner on the river bank, just inside 'Hell Gates' (14), can be seen 'The new milles' (13); to the right between the gates of St. Giles (16) and St. Stephen (17) may be seen an archery contest in the Archery Ground (to-day called Chapel Hill Fields); in the foreground ploughing is going on and sheep are grazing; at the top, in the distance (i.e. east) can be seen the wastes of Mousehold Heath, and nearby, just outside the Bishop's Gate, 'the place where men are customablie burnt.'

The great influx of skilled Flemings and Walloons into Norwich early in Elizabeth's reign increased the city's fame for the manufacture of woven goods, and the 'new milles' near the suburb of Heigham may well be evidence of this flourishing trade.

§ 3 (cf. text p. 4)

*Civitates Orbis Terrarum*, by G. Braun and F. Hohenberg (Cologne, 1577–88 edition). From the copy in the Cambridge University Library. (For general note cf. § 2.)

Labelled by Braun 'florentissimum Angliae Emporium,' Bristol is shown stretching from the former Abbey of St. Augustine's to St. Mary Redcliffe outside the walls. The core of the city lies below the castle and between the two arms of the river Avon (now the floating harbour), with the Temple and St. Thomas's lying beyond the bridge (with its houses spanning the river), but within the outer girdling wall, which stretches across the loop of the river. The churches of St. Nicholas (10) and St. John (5) can be seen actually built into the city walls and across two of the gateways.

Bristol's excellent facilities for a port can be easily assessed from this map. Her woollen industries (like those of Norwich) derived fresh impetus from the immigration of Flemish weavers in Elizabeth's reign.

§ 4 (cf. text p. 4)

*Civitates Orbis Terrarum*, by G. Braun and F. Hohenberg (Cologne, 1577–88 edition). From the copy in the Cambridge University Library. (For general note cf. § 2.)

While illustrating well the extent and character of London at this date surrounded by fields and orchards and with gardens and small open spaces in its heart, this map must not be taken as accurate in all its minute details. Its spelling in many cases is of the peculiar type one might expect from a foreigner with little knowledge of the English language, and Mr. I. A. Shapiro has recently shown in *Shakespeare Survey* I (1948) in his study of early engravings of the Bankside theatres that we cannot rely upon it for its representation of the south bank, for instance. The foreground purports to show the Bear and Bull baitings, but the student of the Elizabethan theatre should look rather at Hollar's Long View of London of 1647 (cf. § 63) for the layout of the south bank.

The Tower, Westminster, Lambeth Palace, London Bridge with its rows of houses and jutting cutwaters, and Old St. Paul's can be picked out, although the latter is shown with its spire, which had already collapsed in 1561.

§ 5 (cf. text p. 9)

Crowland, Lincolnshire, during the floods of 1947. From an air photograph by Aerofilms, Ltd.

The background of this photograph helps to recapture some idea of what the mediaeval fen must have looked like, with its 'watery solitudes' and small 'oozy islands' here and there. The great Abbey of Crowland, whose ruins (used as the parish church) can be seen on the edge of the modern town, was set on the highest land thus taking advantage of the rich fertile soil for its fields and vineyards without danger of inundation.

§ 6 (cf. text p. 11)

Map of the Fen round Wisbech. From a MS. map of 1597 in the Wisbech Museum, Cambridgeshire.

This map, probably a revised copy of an earlier one, gives clear evidence of the system of embankment and 'sewerage' already evolved by this time. The dykes and banks, notably the 'Magna Ripa de Wisebech' can be traced, together with several windmills, which were used for draining the land. The number of churches on even this small portion is some evidence of the wealth of the area at this date. (For further note on fen drainage cf. note to § 67–69.)

§ 7 (cf. text p. 11)

Ely Cathedral. From an air photograph by Aerofilms, Ltd.

Ely Cathedral was preceded by a monastery, which was burnt by the Danes in 870 but restored by King Edgar for the Benedictines in 970. After the Conquest the great Abbey Church began to rise, consisting at first of the choir, tower and transepts, the nave being erected in the XIIth century. During the next century the Norman eastern end was demolished and the presbytery built in its stead; in the XIVth century the

Norman tower fell, damaging the old Norman choir, and it was then that the Octagon Tower and Lantern and the Lady Chapel were built. By the end of the XIVth century the Abbey Church was virtually the same in its main structure as we see it to-day. In 1539 the monastery surrendered to the King, and was dissolved, its church becoming the cathedral. Some of the monastic buildings were destroyed and the others used as houses for the officers of 'the king's new college at Ely.' In the foreground of the illustration can be seen, on the extreme right the remains of the infirmary; the deanery (part of which was the monastery guest hall) and its garden (the former cloister garth); and on the left, just by the west door of the cathedral, the Bishop's palace.

§ 8 (cf. text p. 15)
The Cheviots. From an air photograph by Aerofilms, Ltd.
The air of remote desolation which pervades this scene is probably little altered from Tudor times—it is rather the state of society which has changed.

§ 9 and 10 (cf. text pp. 17, 18)
Newark Castle, Selkirkshire (XVth century). From an air photograph by Aerofilms, Ltd.
Darnick Tower, near Melrose (1569). From a drawing by Edward Blore (1787–1879). B.M. MS. Add. 42,022, f. 24.
Darnick Tower, built in 1569 to replace an earlier tower burnt by the Earl of Hertford, is not very different from the XVth century peel tower of Newark and both should be contrasted with what was happening in Elizabethan England (cf. § 11 and 12 below).

§ 11 (cf. text p. 18)
Stokesay Castle, Shropshire. From a drawing by Edward Blore (1787–1879). B.M. MS. Add. 42,017, f. 40.
This drawing of a XIIIth century half-fortified manor house, with its strong tower and fortress-like aspect, but with a timbered Elizabethan gateway, showing that it has reached a time when its fortification is no longer serious, should be contrasted with § 9 and 10 of Darnick and Newark, to show how conversion from even semi-fortification was taking place in England, at a time when fortification was still the main preoccupation in the Borders.

§ 12 (cf. text p. 18)
Charlecote Park, Warwickshire. From an air photograph by Aerofilms, Ltd.
Built in the first year of Elizabeth's reign in the favourite E-form with corner towers, Charlecote Park, in spite of later additions and alterations, is representative of an Elizabethan manor house set peacefully in its gardens, with gatehouse and stables comfortably removed from the main building. Its widespread

lawns and general layout, its many windows, from ground floor to gable, all bespeak an age of 'peace and economic prosperity' far removed in material conditions from the world of Darnick Tower (cf. § 10) where as late as 1569 the rebuilding of a dwelling entailed the same grim, stone fortress-like aspect, the same lack of windows, the same necessity for a self-contained defensive economy; no spreading outbuildings or ornamentation appear and there is little change from XVth century Newark (cf. § 9).

§ 13 (cf. text p. 18)

Montacute House, Somerset. From an air photograph by Aerofilms, Ltd.

Montacute belongs to the closing years of Elizabeth. It was built by Sir Edward Phelips, in the familiar H-form, of Hamdon Hill stone, with generous window space and elaborate gabling. It was completed about 1600. This photograph shows the east side (note the roundels over the windows) including the beautiful Jacobean garden forecourt enclosed by a balustraded wall with delicate cupolas and corner pavilions—all contemporary. The garden beyond, with yews and ornamental pool is late XVIIIth century and probably replaced the earlier formal garden with knots and dials (cf. § 90).

§ 14 (cf. text pp. 18, 19)

Moreton Old Hall, Cheshire. From an air photograph by Aerofilms, Ltd.

This moated, half-timbered manor house was apparently elaborated from an earlier building first by William Moreton, and then by his son, John, between the fifties and eighties of the XVIth century. Its irregular, almost top-heavy appearance, its restricted window space, and the chequer of its black and white, form a striking contrast to the dignified golden unity of Montacute House (cf. § 13).

§ 15 (cf. text p. 19)

The Bradford Table Carpet, Dept. of Textiles, Victoria and Albert Museum.

This late XVIth century table carpet was acquired by the Victoria and Albert Museum in 1928 from the Earl of Bradford's collection at Castle Bromwich Hall. Its centre is worked in a design of trellised vines, while the border shows hunting and pastoral scenes, all kinds of architecture, and wild animals, against a rolling country background. It is worked in silk on linen canvas in tent stitch in many colours. Oriental rugs and carpets, when first imported into England, were frequently used as table, rather than as floor, coverings, and when copied in English embroidery were still used for the same purpose (cf. the table carpet in § 56). It was only when tables themselves became more ornate that table carpets went out, to come back again eventually as floor carpets.

§ 16 (cf. text p. 19)

The Great Hall, Montacute House, Somerset. From a photograph by *The Times*.

The hall is of single storey height, with original stone doorways and chimney piece—the latter supported by plain Ionic columns. Across the upper part of the north wall of the hall can be seen the Elizabethan plaster panel of the 'Skimmity ride.' This tells the story of the henpecked husband who tried to fetch himself some ale while minding the baby. His wife belabours him with her shoe and a neighbour seeing this, collects the villagers, who make him ride the skimmington (or pole) to the general derision of the village. The decorative plaster frieze and the wooden panelling should be noted, though the ceiling is plain. The stone screens are at the other end of the hall and were elaborately plastered and painted at a later period.

§ 17 (cf. text p. 19)

Gallery at Powys Castle, Montgomeryshire (1592/3). From a drawing by William Twopenny (1797–1873). Dept. of Prints and Drawings, British Museum.

Powys Castle, though of early foundation, was largely re-built by the Herberts, to whom it passed in 1587. Abandoned in 1644, when the Parliament forces took it over, and again in 1688 when the Powys family went into exile, it was considerably altered and restored in the ensuing years.

This wide, well-lighted gallery, panelled and decorated with plaster frieze and elaborately ornamented ceiling, is typical of late XVIth and XVIIth century 'long galleries.' It was built by Sir Edward Herbert in 1592, and the richly decorated plasterwork of the ceiling is the original work of 1592/3. The panelling is mid-XVIIth century; the furniture, however, dates from 1722, when the second Marquess of Powys returned from exile. The sashed windows replace earlier mullioned ones and the busts were not brought here from Italy until *c.* 1810.

§ 18 (cf. text p. 18)

Gresham's Royal Exchange. Engraving from London Prospects Portfolio, Vol. V, in the possession of the Society of Antiquaries.

Sir Thomas Gresham (1519–1579), merchant and financier, built the Royal Exchange at his own expense. It was named and opened by the Queen in January 1571, but was destroyed in the Great Fire of 1666. The golden grasshopper, Gresham's crest, can be seen on the column and the cupolas. The open colonnade and the statues in recessed niches should be particularly noticed.

§ 19 (cf. text p. 18)

The Gate of Honour, Gonville and Caius College, Cambridge.
From a photograph by A. F. Kersting.

Founded as the Hall of the Annunciation in 1348 by Edmund
Gonville, Gonville Hall was refounded by John Caius, as
Gonville and Caius College in 1557. Elected Master the following year Dr. Caius, who had travelled in Italy, France and
Germany, was able to devote himself to designing and building
additions to his college. He planned three gates, of Humility,
of Virtue and of Honour, symbolical of the scholar's career,
but the Gate of Honour was not built until 1575 (two years
after Caius' death); it was built, however, as he had himself
planned. Many of its original elaborations have since gone.
Pinnacles surmounted the lowest cornice and the corners of
the hexagonal tower, and sundials decorated the sides of the
hexagon. The arms of Caius can yet be seen in the spandril of
the arch. The details of the gateway were ornamented in colour
and gold on the white stonework. The architect was possibly
Theodore Havens of Cleves.

§ 20 (cf. text p. 26)

The Skynner Monument, Ledbury Church, Herefordshire.
From a photograph by Sydney Pitcher, Gloucester.

The tomb to Edward Skynner, his wife and family in Ledbury
Church was erected in 1630. Edward Skynner was a wealthy
cloth merchant, but his alabaster altar tomb with its kneeling
effigies of himself and his wife, with the baby between them and
their ten other children below, would not have shamed a
nobleman.

§ 21 and 22 (cf. text p. 21)

Sketches from the Album of Tobias Delhafen of Nuremburg
(1623–5). B.M. MS. Egerton 1269, ff. 65 and 54 respectively.

§ 23 and 24 (cf. text p. 5)

Sketches from the Album of George Holzschuher, also of
Nuremburg (1621–5). B.M. MS. Egerton 1264, ff. 25 and 26
respectively.

These four scenes showing on the one hand, a peasant woman
riding to market with her basket of eggs, and a citizen with his
wife riding pillion, and on the other the pomp and ceremony
which attended the Lord Mayor and his wife, are taken from
two Libri Amicorum—the equivalent of the modern autograph album—belonging to two visitors from Nuremburg to
this country at the beginning of the XVIIth century. The
fashion of such books of blank vellum pages on which one's
friends inscribed their signatures or arms was started about the
middle of the XVIth century by University students and spread
from one University to another. Sometimes they were inter-
leaved printed books, the most popular being those with wood-

cuts or engravings by Jobst Amman and the de Brys. The fashion spread to the court and the professions, and professional illuminators were soon driving a flourishing trade. An engraving was chosen by the friend, who would then have it illuminated and add his autograph or armorial bearings on the opposite page. Sometimes notes of his friend's later career would be added by the owner of the album.

The subjects illustrated here occur in both these MSS. with slight variations, and over a wide range of these Libri Amicorum (belonging usually to Germans or Swiss) similar subjects repeat themselves again and again. The style and content steadily degenerated throughout the XVIIth century, heraldic paintings disappeared and by the XVIIIth century these books of friendship had become, in many instances, mere records of ribaldry and debauchery, interspersed with miniature portraits and later with silhouettes.

A very full study of the subject will be found in *Archaeologia*, vol. xii, 1910, by Max Rosenheim.

§ 25–28 (cf. text pp. 7, 23)

These four woodcuts are taken from ballads in the Roxburghe Collection, Dept. of Printed Books, British Museum.

This collection consists of 'antient songs and ballads written on various subjects and printed between the years MDLX and MDCC chiefly collected by Robert [Harley], Earl of Oxford and purchased in the sale of the late Mr. West's Library in the year 1773. Encreased by several Additions in two volumes. London. Arranged and bound 1774.'

These ballads with their rough woodcuts are typical of those that were hawked about by Autolycus and his fellows (cf. text p. 62) in city street and on village green. The type of pedlar who sold them can be seen in text illustration (p. 61). The cuts are stereotyped and occur again and again in varying states and attached to various ballads throughout the century, many of them bearing little relation to the ballads they adorn.

§ 25. From 'A Dialogue betweene Master Guesright and poore Neighour Needy OR A few proofs both reall and true Shewing what men for money will doe. To a pleasant new tune called, But I know what I know. Printed at London for F. Cowles.' Roxburghe Collection, I, 74, 75.

§ 26. From 'A Bill of Fare, For, A Saturday Night's Supper, A Sunday morning Breakfast, and A Munday Dinner. Described in a pleasant new Merry Dittie. To the tune of Cooke Laurell or Michelmas Terme. London. Printed by H. P. for Fr. Grove, neare the Sarazens Head without Newgate.' Roxburghe Collection, I, 18, 19.

§ 27. From 'A pleasant Countrey new Ditty: Merrily showing how to drive the cold Winter away. To the tune of

When Phoebus did rest; &c. Printed at London for H.G.'
Roxburghe Collection, I, 24, 25.

§ 28. From 'All is ours and our Husbands or the Country
Hostesses Vindication. To the tune of the Carmens Whistle
or High Boys up go we. Printed for P. Brooksby at the
Golden Ball in Pye Corner.' Roxburghe Collection, II, 8.

These four cuts illustrate eating and drinking at home or at the
inn. The ballad to § 25 proclaims:—

'What makes your In-keeper to harbour the pore,
And unto all comers set open his dore,
But that he intends if possible can,
To have his reward of every man.'

While that to § 26 tells of all the good things the company had
to eat one Saturday night when the 'Master of the Feast' paid
the score for all, till 'We rose from our mirthe with the 12 oclock
Chimes, Went everyone home as his way did direct.' The
ballad concludes by describing the sort of breakfast his wife
gave the singer of the ballad next morning 'because she was not
bidden to supper.'

§ 27 illustrates a ballad of winter revels in the country, which
tells how everyone gathers with 'carols and songs to drive the
cold winter away.'

'This time of the yeare
Is spent in good cheare kind neighbours together meete
To sit by the fire
With friendly desire each other in love to greet.'

§ 28 illustrates a very different scene on which mine hostess
sings:—

'For if an honest company
Of boone good fellows come:
And call for Liquor merrily
In any private Room:
Then if I fill the Juggs with Froth
Or cheat them of one or two
If I can swear them out of both
The reckoning is my due, etc.'

§ 29 and 30 (cf. text p. 29)
Woodcut from a broadside (no. 239) in the possession of the
Society of Antiquaries, entitled 'A Schoole for Young Soldiers,
containing in breife the whole Discipline of warre, especially
so much as is meet for Captains to teach, or the Soldier to
learne, that is, to trayne or to be trayned. Fit to be taught
throughout England. London. Printed for John Trundle
dwelling in Barbican at the signe of Nobody.'

This broadside (*temp.* James I) consists of directions for the sorting of arms and the forming of the company itself in squadrons, files, etc. It then gives the various 'postures of the pike, the Musket & Harquebuse' in turn and ends with the words of command to be used in drilling. The posture directions explain loading and unloading, firing, etc. and show how to carry the weapon.

§ 31 and 32 (cf. text p. 29)

*The Arte of Gunnery* (3 Sept. 1608). B.M. MS. Cott. Julius F. iv, ff. 18 and 26.

This MS. is a treatise in English on gunnery and the theory of ballistics, and is illustrated by crude diagrams to point the text. § 32 is concerned with demonstrating the angle of fire of a demi-culverin, while § 31 illustrates concentration of fire on a target, with the guns of the defenders replying.

§ 33 (cf. text p. 3)

Michael Drayton. From the portrait by an unknown artist in the National Portrait Gallery.

The Warwickshire born poet, Michael Drayton (1563–1631), is illustrated here as the poet who sang of England's beauties and her noble past. In his poetic topography of England the *Polyolbion* (1613–22), (from the Greek meaning 'having many blessings'), he set out to bring before his readers the native beauties of their country.

As Camden (cf. § 34) in his *Britannia* detailed for a slightly earlier generation each county and its principal features, geographical, historical or antiquarian, so Drayton in his travels through England displays the streams and rivers of the countryside with their legends and historical associations and all kinds of lore about their flora and fauna as well.

§ 34 (cf. text p. 3)

William Camden. From the portrait by an unknown artist in the National Portrait Gallery.

William Camden (1551–1623), headmaster of Westminster School, herald, antiquary and historian, published his *Britannia* in 1586. This record of his famous journey through England, by which (said Fuller) 'he restored Britain to herself,' used Leland's notes to some extent, but built up a panorama of the cities and towns he visited, as well as of the scenery and antiquities he saw on his way. The scholar and topographer in his survey of England succeeded in enshrining his greatness in a prose work of high literary achievement; originally published in Latin, it was not translated into English until 1610 when Philemon Holland gave it afresh to the world.

§ 35 and 36 (cf. text p. 39)

*The Whole Psalms in foure partes* by John Day (September 1563). From a copy in the Dept. of Printed Books, British Museum.

John Day printed the first collection of psalm tunes in England. § 35 shows the frontispiece to his four oblong little volumes devoted to Tenor, Contra Tenor, Bassus and Medius 'which' (he says in his title) 'may be song to al musicall instruments, set forth for the encrease of vertue: & abolishing of other vayne & triflying ballades.' § 36 is the first page of the Contra Tenor part of the *Veni creator* in the same book.

§ 37 (cf. text pp. 39, 40)

A Preaching at Old St. Paul's, *c.* 1616. From the original painting in the possession of the Society of Antiquaries.

This painting (part of a wooden diptych) gives us a good idea (in spite of some difficulty with perspective) of what Old St. Paul's looked like in the reign of James I. It shows Paul's Cross in the foreground with a Bishop preaching before the King, whose court, judges and officials can be seen seated in the galleries flanking the royal box. (Note the houses built under the transept wall.)

The preaching is probably an imaginary one and not an actual record, as the famous preaching by Bishop John King before the King, which might well be thought to have been the inspiration for this did not take place until 1620 and this diptych is dated 1616.

(For a full discussion of this picture, see *Catalogue of Pictures belonging to the Society of Antiquaries*, by George Scharf (1865).)

§ 38 and 39 (cf. text p. 39)

Illustration from a broadside (no. 231) in the possession of the Society of Antiquaries, entitled 'The Christian's Jewell—how to adorne the Heart and decke the House of every Protestant. Taken out of St. Mary Overis Church in the Lectureship of the late deceased Doctor Sutton. 1624. Are to be sold by Tho. Iener at the exchange.'

This broadside sets out the Ten Commandments above the Lord's Prayer and the Creed. In the corners are four small engravings of Circumcision and Baptism, the Passover and the Lord's Supper, with texts setting out the authority for Baptism and Communion. At the bottom is a medallion portrait of Dr. Sutton.

Note the swaddling clothes of the child being christened and the way in which communion is being administered. The table is in the body of the church, with the communicants kneeling all round it—the priest seems to be on the right (in the middle) with his clerk opposite him.

§ 40 (cf. text p. 42)

Richard Lyne's Map of Cambridge (1574). From the copy in the Cambridge University Library.

This beautiful copper engraving illustrates a university town in Elizabeth's day. It was drawn and engraved by Richard Lyne (fl. 1570–1600), who was employed by Matthew Parker, Archbishop of Canterbury and benefactor of the University of Cambridge.

In factual accuracy this map cannot be compared with John Hammond's plan of 1592, but it gives a vivid pictorial impression of XVIth-century Cambridge, and though we may not accept his Castle or the relative scales of his buildings, we do spy with pleasure the angler on the Backs just by Clare Hall, and the boat with the drag-net coming from the bridge and drawing level with John's; otherwise the streets are empty, though he fills the meadows with sheep and cows, pigs and horses.

§ 41 (cf. text p. 42)

*Civitates Orbis Terrarum*, by G. Braun and F. Hohenberg (Cologne, 1577–88). From the copy in the Cambridge University Library. (For general note cf. § 2.)

Besides the large maps reproduced in § 2, 3 and 4 there are many delightful long views of such towns of interest as Windsor or Oxford, and in these as well as in the maps groups of people appear. In this illustration the two scholars 'disputing' as they look down on Oxford towers, wear the long clerical gown common to every European university town of the time.

§ 42 (cf. text p. 45)

From Holinshed's *Chronicle* (1577). From the copy in the Cambridge University Library.

This picture of work at the Mint accompanies Holinshed's account of how on the 15 November 1561 the Queen 'restored to the Realme diverse small peeces of silver money ... And also forbad all foreyne coynes to bee currant within the same Realme, as well golde as silver, calling them to hir Maiesties Myntes, except two sortes of Crownes of Golde, the one the Frenche Crowne, the other the Flemish Crowne.'

§ 43–45 (cf. text pp. 46, 47)

From Agricola's *De Re Metallica* (Basle, 1561). From the copy in the Cambridge University Library.

Georg Bauer (whose name was Latinised as Agricola) (1490–1555) was regarded by German writers as the father of mineralogy. He practised as a doctor of medicine but his great work the *De Re Metallica* (in twelve books) was on mining and metallurgy.

§ 43. In the second book Agricola discusses the use of the wand or twig from Circe's turning Ulysses' men into swine with it to its use as a divining rod for finding metals. This illustration shows prospecting by means of a divining rod and 'open cast' mining.

§ 44. In the fifth book he discusses the methods of mining—the sinking of shafts, the height and width of the galleries, etc.

The illustration shows a mine with timbered shafts (shown in section). Note the winding mechanism on the right and the men pushing barrows through the underground galleries. Both this and § 43 show how quickly the timber is being used up in the vicinity of such workings.

§ 45. In the sixth book he discusses how metals occur in the earth, how they are extracted and transported, and afterwards the many ways of working them. This illustration depicts mining in difficult mountainous country, and can be taken as showing the kind of methods probably employed by German miners in the Lake District. In the background can be seen packhorses, while in the foreground the busy scene of activity at the mine itself is shown. In the centre stands the overseer marking off the number of cartloads of ore on his tally stick. An interesting feature is the two-wheeled cart on the right drawn over a track of tree trunks (for easy and smooth running on steep rough ground). On the left is a heap of ore, while further back men can be seen with wheelbarrows and boxes into which they are emptying the metal. The subject of this picture is the treatment of gold-bearing ores and therefore shows a stream for washing the ore.

§ 46 (cf. text pp. 47, 48)
An Elizabethan cast-iron fire-back. From the Dept. of Metalwork, Victoria and Albert Museum.

Cast-iron fire-backs and andirons first appeared in the late XVth century and were then mainly for royal use. The industry of iron casting originated in the Weald and received great impetus in the reign of Henry VIII, when Ralph Hogge or Hugge offered to cast cannon in iron (instead of bronze) for the King. This proved a great success; besides cannon, fire-backs with elaborate and accurate heraldic designs were also cast for the King. From now on fire-backs were produced for the court; Elizabeth used the old Tudor supporters for her royal arms, the lion and the greyhound, as shown in this fine example.

§ 47 (cf. text p. 47)
From *Silva* by John Evelyn (1679 edition). From a copy in the Cambridge University Library.

This book (first published in 1664) on tree culture first drew attention in England to the importance of forestry. In this illustration Evelyn (for whom see note to § 83) is concerned with showing the method of charcoal burning in XVIIth century England,—doubtless the same as had been practised for many centuries before.

In the central clearing wood is placed in a triangle round a pole, and on this foundation timber is piled up to form a beehive shape. It is then covered with earth or clay (as on the right) and set fire to.

§ 48 (cf. text p. 49)

From a broadside (no. 92) in the possession of the Society of Antiquaries, entitled 'A brief note of the benefits that growe to this Realme by the observance of Fish-daies: with a reason and cause wherefore the lawe in that behalf made, is ordained. Very necessary to be placed in the houses of all men, specially *common* victualers. Seene and allowed by the most honorable privie Counsell, in the yeare of our Lord God, 1593. The 20 of March. AT LONDON. Printed by Roger Warde dwelling in Fleete Streete over against the Conduit at the signe of the Castle.' This broadside sets out the law that only fish may be served by victuallers, innkeepers etc., on the fish-days appointed. It then explains the reason for this law, namely, that England is surrounded by the sea, and her coast towns and villages are decayed and need to be rehabilitated, so that fishing and all allied trades of sail and rope making may flourish. It concludes with an estimate of how much beef can be saved thereby, as the increased eating of flesh is a cause of great concern to the country.

§ 49 (cf. text p. 56)

Calais. From a chart of the harbour and road of Calais, XVIth century. B.M. MS. Cott. Aug. I. ii. 70.
This chart shows ships in full sail making up the roads to Calais harbour, with the town above; beyond, eastwards, stretch the cliffs crowned with fortifications, with houses and windmills interspersed.

§ 50 (cf. text p. 55)

The 'Ark Royal' (Lord Howard of Effingham's flagship against the Armada). Woodcut, anonymous, *c.* 1588. Dept. of Prints and Drawings, British Museum.
Built by Sir Walter Raleigh for his own use this ship (originally known as the 'Ark Raleigh') was sold to the Queen as her flagship against the Armada. J. S. Corbett in *Drake and the Tudor Navy*, vol. ii (1899), p. 127, quotes Wynter, the Vice Admiral, writing from the Downs:—'I pray you tell her Majesty from me that her money was well given for the 'Ark Raleigh'—for I think her the odd ship in all the world for all conditions. . . . We can see no sail great or small but how far soever they are we fetch them and speak with them.'

§ 51 (cf. text p. 51)

Sir Walter Raleigh. From the portrait by an unknown artist in the National Portrait Gallery.
Sir Walter Raleigh (?1552–1618) forms a complete contrast to Drake, no less in physical appearance than in character and attainments. A soldier and explorer, he was also a poet and scholar, as well as a courtier. But falling under the Queen's displeasure (on account of his marriage) he was imprisoned, and

freed again only to be re-imprisoned by James I on a charge of treason. Inspired by romantic dreams of re-discovering the city of Manoa, he was permitted to undertake an expedition in search of its gold. His failure was rewarded by arrest and execution (at the instance of the Spanish Ambassador). Most of his prose writing dated from his years of imprisonment, including his *History of the World*, of which only one volume was completed, but the general purpose of which was to show the judgment of God against the wicked.

§ 52 and 53 (cf. text p. 55)
From *Expeditionis Hispanorum in Angliam vera descriptio* (1588). Line engravings by Augustine Ryther (fl. 1575–92) after Robert Adams. The accompanying text by Petruccio Ubaldini was published as *Discourse concerninge the Spanishe Fleete* in 1590. From the copy in the Dept. of Printed Books, British Museum. These beautiful handcoloured plates are a contemporary authority based on Howard's own narrative and show the successive positions of the English and Spanish fleets from the first sighting of the Spaniards off the Cornish coast, until the moment when, driven through the Straits, the latter are being forced northwards to the open sea.

§ 52 (the second of the series) shows the English fleet hurrying out of Plymouth harbour on the night of July 20th 1588; some are seen beating to windward inshore and taking up positions in the rear of the Spanish fleet, while others make straight out to sea in line across the Spanish van, thus leading Medina Sidonia to believe himself caught between two squadrons, whereas the latter ships were actually making for the main body in the Spanish rear, preparatory to falling upon their starboard and leeward wings.

§ 53 (the tenth of the series) shows the final battle of Gravelines which developed into a running fight, the Spaniards trying to keep close formation and escape to the open sea, while the English try to cut off their foremost ships and drive the rest on the Zeeland banks. Apart from the main action some of the English ships can be seen endeavouring to secure a disabled Spanish ship off Calais and subsequently rejoining the main fleet, after having had to abandon her capture. In this final action the Spaniards were eventually driven out of the Channel and forced northwards in disordered flight.

§ 54 (cf. text p. 51)
Sir Francis Drake. From the contemporary engraving in the Dept. of Prints and Drawings, British Museum.
Sir Francis Drake (?1540–96), circumnavigator of the globe, builder of English naval supremacy, implacable enemy of Spain, pirate, adventurer and explorer, was typical of his age,

in his capacity for hard work and untiring enterprise, his flamboyance and imaginative shrewdness. A firm believer in the theory that attack is the best form of defence, he advised the Queen to forestall a Spanish invasion by herself attacking Spain, and his action at Cadiz postponed the coming of the Armada for a year.

§ 55 (cf. text p. 67)

Frontispiece of *The Generall Historie of Virginia, New England & the Summer Isles,* etc. by Capt. John Smith. London, 1624. From the copy in the Cambridge University Library.

Capt. John Smith (1580–1631) made one of the party which set out to colonise Virginia in 1606. Everyone is familiar with the story of how he was rescued from the Indians through the good offices of their princess, Pocahontas (who later married John Rolfe). Smith became governor of the colony of Virginia in 1608, and was active in further explorations. He published this book in 1624. The engraved title page is by Jan Barra (probably of Middelburg). Medallions of Elizabeth, James I and Charles I appear at the top superimposed on a map, and at the foot a landscape in which can be seen Indians, their dwellings and a party in a dug-out canoe.

§ 56 (cf. text p. 68)

The Somerset House Conference (1604). From the portrait group attributed to Marc Gheeraedts II, in the National Portrait Gallery.

The commissioners of England, Spain and the Netherlands met to discuss at this conference the future relations of England with Holland and the Indies. The English representatives are seated on the right of the picture, the figure in the foreground being Robert Cecil, Earl of Salisbury. (Cf. note to § 15 for a note on table carpets.)

§ 57 (cf. text pp. 67, 68)

From *A Brief and true report of the new found land of Virginia,* by Thomas Hariot, with engravings by Theodore de Bry from drawings by John White. (Frankfurt, 1590.) (English translation by Richard Hakluyt.) From a copy in the Dept. of Printed Books, British Museum.

Theodore de Bry (1528–98) settled in Strasbourg about 1560 and worked there as goldsmith and engraver. During visits to England in 1586 and 1588 he met Hakluyt who inspired the idea of the great work of illustrated travels and voyages. De Bry began with this volume, the report on Virginia by Thomas Hariot, who was with the expedition sent out in 1585/6 by Raleigh; John White (also attached to the expedition) had made the series of drawings, which de Bry, after having been introduced to White, used for these engravings. The great illustrated series of American and African travels was thus begun (in Latin, German, French and English editions), the work occupying the rest of de Bry's life and being continued after his death by his sons.

This plate is entitled 'The Arrival of the Englishmen in Virginia.' It shows how the coast is bordered by islands which make access difficult, and the small pinnaces with which trial was made to find entrance and to try the sandy shallows of the rivers.

§ 58 (cf. text p. 68)

From a broadside (no. 151) in the possession of the Society of Antiquaries, entitled 'A Declaration for the certaine time of drawing the great standing Lottery. Imprinted at London by Felix Kyngston, for William Welby, the 22 of Februarie, 1615.' This broadside is of particular interest in showing one way in which money for colonisation was raised and also in depicting the type of lottery boxes used. The broadside sets out the various prizes and rewards which will be paid out by the treasurer for Virginia, Sir Thomas Smith, Knight, and details the arrangements by which the money for 'Adventures' can be entered. Everyone is invited to adventure money in this way to help bring much-needed supplies to the colony as quickly as possible. It is stated, moreover, that anyone leaving (on a venture of £12.10 and upwards) his prizes in, shall have a bill of Adventure to Virginia and shall be free of that company and have his part in lands and all other profits according to his first venture. The figures of Red Indians in the top corners of this broadside seem to be based on John White's drawings (cf. note on § 57 on de Bry's Virginia).

§ 59 (cf. text p. 76)

Title-page from *An Embassy sent by the East India Co. of the United Provinces to the Grand Tartar Cham or Emperor of China*, described by J. Nieuhoff. Translated by J. Ogilby (1673). Engraving by W. Hollar (1668). From the copy of the second edition (1673), Dept. of Printed Books, British Museum.

This fascinating book tells of the Dutch embassy to the Emperor of China in 1655 to procure free trade for Holland in China, and of how the Jesuits already in Peking tried to prevent the Emperor granting the Hollanders what they sought. Richly illustrated with engravings of the places and people the embassy saw on its way from Canton to Peking, the book covers all their difficulties and delays, the strange customs they witnessed and the treatment they met with, until they came at last to their audience with the Emperor.

Hollar's frontispiece reproduced here was apparently meant to illustrate their description of the audience with the Emperor, but also shows a globe giving the position of China, and a prisoner or two to represent the power of the Cham. In their own words the Dutchmen's sight of the Emperor was as follows:—'On each side of the throne stood 112 soldiers, each whereof bore a several Flag and likewise wore coloured Habits suitable to his Ensign, only they had all black Hats with yellow Feathers. Next to the Emperors Throne stood twenty two Gentlemen, each with a Yellow skreen or Umbrillo in his hand; next these stood ten other persons, each holding a Gilt Radiant Circle in his hand, resembling the Sun; next to these stood six others with Circles imitating the Moon at the Full; after these, were standing sixteen other persons, with half Pikes or Poles in their hands, hung full of silk Tassels of several colours, near to these stood thirty six more, each holding a Standard, curiously adorned with Dragons (the Emperors Coat of Arms) and other such Monsters after the Chinese fashion. And in this manner were both sides of the Emperors Throne Guarded and Adorned adding an infinite number of Courtiers, all of them in very rich Habits, all of one Colour and silk, as of a Livery; which added very much to the splendour of the place.'

§ 60 (cf. text p. 61)
William Shakespeare. From the engraving by Martin Droeshout for the title-page of the first folio edition of the plays, 1623. From the National Portrait Gallery.
William Shakespeare (1564–1616), dramatist, poet and actor, became a member of the Lord Chamberlain's company of players in London and acted at the Globe as well as at other theatres. His acting experience and early journeyman work in revising and reshaping plays for his company gave him a useful apprenticeship in the technical details of his art, which came to its full fruition in the great series of tragedies, comedies and chronicle plays, which still bring glory to his name. The plots and stories of his plays might be drawn from or based on Italian romances, mediaeval collections of stories, Plutarch's lives or Holinshed's histories, but his dramatic power and poetic genius gave them new being and significance. The taste of his times is reflected in his free mingling of tragedy and comedy, of rustic by-play with courtly plot, while the Elizabethan love of rich imagery and sensuous language combines with psychological insight, wide range of emotion and a powerful feeling for action and interplay, to make him the chief dramatist of the English theatre in his own and subsequent times.

§ 61 (cf. text p. 62)
The New Inn, Gloucester. From a photograph by R. A. (Postcards) Ltd.
The XVth and XVIth century inn (the prototype of the Elizabethan theatre) was built round three sides of a courtyard, the guests' rooms opening on to the galleries, which thus gave a view

on to the yard itself. A rough temporary stage on trestles would be set up by the players in the yard. They would probably also utilise the staircase, archway and upper gallery as shown in this illustration. The 'groundlings' would crowd about the stage and those of higher position would watch from the galleries. Plays were also acted in the halls of schools and colleges, or great houses, where the 'screens' at one end (often below a minstrels' gallery), faced the dais at the other end of the hall; through the 'screens' doors led to the kitchens. The analogy with the innyard and the early theatre is easy to see (cf. § 62).

§ 62 (cf. text p. 62)

Interior of the Swan Theatre. From a sketch by Johannes de Witt, made during a visit to London in 1596. MS. 842 (Var. 355), f. 132 in the University Library, Utrecht.

This sketch, originally made by the Dutchman de Witt on a visit to London, and recopied by his friend Arend van Buchel, is now at Utrecht. It is the only contemporary picture of the interior of an Elizabethan theatre, the Swan, which had only been built in 1595. It shows a circular building, with close affinities to the structure of the inn yard (cf. § 61). The platform stage juts out into the auditorium, where the ' groundlings ' would be crowded, the whole enclosed by the covered, galleried, circular wall. The back of the stage consists of a roofed structure supported on pillars and having two doors, which concealed the 'tiring' room but which could be opened to reveal an inner room (thus extending the stage to portray, for instance, the interior of a house). Above these doors the first gallery is continued right across the rear of the stage and could be used either for spectators or as an upper stage (cf. the close similarity here with the innyard in § 61). From what we learn from the agreement drawn up in 1600 when the Fortune Theatre was to be built (on the lines of the Globe of 1599) it would seem that de Witt's drawing is not wholly accurate, since it does not provide for the 'shadow' to cover in the whole platform, and to judge from stage directions of the time it appears more likely that the doors for entrances and exits were further to the side and that a curtain between them gave access to the tiring room and could be drawn back to give a view of an inner stage, if so required by the plot.

§ 63 (cf. text p. 62)

From Wenceslaus Hollar's Long View of London, Amsterdam, 1647. From the copy in the Guildhall Library, London.

Wenceslaus Hollar, a native of Bohemia, worked in England from 1635 until his capture by the Parliamentary forces at Basing and subsequent escape to Antwerp. He returned to

England in 1652. His delicate topographical and costume drawings build up a rich visual background to the period. Mr. I. A. Shapiro's studies of 'The Bankside Theatres: Early Engravings' and 'An Original Drawing of the Globe Theatre' in *Shakespeare Survey*, I and II (1948 and 1949) should be referred to for the arguments assessing this view as the most accurate of the pre-Restoration representations of the Bankside theatres. Even so it has to be remembered that Hollar (as Mr. Shapiro proves) accidentally interchanged the names, so that the building with the flag is really the Beargarden and the one to the left, showing twin gables, is the Globe (the second theatre of that name but already pulled down in 1644). From all the evidence available it appears that both the second Globe and the Beargarden were circular buildings as was the Swan also (cf. § 62) and that Hollar's view gives us a reliable glimpse of what the interior of the Globe (between 1614–44) was like, at least in so far as the gabled half roof of the 'Heavens' is concerned, which must have been carried on pillars (cf. de Witt's drawing of the interior of the Swan § 62).

§ 64 and 65 (cf. text pp. 44, 56)

Sir Philip Sidney and Sir Richard Grenville from portraits by unknown artists (1571 and 1577 respectively) in the National Portrait Gallery.

§ 64. Sir Philip Sidney (1554–86) is the epitome of the Elizabethan ideal of nobility. As poet and statesman he was intimate with Edmund Spenser and Fulke Greville and a favourite of Burghley. The range of his interests is evidenced by the fact that both Spenser's *Shepheardes Calendar* and Halkuyt's *Voyages* were dedicated to him. He was known to be deeply interested in the colonisation of America and enthusiastic for Drake's aggressive policy against Spain. Made governor of Flushing he was wounded in fighting the Spaniards at Zutphen and died at Arnhem. His prose romance of *Arcadia*, his *Apologie for Poetrie* and the *Astrophel and Stella* sonnet sequence were not published until after his death.

§ 65. Sir Richard Grenville (?1541–91), cousin of Sir Walter Raleigh, commanded the fleet which set out to colonise Virginia, and was afterwards concerned in various measures for strengthening English defences in the west immediately prior to the coming of the Armada. He became second in command of the Azores fleet under Lord Thomas Howard and in 1591 his ship, the 'Revenge,' fought the Spanish fleet for fifteen hours (cf. § 66 for this action), in which great sea fight he died.

§ 66 (cf. text p. 56)

The last fight of the 'Revenge,' August 1591. From the original tapestry (dated 1598) formerly lent by Monsieur Hypolite Worms to the National Maritime Museum, Greenwich.

The 'Revenge' was Drake's flagship against the Armada and later under Sir Richard Grenville (cf. § 65) played her part in harrying Spanish ships returning home laden with the spoils of the Indies. This contemporary tapestry shows the 'Revenge,' her foremast already shot away, hemmed in by four Spanish ships, with the rest of the Spanish fleet standing by to the left, while in the right background the English fleet (under Lord Thomas Howard) is in retreat. The islands of the Azores can be seen in the far distance.

§ 67–69 (cf. text pp. 83, 84, 85)
Windmills and Trenching Tools. From *The English Improver Improved*, etc., by Wa: Blith (1652). From the copy in the Cambridge University Library.

This 'survey of husbandry' was dedicated by its author 'a lover of ingenuity' to the 'Lord General Cromwell, the Right Honourable the Lord President and the rest of the Council of State.' It is divided into two parts, called 'Six Peeces of Improvement' and 'Six Newer Peeces of Improvement.' The first part covers in its second section the improvement of land 'By Draining Fen, Reducing Bog and Regaining Sea-lands,' with supplementary information on the tools with which to achieve this. After describing the causes of bogs and the nature of the Fen, the author details the chief hindrances to the work of drainage. He advocates the drawing-off of the land floods from the high lands outside the Fen before they reach the Fen itself, and dealing with the Fen-water itself by straight, well-cut drains, embanking and windmills (he has cautionary remarks to make on watermills which he thinks may cause more harm than good by being dammed too high and thus keeping all lands that lie under their mill head boggy). He then describes the windmills (as illustrated):—'Thy Engines may also be divers; as an Engine or Windmill made with a water wheel, planted in thy water course, or Master drain, or very near unto it, which water wheel must be made to that height as may be sure to take out the bottom of the water, and deliver it at the middle of the wheel, which wheel may be contrived into such a form, as that the Ladles, as I may call them, or Peals or Scoops, as others call them, will cast up, and cast out the water to a considerable height, as a man doth with a hand scoop, pail or kit, cast water out of a ditch . . . or else by a good chain pump or bucket work, both which may be made into a wind-mill Engine, or else with an Engine made with a perpetual Screw; all which for that height as is requirable to the draining of such a work, will lay a good compass of land dry in a few daies.' He completes this section by describing turving and burning of the Fen, the crops to plant afterwards, and so on. He then lists the tools necessary,—line and water level, a trenching plough or coulter to cut out the trench—this should be made from willow and shod with iron and fitted with a 'little brazen wheel' to bear upon with the foot that 'it may run more pleasantly.' A turfing spade and a trenching spade, the latter fitted with broad up-curving knife blades or 'Langets' to cut a clean deep furrow and lastly a paring spade wholly of iron—to cut out a trench in shallow places (where the plough cannot work) or to pare old trenches, whose sides are grown thick with grass.

§ 70 (cf. text p. 105)

Inigo Jones.    From the portrait by Van Dyck, in the Hermitage.

Inigo Jones (1573–1652), architect, surveyor of works to James I and Charles I and designer of masques, travelled extensively in Italy under the patronage of William Herbert, 3rd Earl of Pembroke, and while there purchased works of art for both Lord Pembroke and Lord Arundel. By his graceful and imaginative interpretation he established a taste for classicism in England, designing such buildings as the Queen's House at Greenwich (1617–35) (cf. § 71), the Banqueting Hall in Whitehall (1619–22), envisaged as part of a new palace, the Piazza of Covent Garden, and (at the end of his life and with the help of John Webb) such interiors as those for Wilton House (1648) (cf. § 72), besides superintending repairs to Old St. Paul's.

§ 71 (cf. text p. 105)

The Queen's House, Greenwich (1617–35). From an air photograph by Aerofilms, Ltd. (cf. note on Inigo Jones § 70). In complete contrast to Wilton House (cf. § 72) is the dignified simplicity of Inigo Jones' work in the Queen's House at Greenwich. Completed thirteen years before Wilton, the decoration is mostly concentrated in the elaborate ceilings, the walls being plain, occasionally relieved by the elaboration of the fireplaces. The exterior is classically simple, the only decoration being a plain balustrade round the roof, and balusters beneath the windows, and a pillared loggia on the first floor. In the background of this illustration can be seen Greenwich Hospital with its twin domes designed by Sir Christopher Wren (for whom cf. note under Colour Plate IV), to harmonise with the already existing Queen's House.

§ 72 (cf. text p. 105)

The Double Cube Room, Wilton House (1648). From a photograph by Country Life, Ltd. (cf. with § 87 of the Grinling Gibbons room at Petworth House).

The Italianate magnificence of the great suite of rooms along the south front of Wilton House owes its inception at least to Inigo Jones, though most of the work was actually carried out under John Webb's direction. The whole decoration of the double cube room is in plaster (cf. with Grinling Gibbons' carved woodwork at Petworth § 87) in gold and white, the walls being divided into panels by swags of fruit and flowers depending from masks. The decoration forms an elaborately designed setting for the great Van Dyck portraits; the doorways are pillared and surmounted by broken pediments, upon which recline sculptured figures; the carved mantelpiece supports an elaborate arrangement of pilasters and figures framing a picture; and upon the whole looks down de Critz's painted ceiling. When we remember that this was accomplished in the disturbed period of the Civil War, the achievement seems the more astonishing (cf. § 91 for de Caus' garden plan for Wilton).

§ 73 (cf. text pp. 89, 90)

Title-page from 'The Lamentable complaints of Nick Froth the Tapster and Rulerost the Cooke. Concerning the restraint lately set forth against drinking, potting, and piping on the Sabbath day, and against selling meate' (1641). From the Thomason Tracts, Dept. of Printed Books, British Museum.

This tract takes the form of a dialogue between the tapster and the cook concerning the new regulations 'whereby we are commanded not to sell meat nor draw drink upon Sundays.' They both defend their trades and the cook bemoans 'the lusty Surloines of roast Beefe which I with much policy divided into an innumerable company of semi-slices, by which, with my provident wife, I used to make eighteene pence of that which cost me but a groat (provided that I sold it in service time).' The tapster says that after all there's one good thing about the new law, that whereas previously he had had to pay a fee to the Apparitors so that he shouldn't be brought into Court and prosecuted for selling drink on Sunday, now he will be able to save a Noble a quarter (cf. note to § 74). The cook agrees but says he paid in kind and 'a stone of beef was no more in one of their bellies than a man in Pauls.' They get some comfort from the thought that they're all out of a job together.

§ 74 (cf. text pp. 89, 90)

Title-page from 'The Proctor and Parator their mourning: or, The Lamentations of the Doctors Commons for their Downfall. Being a true Dialogue, Relating the fearful abuses and exorbitancies of those Spirituall Courts, under the names of Sponge the Proctor, and Hunter the Parator' (1641). From the Thomason Tracts, Dept. of Printed Books, British Museum.

This dialogue gives the other side of the picture to that described in the note to § 73 above. The two rascals discuss how business is going and Parator describes how he went out and found transgressors among 'Chandlers, Alehouses, Tavernes, Tobacco-shops, Butchers, Comfit-makers, Gunsmiths, Bakers, Brokers, Cookes, Weavers, etc.' while the Proctor sat at home and 'framed interrogations against them.' They gloat together over their ways of getting wealth from 'Popish recusants and Seminary Priests for concealing their haunts, as well as from Nuns and Novices . . . Brownists, Anabaptists, etc.' in fact, from all those who want to keep out of the spiritual courts. Now, however, times are not what they were and they decide finally they'd 'better turn journey-man to Gregory the hangman, for it is reported he has great trading, anything rather than stand out, better live by a Rope, than by the Pope.'

**§ 75 (cf. text pp. 89, 90)**
From 'The Ploughman's Reply to the Merry Milk-maid's Delight.'

> 'I am a ploughman brisk and young
> And well I like the Milkmaid's Song.'

Tune of: I am a Weaver to my Trade, printed for William Thackeray, T. Passenger and W. Whitwood.' Douce Collection, ii, 177ᵛ, Bodleian Library, Oxford. Reproduced from *The Bagford Ballads*, collected by J. W. Ebsworth, (1876–8), from the copy in the Cambridge University Library.

**§ 76 (cf. text pp. 90, 91)**
From 'A Glasse for the Times, by which according to the Scriptures, you may clearly behold the True Ministers of Christ, how farre differing from false Teachers—with a brief Collection of the Errors of our Times, and their Authors names—drawn from their own writings, also proofs of scripture by way of comfutation of them by Sundry Able Ministers. Collected by T. C. a Friend to Truth. Printed by Robt. Ibbitson, 1648.' From the Thomason Tracts, Dept. of Printed Books, British Museum.
The illustration to this tract of error corrected contrasts the orthodox minister with the canting imposter, whose sayings are confuted in the body of the text.

**§ 77 (cf. text p. 92). The House of Commons in 1651.**
From the reverse of the second Great Seal of the Commonwealth (1651). Seal XXXIV. 17. Dept. of MSS., British Museum.
This seal, the work of Thomas Simon (1623–65), the medallist and seal engraver, bears on its obverse a map of England, Wales and Ireland, and on its reverse (as shown here) the House of Commons in session, with the Speaker in the chair. A member (said by Vertue to be Harrison (Cromwell's brother-in-law)) with arm outstretched, is speaking to the House. The words round the rim of the seal are: 'In the Third yeare of Freedome by Gods Blessing Restored. 1651.'
The general design is the same as that of the first Great Seal of the Commonwealth, but more carefully elaborated. It was used

from 26 March 1651 to *c.* 1658 and though supplanted by the Seal of Oliver Cromwell as Protector, was again used during the Interregnum 14 May 1659 to 28 May 1660.

§ 78 (cf. text p. 92)

John Bunyan. From the frontispiece to *The Pilgrim's Progress* by John Bunyan. Third Edition, 1679. From the copy in the Dept. of Printed Books, British Museum.

This portrait of Bunyan occurs for the first time in the third edition and is repeated in most of the immediately following editions. Bunyan (1628–88), son of a Bedford tinsmith, himself served in the Parliamentary forces for a time, and undergoing conversion became a preacher and writer of tracts. Since he was an unlicensed preacher he soon found himself in prison, where he remained for some twelve years. While in prison, however, he was allowed to preach to his fellow prisoners and to write. After the Declaration of Indulgence by Charles II in 1672 he was left free to preach and write as he would, and *The Pilgrim's Progress* was first published in 1678.

§ 79 (cf. text p. 99)

The Battle of Naseby. From *Anglia Rediviva*, by Joshua Sprigg, 1647. From the copy in the Dept. of Printed Books, British Museum.

This illustration shows the disposition of the King's and Sir Thomas Fairfax's forces before the Battle of Naseby (14 June 1645). *Anglia Rediviva* (an account of the successes of Fairfax's army) was compiled by Joshua Sprigg, a retainer of Sir Thomas Fairfax. Sprigg relates how on the night of the 13th June the van of the Royalist army was reported at Harborough, the rear within two miles of Naseby. At 3 o'clock on the following morning Fairfax advanced with the intention of retarding the Royalists from going to Leicester, but on seeing the King's Horse advancing towards them on the hill top this side of Harborough, Fairfax drew down into a large fallow field about one mile broad on the N.W. of Naseby, flanked on the left with a hedge, and taking advantage of a ridge of hill running E.W. he drew down behind this and awaited the Royalist attack. The Royalist seeing them draw back thought they were retreating to avoid an engagement and rushed on, leaving most of their ordnance behind them. The main body was repelled, but the right wing under Prince Rupert worsted the left wing of the Parliamentary forces and followed his success up almost to Naseby Town, but on his return he tried to seize the Train of Artillery, but it was strongly defended with 'Firelocks and Rearguard'—and this and the Parliamentary success in the main battle forced Rupert to withdraw hastily to the King's rescue, where the Royalist horse had been worsted and their foot were at Fairfax's mercy. Meanwhile the Parliamentary foot had got left some quarter of a mile behind their horse and Fairfax decided to wait for them before pressing on the attack with horse, foot and artillery. This further attack broke the Royalist forces completely and they were pursued within two miles of Leicester (i.e. says Sprigg some fourteen miles), losing five thousand prisoners, all their artillery, arms and equipment, together with the King's papers and treasure.

This plate shows the Parliamentary army in the foreground, with General Ireton on the left wing, Lt. Colonel Pride in the rearguard and General Fairfax and Lt. General Cromwell on the right wing; in the left foreground can be seen the artillery guarded with firelocks. In the background are opposed the Royalist forces, with the King in the centre, on the left Prince Rupert and Prince Maurice, other Royalist officers on the right, and the King's bodyguard and Prince Rupert's foot behind the main body.

§ 80 (cf. text p. 99)
Oliver Cromwell. From the engraving after William Faithorne for *The Emblem of England's Distraction* (1658). B.M. MS. Add. 32, 352, f. 228.

This symbolical picture shows Oliver Cromwell, attended by Fame and trampling on Error and Faction. In the foreground, to the left is represented 'They shall beat their speares into pruning hooks,' and to the right 'their swords into Plowshears.' In the top left-hand corner is depicted the Ark upon Mount Ararat and below it Abraham about to sacrifice Isaac with the ram caught in the thicket, while in the top right corner are Scylla and Charybdis.

In other versions of the engraving all these symbols or 'emblems' are labelled with their meanings, as was the fashion in the 'emblem-book,' Cromwell's sceptre being labelled 'Pro Deo lege et grege' and the building above the figures of Anglia, Scotia and Hibernia 'Floreant Protector et Parliamentum Angliae,' etc. For a plate giving the emblem inscriptions, cf. S. R. Gardiner's *Oliver Cromwell* (1899), Goupil Monographs.

§ 81 (cf. text p. 103)
From the frontispiece of *The Present State of London*, by T. de Laune (1690). From the copy in the Cambridge University Library.

This book sets out to be a full and succinct account of the 'Ancient and Modern State of London its Original, Government, Rights, Liberties, Charters, Trade, Customs, Priveleges and other Remarkables etc.' Chapter 4 of Section 2 gives an account of the temporal government of London and lists all the Lord Mayors and Sheriffs from 1189 up to 1690. Later follows a brief account of the Court of the Lord Mayor and Aldermen, shown in this illustration, and of the various sub-courts for 'Orphans, Wardmote, Hall-mote, Conservation of the Water and River of Thames, Coroner and Escheaker, Policies and Assurances to Merchants, the Tower, the Common Council, and the Chamberlain.'

The Court of the Aldermen is described as being one of record 'principally instituted for the redressing and correcting the Errors, Defaults and Misprisions which happen in the government of the City. Held on Tuesdays and Thursdays.' Of the temporal government of the City of London De Laune says: 'This great and populous City is governed with that admirable order and Regularity that it is even astonishing. For therein (as in most other things) she excells all other cities of the world.'

§ 82 (cf. text p. 97)

John Milton. From the engraving by William Faithorne (1670) in the National Portrait Gallery.

John Milton (1608–74), poet and scholar, and Latin secretary to the Council of State. The erstwhile 'Lady of Christ's,' the political idealist, the poet who set out 'to justify the ways of God to men,' the pioneer of the liberty of the press, illustrates all that was best on the Parliamentary side, and it is perhaps salutary to set his figure against the preconceived idea that every member of the Parliament side was necessarily a ranting, psalmsinging boor of a Roundhead.

§ 83 (cf. text p. 103)

John Evelyn. From the engraving by Robert Nanteuil in the National Portrait Gallery.

The Royalist, John Evelyn (1620–1706), may similarly (cf. note to § 82 above) be set against the popular picture of the Cavalier, with wanton lovelocks and plumed hat. A man of cultivated tastes and enquiring mind is revealed in his Diaries, which describe his travels and his contemporaries. Apart from the Diaries he is remembered chiefly for his interest in landscape gardening, and for the part he played in promoting the foundation of the Royal Society.

§ 84 (cf. text p. 105)

Ham House, Surrey. From a photograph by Country Life, Ltd. This illustration shows the Jacobean north front built originally about 1610 by Sir Thomas Vavasor, but altered extensively about 1672 when the Countess of Dysart married (as her second husband) the second Earl (later Duke) of Lauderdale. It is thus an example of a traditional house with the additions and alterations of later XVIIth century taste. On this side, roundels have been cut out (after the classical model) above the ground floor windows, the earlier gables have been replaced by a hipped roof and cornice, and bays have been thrown out from the end of the wings. It should be contrasted with the following plate of Coleshill.

§ 85 (cf. text p. 105)

Coleshill House, Berkshire. From a photograph by Country Life, Ltd.

With this illustration we have an example of the later development of the Inigo Jones school in the transference and adaptation of the classical Italian style to England. (It should be contrasted with the foregoing plate of Ham House, which shows classical influence on an existing house in an earlier style.) Built between 1650 and 1664 by Roger Pratt (possibly with some preliminary advice from the aged Inigo Jones (who was dead by 1652)), Coleshill replaced an earlier manor house. Roger Pratt (cousin of Sir George Pratt, for whom Coleshill was built) had returned in 1649 from travels in Italy (in John Evelyn's company), and is said to have persuaded Sir George to pull down the house he was beginning to build (to replace his old manor house which had been recently burnt) and let him design him a house in the Italianate style. The restrained dignity and purity of design of Coleshill was the happy result. The rich cornice, the outstanding chimney stacks and the balustrade and cupola should be noted.

§ 86 (cf. text p. 105)

Staircase at Tythrop House, Oxfordshire (c. 1680). From a photograph by Country Life, Ltd.

Note the beautifully carved balusters and the pierced work of the panels, the wide shallow treads and the broad landings.

§ 87 (cf. text p. 105)

The Grinling Gibbons carved room at Petworth House, Sussex (1689 and after). From a photograph by Country Life, Ltd.

(Cf. with § 72 of the interior of Wilton by Inigo Jones and Webb.)

The splendour to which carved panelling could attain is well illustrated by this room decorated by Grinling Gibbons (1648–1720) for the seventh Duke of Somerset about 1689. The walls are panelled with oak and are decorated with carved swags of fruit and flowers in limewood, which form an elaborate setting for the great portraits, for which he also designed the frames. (Cf. § 99 for the carving in Trinity College Library, Cambridge, which he also carried out.)

§ 88 (cf. text p. 106)

An Elizabethan formal garden with pleached bower (1568), from *The Profitable Arte of Gardening*, by Thomas Hill (1568). From a copy in the Dept. of Printed Books, British Museum.

Thomas Hill compiled and translated many books on gardening. In this little treatise he shows a formal garden, enclosed with pillars and balustrade within a hedged fence. On the right can be seen a pleached arbour and on the left a well and bucket for watering the beds.

§ 89 (cf. text p. 106)

*A New Orchard and Garden*, by William Lawson (1618). From a copy in the Dept. of Printed Books, British Museum.

William Lawson discusses in his book planting and grafting as well as layout. This little plan allows for orchard and kitchen garden, walks and garden knots as well as bees and 'still room houses,' and says Lawson 'if the river run by your door and under your mount, it will be pleasant.'

*Key to illustration.*

'A. All these squares must be set with Trees, the Garden and other Ornaments must stand in spaces betwixt the Trees and in the borders and fences.

B. Trees twenty yards asunder.

C. Garden Knots.

D. Kitching Garden.

E. Bridge.

F. Conduit.

G. Stairs.

H. Walks set with great wood thicke.

I. Walks set with great wood round about your orchard.

K. The out fence.

L. The out fence set with stone fruit.

M. Mount. To force Earth for a mount or such like, set it round with quick and lay boughs of Trees strangely intermingled, the tops inward, with the Earth in the middle.

N. Still house.

O. Good standing for Bees, if you have an house.

P. If the River run by your door and under your mount, it will be pleasant.'

§ 90 (cf. text p. 106)

*The Country Housewife's Garden*, bound up with *A New Orchard and Garden* (cf. note to § 89 above), and *The husbandry of Bees* . . . 'being the labours of forty eight yeares of William Lawson' (1618). In spite of Lawson's statement, *The Country Housewife's Garden* is Gervase Markham's, being reprinted from his *Country Contentments* of 1611. From a copy in the Dept. of Printed Books, British Museum.

The author says engagingly that 'the number of mazes and knots is so great and men are so diversely delighted that I leave every housewife to herselfe, especially seeing to set downe many had bin butt to fill much paper, yet lest I deprive her of all delight and direction let her view these few choice, new, formes.' He gives several pages of diagrams of the ground plans for knots: cinkfoyle, Flower deluce, Trefoyle, Frette, Lozenges, Croseboowe, Diamond, ovall and maze, of which four are shown in this illustration.

§ 91 (cf. text p. 106)

*Plan of Wilton Garden*, by Isaac de Caus (1645). From a copy in the Dept. of Printed Books, British Museum.

The *Hortus Pembrochianus* shown in this plate was designed by Isaac de Caus, who may have been the nephew of the Norman architect and engineer, Salomon de Caus, one of whose particular studies was the motive power of water. Isaac was primarily a mathematician, also interested in hydraulic problems. During the Civil War years while John Webb was occupied on Wilton House, Isaac de Caus laid out the gardens. In this plate can be seen (in the extreme distance) the orchard, divided from the enclosed garden by a raised terrace and balustrade with a small building, having a flat roof and arches. The garden is divided into three parts, the furthest of which is laid out with trees and grass, round a central gravelled space and statue. Along the sides run pleached alleys, which are repeated in the middle section of the garden, which is mainly given up to a plantation of trees, through which runs a stream. In the foreground are the knots (cf. § 90) laid out in formal evergreens, with fountains and statues.

§ 92 (cf. text pp. 108, 109)

From the frontispiece by Wenceslaus Hollar to *Britannia*, by John Ogilby (1675). From a copy in the Map Room, British Museum.

This road book of England and Wales is the forerunner of the sectional map book. At the top of the plate can be seen three cherubs who have scrolls showing sections of road, while below can be seen a fortress, in the foreground a number of men occupied at a table with a globe and numerous mathematical instruments, while a couple more set out on the long winding road, with a road map for guidance. On every side men can be seen carrying on their daily jobs, some are fishing in the river, a stag hunt is in progress through quite undisturbed sheep, horses and cattle, ships are putting out from the castellated port, and far up the road, climbing towards the windmill on the summit, is a travelling coach.

§ 93 (cf. text p. 118)

Frontispiece to *Comical Romance of A Company of Stage Players*, the English translation of Paul Scarron's *Roman Comique*, engraved by W. Faithorne (1676). From a copy in the Cambridge University Library.

Scarron was a crippled French burlesque dramatist (his wife later became Mme. de Maintenon), whose travesties of Virgil, etc., had a great influence on the burlesque writers and translators of the later XVIIth century in England. The frontispiece depicts a touring company of players arriving for a performance in a provincial town. In the background can be seen their stage already set up, with a play in progress before an audience of townspeople. In the foreground, one of the actresses is just drawing up at the inn; she rides, seated high on the 'props,' in a cart drawn by two bullocks, with a horse and pony running alongside; beside her walk an old man with a bass viol on his back, and an actor with sword and gun, and a brace of birds slung at his hip.

§ 94 (cf. text p. 118)

The Stage of the Red Bull (or possibly of the Cockpit) from *The Wits, or Sport upon Sport,* by Francis Kirkman (1673). Reproduced by permission of Messrs. Duckworth from Karl Mantzius' *History of the Drama* (1904).

In the early years of the Restoration, with the raising of the Puritan ban on the theatre and before new theatres such as the Theatre Royal in Drury Lane (1674) and the Duke's Theatre in Dorset Gardens (1671) were opened, some old theatres, notably the Red Bull (1605) and the Cockpit (1617), were utilised. Our illustration thus shows a stage of the interesting intermediate period, completely roofed in, with candelabra and footlights, but retaining the old platform stage with the audience still surrounding the players. It does not yet have the proscenium arch, drop curtains and scenery and modified apron stage of the Restoration theatre proper, which owed its development to the influence of the court masque brought into England by Inigo Jones during the early years of the XVIIth century.

The play being enacted is one of the short 'drolls' which managed to sustain a precarious existence even during the Commonwealth itself. These were usually one act farces made out of incidents in full length plays (Falstaff and mine hostess can be seen in the left foreground). *The Wits,* published in 1673, was a collection of these drolls.

§ 95 (cf. text p. 128)

From *Systema Agriculturae, being the Mystery of Husbandry Discovered and layd open,* by J[ohn] W[orlidge] (1669). From a copy of the second edition (1675) in the Dept. of Printed Books, British Museum.

This book 'published for the common good by J. W. Gent' (as the title-page runs) was the first attempt to advise on agricultural methods on a large scale. The explanation of the frontispiece is worth quoting:

'First cast your eye upon a Rustick seat,
Built strong and plain, yet well contriv'd and neat,
And situated on a healthy Soyl,
Yielding much Wealth with little cost, or toyl.
Near by it stand the Barns fram'd to contain
Enriching stores of Hay, Pulse, Corn and Grain;
With Battons large, and places where to feed

Your Oxen, Cows, Swine, Poultrey, with their breed,
On th'other side hard by the House, you see
Th' Apiary for th' industrious Bee.
Walk on a little farther, and behold
A pleasant Garden from high Winds and cold
Defended (by a spreading, fruitful wall
With Rows of Lime, and Fir trees straight and tall),
Full fraught with necessary Flow'res and Fruits,
And Nature's choicest sorts of Plants, and Roots,
Beyond the same are crops of Beans and Pease,
Saffron and Liquorice, or such as these;
Then Orchards so enriched with fruitful store,
Nature could give (nor they receive) no more,
Each Tree stands bending with the weight it bears
Of Cherries some, of Apples, Plums and Pears;
Not far from thence see other Walks and Rows
Of Cyder-fruits, near unto which there flows
A Gliding Stream; the next place you discover
Is where St. Foyn, La Lucern, Hops and Clover
Are propagated: Near unto those Fields,
Stands a large Wood, Mast, Fewel, Timber yields,
In yonder Vale hard by the River stands
A Water Engine, which the Winde commands
To fertilise the Meads, on t'other side
A Persian Wheel is plac't both large and wide
To th' same intent; Then do the Fields appear
Cloathed with Corn, and Grain, for th' ensuing year,
The Pastures stockt with Beasts, the Down with Sheep,
The Cart, the Plough, and all good order keep;
Plenty unto the Husbandman, and Gains
Are his Rewards for's Industry and Pains,
     Peruse this Book, for here you onely see
     Th' following subject in Epitomy.'

Other plates in the book show in detail the Persian Wheel, farm implements, etc.

§ 96 (cf. text pp. 115, 116)

Isaac Newton. From the portrait by Kneller (1689) in the possession of the Earl of Portsmouth.

Isaac Newton (1642–1727), the natural philosopher and mathematician, was the first to grasp the idea of a law of universal gravitation, which is considered in his *Philosophiae Naturalis Principia Mathematica* (1687). Besides becoming Master of the Mint and President of the Royal Society, he also wrote on theological subjects and submitted reports on the coinage.

§ 97 (cf. text pp. 115, 116)

Robert Boyle. From the portrait by Frederic Kerseboom in the possession of the Royal Society.

Robert Boyle (1627–91), chemist and natural philosopher, the promulgator of 'Boyle's Law' (of which he gave experimental proof in his *Defence against Linus*, which was appended to the second edition of his *New Experiments Physico-Mechanical* (1662)), combined these studies with a pious fervour for the propagation of Christian doctrine. He was a governor of the Corporation for the Spread of the Gospel in New England, a founder of the Royal Society and a director of the East India Company.

§ 98 (cf. text p. 122)

Pepys' bookcases at Magdalene College, Cambridge. From a photograph by A. F. Kersting.

Samuel Pepys (1633–1703), the diarist and Secretary to the Admiralty, left his library to Magdalene (where he had been a sizar), with instructions that it should be housed in the new building (not finished until 1703), now accordingly known as the Pepysian Library.

This illustration shows some of his books in Pepys' own fine mahogany glazed bookcases, in which he had had them placed in 1666, when he wrote in his *Diary* (24 August 1666): 'Comes Sympson, to set up my other new presses for my books, to my most extraordinary satisfaction; so that I think it will be as noble a closet as any man hath; though, indeed, it would have been better to have had a little more light.' (It is of interest to note that on 5 October 1665, Pepys had been reading John Evelyn's translation (1661) from the French, called *Instructions concerning Erecting of a Library* (which had been sent him), and had noted 'but the book is above my reach.'

§ 99 (cf. text p. 123)

Grinling Gibbons' carving on bookcases in Trinity College library, Cambridge. From a photograph by A. F. Kersting.

When Wren planned the library of Trinity he is thought to have borrowed the general design from that of the library of St. Mark's at Venice, where the library is also raised above a cloister (cf. J. W. Clark's *The Care of Books* (1902)). But Wren also paid great attention to the interior arrangement and fittings of his library; in his Memoir he writes: 'The disposition of the shelves both along the walls and breaking out from the walls ... must needs prove very convenient and gracefull, and the best way for the students will be to have a little square table in each Celle with 2 chaires' (*v*. Clark, p. 280 f.). Even the bookcases themselves were designed by him as well as stools and tables. The bookcases were intended to carry statues, but instead are surmounted by busts introduced by Grinling Gibbons, who also carved the panels of fruit and flowers (which carry the monograms of those who subscribed to the building of the library) on the ends of the bookcases.

§ 100-103 (cf. text pp. 108, 109, 144)

Road and river transport. Details from D. Loggan's *Cantabrigia Illustrata* (1690) and *Oxonia Illustrata* (1675). From copies in the Cambridge University Library.

§ 100. Detail from plate of Magdalene College, Cambridge, showing barges and 'tilt boats,' the former carrying coal, while the latter had canopies and carried passengers for fares.

§ 101. Detail from plate of University College, Oxford, showing a stage waggon drawn by six horses. This was an ordinary cart covered over with cloth and carried goods and passengers together, rather like a carrier's cart.

§ 102. Detail from plate of St. Mary's Church, Oxford, showing a string of loaded packhorses.

§ 103. Detail from plate of Exeter College, Oxford, showing a dray loaded with barrels, as well as a horse with panniers.

§ 104 and 105 (cf. text p. 109)

Coaches.

§ 104. Detail from D. Loggan's *Oxonia Illustrata* (1675). From a copy in the Cambridge University Library.

This shows a coach and four arriving at the Sheldonian Theatre. Note how low the coach is swung between the great wheels, and the lack of window space.

§ 105. From an engraving by John Dunstall (fl. 1644-75) in the London Prospects Portfolio, Vol. V, in the possession of the Society of Antiquaries.

This plate shows an ornate travelling coach, with its leather curtains let down. In the distance can be seen Old St. Paul's (which would seem to place the engraving prior to the Great Fire of 1666). Across the bottom of the plate the coach can be seen on the open road, drawn by six horses and with a mounted escort. I have not been able to identify the occupants of the coach, though it would seem that the engraving is meant to portray some particular event.

§ 106-111 (cf. text pp. 136, 137, 138, 139)

Sport in the XVIIth century. Engravings from *The Gentleman's Recreation*, published by R. Blome (1686). From a copy in the Dept. of Printed Books, British Museum.

Every branch of XVIIth century sport and pastime is covered by the engravings in this book, which are mostly the work of Francis Barlow (1626-1704), the earliest English artist to delineate sporting subjects. The engravings speak for themselves and form an interesting commentary on sporting usage as shooting supersedes hawking, 'shooting flying' vies with 'perching the pheasant' or hunting partridge with dogs and net. Hunting the hare and the stag are both here: some of the plates, notably § 110, 'Hunting the hare with deep mouthed hounds,' have a delightful sense of pattern and movement.

§ 112 (cf. text p. 139)

The Last Horse Race run before Charles II at Dorsett (=Datchet) Ferry, 1684. Etching by Francis Barlow (1687). From the Dept. of Prints and Drawings, British Museum.

This etching by Francis Barlow (1626–1704) (cf. note under § 106–111) shows the king watching for the last time the racing he had himself inaugurated at Windsor; as the caption indicates the race at this time was run at Datchet Ferry (not until Queen Anne's time was it changed to Ascot).

§ 113 (cf. text p. 145)

Flying from the Plague in 1630. From a broadside (no. 304) in the possession of the Society of Antiquaries, entitled 'London Soundes a Trumpet, that the countrey may hear it.'

'When death drives, the Grave thrives,
 Coachman, Runne thou away, never so fast
One stride of mine, cuts off the Nimblest haste.
Printed for Henry Gosson, 1630. London.'

This same illustration is also used for a similar broadside (no. 303) entitled 'A Looking Glasse for City and Countrey.' Both broadsides are concerned with the flight of the townspeople to the country. The first apostrophises London: 'Now doe thy coaches . . . runne thorow thy streets, and so out at thy gates, full of brave rich people, to live safe (as they hope) in the Countrey; not caring how sorrowful a life thou leadest here in their absence. How little doe they regard the poore, which they leave behind them. . . .' It then goes on to admonish the country people to show more kindness to the sick coming from the towns, and continues by comparing the lot of London with such cities as Mantua, Parma, etc., where plague mortality is much higher and more frequently experienced. It concludes with a prayer that the whole land as well as the city may prosper again soon and the plague be removed from them.

§ 114 (cf. text p. 139)

Bathing in the King's Bath at Bath in 1675. From an engraving by Thomas Johnson (1675) in the Dept. of Prints and Drawings, British Museum.

Thomas Johnson was a follower of Hollar, the Bohemian engraver, whose careful topographical and costume drawings of England and the English people of the middle XVIIth century, have added so much to our visual knowledge of the period (cf. note to § 63). Johnson's engraving gives a very vivid picture of what a visit to Bath for one's health entailed in the 1670's. It shows the oldest of the baths—the King's

Bath, with the Queen's Bath adjoining it on the left. In the middle of the King's Bath is a wooden pavilion, called the Cross, which had been built over the hot water spring itself in 1664. Here the water was naturally hottest and the recesses below were known as the Kitchen. Obviously the bath attracted many onlookers and there is hardly a window without a spectator or two. Mixed bathing is the rule and people duck or wade as they choose: one woman appears to be towing her two children along behind her, while another (in the lower right-hand corner) is taking a glass of the waters, as she bathes.

§ 115 and 116 (cf. text pp. 146, 147)

London after the Fire, from an engraving in the London Prospects Portfolio, Vol. V, in the possession of the Society of Antiquaries.

This is an XVIIIth century engraving after Hollar's 'True and exact prospect' of London after the Fire (1667). (For note on Hollar cf. § 63). The shell of Old St. Paul's can be distinguished clearly and the gutted ruins of churches and houses can be traced along the river-bank beyond London Bridge to the Tower. On London Bridge itself the houses at the northern end had been burnt down in 1632 and later rebuilt, only to suffer again in 1666; the extent can be seen here.

The diaries of John Evelyn and Samuel Pepys give vivid eye-witness accounts of the Fire, and a very full discussion of it, with plans and prints, can be found in *The Great Fire of London in 1666*, by W. G. Bell (1920).

§ 117 (cf. text p. 147)

John Lofting's Fire Engine (1689/90). From an engraving by J. Kip in the London Prospects Portfolio, Vol. V, in the possession of the Society of Antiquaries.

John Lofting (?1659–1742), a Dutchman, settled in London as a manufacturer of fire engines, patented this one in 1690. The engraver has shown the engine being tried out on the new Royal Exchange (which had been built in 1669 to replace Gresham's Royal Exchange, destroyed in the Great Fire,—the second building was itself destroyed by fire in 1838). Presumably it was chosen to test the height to which the jet could be thrown, in view of the height of the tower (160 feet to the grasshopper at the top). In another later and more elaborate plate (in the same portfolio) Lofting describes by means of a series of small inset pictures (with a key) how his 'new sucking worm fire engine' worked. This plate is apparently imitated from illustrations in Jan Van der Heyde's book on fire engines with leather hose (published 1690); it shows sections of a house on fire, and different ways of treating fires, from those in ships to those in cellars. The engine could either be worked direct

from a pool of water or a river, or could be supplied with
water at a greater distance by the help of the smaller engine and
the long canvas or leather pipes.

§ 118 and 119 (cf. text p. 148)
Portland Quarries. From drawings by S. H. Grimm (1790).
B.M. MS. Add. 15,537, ff. 158 and 198.
These drawings by the Swiss artist Samuel Hieronymus Grimm
(1734–94) show the galleries of a Portland stone quarry and
the method for transporting the great unfashioned blocks
across to the mainland. Though they are of a century later, it
is unlikely that there had been much change in the interval in
either the method of quarrying or in that of transport.

§ 120 (cf. text p. 148)
St. Paul's Cathedral. From an air photograph by Aerofilms, Ltd.
The splendour of Wren's design can perhaps be most truly
appreciated from this angle, for in spite of the devastation of
1940, it is still difficult to get an uninterrupted view of its proportions from ground level. (For a note on Wren cf. note to
Colour Plate IV.)
After the Great Fire Wren produced his plan for the rebuilding
of London, which owing to the private haste and self-interest
of property owners was never implemented. His earliest
design for St. Paul's itself was rejected and it was not until
1675 that a second design was granted the royal warrant, and
with certain alterations (principally the substitution of the
present dome) the building was finally completed in 1710,
although it was usable for services some thirteen years earlier.
Its classical beauty is in striking contrast to the Gothic of Old
St. Paul's (cf. § 37). Wren's complete break with the mediaeval
can be seen also in his City churches (cf. § 121 and 122).

§ 121 (cf. text p. 148)
St. Bride's Church, Fleet St. From a photograph by A. F.
Kersting.
Built by Wren (cf. note under Colour Plate IV) in 1680 to
replace the earlier church destroyed in the Great Fire, St.
Bride's was itself destroyed in the blitz of 1940, though its
gutted steeple still survives. This steeple with its lovely
diminishing tiers was not completed until the turn of the
XVIIth century.

§ 122 (cf. text p. 148)
Church of St. Magnus the Martyr. From a photograph by
A. F. Kersting.
Rebuilt by Wren (cf. note under Colour Plate IV) in 1676 after
the destruction of the earlier church in the Great Fire, St.
Magnus, though damaged, survived the 1940 blitz. Note in
this interior how completely the columns and ceiling break away
from the Gothic conception of a church.

§ 123 (cf. text p. 139)

Church of King Charles the Martyr, Tunbridge Wells. **From** a photograph by A. F. Kersting.

Built in 1685 the plain brick exterior of this church conceals an ornate plaster ceiling of great beauty and sophistication as shown in this illustration.

§ 124 (cf. text p. 148)

The Chapel, Petworth House, Sussex. From a photograph by Country Life, Ltd.

The only part of Petworth House, which is earlier than the late XVIIth century is the chapel (*c.* 1250) and this was also redecorated when the Duke of Somerset was rebuilding the rest of the house (1688–96). It forms an interesting example of the change of taste, the XIIIth century pointed windows and slender shafts retiring oddly behind the heavy panelling, while the gallery with its great carved canopy and the pillared screen below might almost belong to a college hall.

Text illustration, p. 3 (cf. text p. 2)

Woodcut from 'The most rare and excellent History of the Dutchesse of Suffolke's Calamity. To the tune of Q. Dido. London. Printed for Ed. Wright. Dwelling at Christ Church Gate.' Roxburghe Collection of Ballads, I, 94. Dept. of Printed Books, British Museum.

(For general note on the Roxburghe Collection cf. note on § 25–28 above.)

After detailing a list of martyrs this ballad tells how the Duchess of Suffolk escaped with her husband, nurse and child from Gravesend for Germany, where they stayed, suffering many hardships, until Elizabeth came to the throne and they could return to England.

Text illustration, p. 48 (cf. text p. 48)

From a Broadside (no. 291) in the possession of the Society of Antiquaries, entitled: 'A most Excellent offer of a certaine Invention for a new kind of fire, being both cheape and Good, and most necessary for all men, especially in these deare times of Fuell. Printed at London, by T. C. for M. S. 1628.'

The scarcity and expense of fuel is pointed by this broadside, which described 'an artificial fire (or coale) for rich and poore.' It claims that by mixing stiff mortar, water and small sea-coal, rolling the mixture into round balls and 'piling them in a handsome manner, . . . in 4 Chaldren there may be saved 3 load, which at thirty shillings a Chaldren, 4 Chaldren comes to six pounds, and there may be saved in that forty-five shillings, which I thinke being cast up in Brewhouses, Dyehouses, Bakers, Cookes and private houses, would rise to a large summe in a yeare.'

Among such qualities in its favour as its durability, lack of smoke or cinder, saving of timber for ships, etc., the author claims that it will give employment in the making of it to maimed soldiers and orphans 'and thus might our poor idle children be employed to work, to save the citie store, and parish Churche stocks of coals.'

Text illustration, p. 58 (cf. text p. 59)
From the title-page of *The Roaring Girle or Moll Cut-Purse*, by T. Middleton and T. Dekker (1611). From a copy in the Dept. of Printed Books, British Museum.
Moll Cutpurse was a real person, a thief and a forger, but Middleton and Dekker make of her an honest, well-meaning, swaggering wench, who wears breeches and smokes tobacco, and the plot of their play turns on her success in bringing together the lovers, who have been kept apart by a covetous father. There are frequent references throughout the play to smoking and tobacco, showing how common a habit it had become by this date.

Text illustration, p. 61 (cf. text pp. 61, 62)
Woodcut from 'The Sorrowful Lamentation of the Pedlars, and Petty Chapmen for the hardness of the times and the decay of Trade. To the tune of My Life and My Death. This may be printed. R .P. Printed for I. Back at the Black-boy at London-bridge.' Roxburghe Collection of Ballads, II, 404. Dept. of Printed Books, British Museum.
(For general note on the Roxburghe Collection cf. note to § 25–28 above.)
A typical Autolycus with pack on back and his dinner in his hand calls

'Then Maidens and Men
Come see what you lack
And buy the fine toys that I have in my pack.'

He recounts all the things he has to sell, points and garters, pins and cotton, bodkins and lace and songs 'all Pleasant, Witty, Delightful and New,' and concludes with the frank statement 'To buy a new Licence, your money I crave.'

Text illustration, p. 71 (cf. text p. 72)
Woodcut from 'A merry new Ballad, both pleasant and sweete In praise of the Blacksmith, which is very mete. To the tune of Greensleeves, etc.' Roxburghe Collection of Ballads, I, 250, 251. Dept. of Printed Books, British Museum.
(For general note on the Roxburghe Collection cf. note to § 25–28 above.)
This rollicking ditty begins by retailing that a blacksmith's trade is the best of all; traces it back to Cyclops and Vulcan; and tells how many proverbs arise from a blacksmith's trade and how useful a trade it is.

Text illustration, p. 71 (cf. text p. 72)

> Woodcut from 'Ragged and Torne and True. To the tune of Old Simon the King. Printed by the Assignes of Thomas Symcocke.' Roxburghe Collection of Ballads, I, 352, 353. Dept. of Printed Books, British Museum.
>
> (For general note on the Roxburghe Collection cf. note to § 25–28 above.)
>
> The housewife sits spinning at her door, while a stag hunt goes by (rather improbably) in the background. The woodcut is not directly illustrative of the ballad, which is a somewhat smug song by a young man, who though poor and ragged, is contented, and therefore better off than everyone else:—
>
> > 'What though my backe goes bare
> > I'm ragged and torne and true.'

Text illustration, p. 71 (cf. text p. 72)

> Woodcut from 'A lanthorne for Landlords. To the tune of the Duke of Norfolk. London. Printed for John Wright.' Roxburghe Collection of Ballads, I, 180, 181. Dept. of Printed Books, British Museum.
>
> (For general note on the Roxburghe Collection cf. note to § 25–28 above.)
>
> This doleful ballad tells how a poor widow helped in the harvesting near Norwich and of how her two little children wandered away among the broad cornfields and were lost and miserably died. The woodcut shows haymaking instead of harvesting.

Text illustration, p. 95 (cf. text p. 96)

> Woodcut from *The Shepheardes Calendar*, by Edmund Spenser (1581 edition). From a copy in the Dept. of Printed Books, British Museum.
>
> This woodcut for the month of May may be described in Spenser's own words from the dialogue between Piers and Palinodie. The dialogue treats actually of a discourse between Protestant and Catholic, but disregarding this we may take the following passage purely for its description of the English countryside on May morning and the doings of the country youth.
>
> > 'Is not thilke the mery month of May,
> > When love lads masken in fresh aray?
> > . . .
> > Yongthes folke now flocken in everywhere,
> > To gather may buskets and smelling brere:
> > And home they hasten the postes to dight,
> > And all the Kirke pillours eare day light
> > With Hawthorne buds, and swete Eglantine,
> > And girlonds of roses and Sopps in wine.

: : :

Sicker this morrowe, ne longer agoe,
I saw a shole of shepheardes outgoe,
With singing, and shouting, and jolly chere:
Before them yode a lusty Tabrere,
That to the many a Horne pype played,
Whereto they dauncen eche one with his mayd.
To see those folkes make such iouysaunce,
Made my heart after the pipe to daunce.
Then to the greene wood they speeded hem all,
To fetchen home May with their musicall:
And home they bringen in a royall throne,
Crowned as king: and his Queene attone
Was Lady Flora, on whom did attend
A fayre flock of Faeries, and a fresh bend
Of lovely Nymphs. (O that I were there,
To helpen the Ladyes their Maybush beare).'

Text illustration, p. 96 (cf. text p. 96)
Woodcut from 'The Milkmaid's Life; or, A pretty new Ditty,
Composed and Pend, The praise of the Milking paile to defend.
To a curious new tune called The Milkmaids Dumps. Printed
at London for T. Lambert.' Roxburghe Collection of Ballads,
I. 244, 245. Dept. of Printed Books, British Museum.
(For general note on the Roxburghe Collection cf. note to
§ 25–28 above.)

Text illustration, p. 97 (cf. text p. 96)
Woodcut from 'The Merry conceited Lasse. To a pleasant
northern tune. Printed at London for Thomas Lambert at the
signe of the Horse-shoe in Smithfield.' Roxburghe Collection
of Ballads, I, 240, 241. Dept. of Printed Books, British Museum.
(For general note on the Roxburghe Collection cf. note to
§ 25–28 above.)

Text illustration, p. 109 (cf. text p. 109)
Woodcut from 'The Coaches overthrow or A Ioviall Exalta-
tion of divers Tradesmen, and others, for the suppression of
troublesome hackney Coaches. To the tune of old King
Harry.' Roxburghe Collection of Ballads, I, 546, 547. Dept.
of Printed Books, British Museum.
(For general note on the Roxburghe Collection cf. note on
§ 25–28 above.)
The ballad is all for the suppression of hackney coaches for

'They make such a crowde
Men cannot passe the towne.'

It calls for room for 'the Carmens Cars and the Merchants
Wares,' and in one verse declares

'Arise Sedan
Thou shalt be the Man
To beare us about the Towne.'

The oft repeated refrain is
'Heigh downe, dery dery downe, with the hackney coaches
downe.'

(For other illustrations of different types of road traffic cf.
§ 100–105.)

# INDEX

ACT of Settlement, 136
Acting, Actors, 62-3, 118; Elizabethan, 62-3
Addison, Joseph, Sir Roger de Coverley of, 112-13, 137
Admiralty Court, 104
Adultery, Puritan Act against, 90
African Company, the, 60, 130
Agincourt, battle, 9, 52
Agricultural labourer, wages, 133 *and n.*
Agricultural revolution, 127
Agriculture, open field cultivation, 7, 8, 128; enclosure, 7-8, 28, 127; subsistence agriculture, 7; industrial crops, 7; in time of Charles II, 127-129; improvement in, 127-8; land improvement, 128; great estate system, 128
Ale and Beer, the ale bench, 23
Alva, Duke of, 53, 58
Amboyna, 79
American Colonies, the, 53, 67-74
Amsterdam, 58
*Ancien régime*, 88
Anglicanism, 38, 111-13, 123
Anticlericalism, in reign of Henry VIII, 91; subsides, 35-6; in Elizabeth's days, 91; the Laudian church, 91; reacts against Puritanism, 91.
Antwerp, 31, 56, 58
Apprentices, 24; of London, 25; pauper apprentices, 51
Apprenticeship, national system, 50-1; indentures, 51; of younger sons, 24-5
Archery, 28
Architecture, Gothic, 17, 18; Italianate, 18; Elizabethan, 17-19; Early Stuart, 105; the Jacobean mansion, 105; Ecclesiastical, 18, 148; Wren's churches, 148; Public buildings, 18
Arden, Forest of, 6, 47, 141
Aristocracy: Tudor, 24; Restoration epoch, 126. *See also* Nobility
Armada, Spanish, the, 28, 29, 37, 52-5
Army: development, 28-9
Artificers, Statue of, 51, 133
Arundel, Earl of, 105
Ascham, Roger: *Schoolmaster* of, 40
Atheism, 115

Audley End, 18, 103
Austen, Jane, 139; novels of, 23, 37, 64
Australia, 53

BACON, Sir Francis, 42, 106
Bacon, Sir Nicholas, 42
Ballads, 2, 62, 96-8; Border Ballads, 16
Baltic Trading Company, 60
Baltimore, Lord, 69
Banking Trade, 81-2
Banks, 81
Baptists, 92, 113
Barbados, 67, 70
Barley, 5, 6
Barrow, Isaac, 123
Bath, 21, 139
Beards, wearing of, 20
Bedford, Earls and Dukes of, 24, 81-7, 101, 127
Beds and Bedding, 106
Beggars, 31; in continental countries, 88. *See* Sturdy beggars
'Belted Will Howard,' 17
Bentley, Richard, 124; *Letters of Phalaris*, 124
Berry, Maj.-Gen., 12
Bible, the, 1, 40, 62, 92-3; reading of, and religion, 40; in American colonies, 74; in Puritan epoch, 92-3; scientific enquiry and, 115-16
Bideford, 4, 145
Birch, Colonel, 111
Birmingham, 100, 141
Bishops, the: denounced by Puritan clergy, 37, 38; under Charles I, 91
Black Death, the, 145
Blackwell, Aldermen, 83*n.*
Blake, William, 94
Bombay, 75*n.*
Books and reading, 97-9
Border Ballads, 16
Border Country, the, 14-16
Boswell, James: *Life of Johnson*, 64
Bosworth field, 12
Boyle, Robert, 115
Bread, 6 *and n.*
Bridgewater, Lord (1634), 97
Bristol, 4, 59, 77, 144

Browning, Robert, 33
'Brownists,' the, 38
Bruges, 56
Building, ecclesiastical, 18
Bullion export, 77
Bunyan, John, 92, 113; *Pilgrim's Progress*, 92, 93-4, 121
Burbage, actor, 62
Burial shrouds, 130
Burnet, Bishop, 86, 123
Buxton resort, 21, 139

CALAIS, 51, 56
Calvinists, 35, 40
Cambridge, 43-5; town and gown riots, 44
Cambridge Fair, 45
Cambridge University, Nineteenth and Twentieth centuries, 44; Colleges mentioned: Caius, 18; Clare, 44; St. John's, 43; Trinity, 18, 43, 123, 124
Camden, William, 3, 16, 42; his *Britannia* cited, 6, 21, 47, 48-9, 140. *See also under* Gibson
Canada, 53 *and n.*, 73
Canals, 84, 85
Capitalism, 59; merchant capitalism, 59
Carlisle, Bishops of, 16
Carpets, 105
Carriers, 5
Cattle, 8; breeding of, 8; fairs, 8
Cattle raiding, 14
Cavalier Parliament, the, 136, 137
Cavaliers, 101, 102, 112, 114; changing fortunes of, 125-7
Cecil, William: Lord Burleigh, 35, 42, 49, 55; the Cecils, 42
Ceilings, 105
Celibacy of the clergy, 36
Censorship (Licensing Act, 1663), 121-122 *and n.*
Census figures (1801-1831), 134-5
Chairs, 106
Chancery Court, 29, 104
Charcoal, 46, 47
Charity Schools, 23
Charles I, 78, 90, 91, 104; and monopolies, 78; Church under, 91; and the Tower Mint, 81
Charles II, 74, 118; Court of, 118-19; acquisitions from the Dutch, 74; patronage of science, 115, 118
Charltons, the: Border clan, 15

Chartered Company, the, 60
Chaucer, Geoffrey: *Canterbury Tales* of, 63
Cheques, 82n.
Chester, 3
Child, Sir Josiah, 79, 80, 86
Child betrothal and marriage, 86-7
Chimneys and increased use of coal, 48
China (or Cathay), 76
China porcelain, 77
Chipchase Castle, 15
Christ Church, Oxford, 43
Church, the: Anglican, under Elizabeth, 11, 33-41; and Stuarts, 69, 91, 93; at Restoration, 111-13, 123. *See Subject Headings*
Church architecture, 18, 148
Church attendance, enforced, 40
Church Courts, 90
Church Service: Elizabethan, 39-40; Hanoverian, 39n.
Cider, 6
Civil Wars, the, 99-102, 111, 138; economic causes, 87; fines and losses, 127; London in, 4, 77-8, 92, 99-100
Clarendon Code, the, 112, 124; object of, 114
Clarendon, Earl of, 36
Classical scholarship, 124; classicism in the England of Shakespeare, 1-2
Clergy: Anglican, under Elizabeth, 11, 33-6, 39-41; under Stuarts, 36; the release from celibacy, 36; rise in status, 37; under Commonwealth, 119
Clive, Robert, 75, 87
Cloth manufacture, 4; periodical unemployment in, 31, 57
Cloth trade, 56-9; fostered by Government, 130; affecting foreign policy, 56-8; Far East market, 78; Irish cloth trade, 130
Coal, Coal trade, 17, 47-8, 141-4; seacoal, 17, 47-8, 144; as domestic fuel, 47-8, 141; export of, 48; transport of, 144; trade development Stuart era, 141; production advance, 142n.; coalfields distribution, 142n.; applied in smelting of iron, 48; coal and iron age, 142
Coal-mining, 17; surface mining 17; miners' conditions, 142-3; fire damp explosion, 142; female and child labour, 142; the 'bondmen' in Scotland, 142

Cock-fighting, 139
Cod-fishing, 48
Coffee, 77
Coinage: debasement of, by Henry VIII,
    45; restored under Elizabeth, 45-6;
    and rise of prices, 6
Coke, Edward, 104
Coke, Thomas, of, Norfolk, 128
Collier, Jeremy, 123
Colonial expansion, 51, 52-3, 67-70
Common Law of England, 29-30, 74,
    104; and Prerogative Courts, 29, 104
Commonwealth, the: social cleavage,
    101-2; upper classes and, 111
Congregational singing, 39
Congregationalists, 92
Congreve, William, 120
Connecticut, 69
Conventicles, Puritan, the, 112
Cook, Captain James, 76
Cooking, 7
Cooper, Anthony Ashley, 1st Earl
    Shaftesbury, 111, 112
Corn, export, 5-6; bounties, 128, 129
    and n.
Corn Laws, 129
Corneille, 120
Cosway, Richard, 20
Cotton family library, 122
Country gentleman, the 24-5, 31, 65,
    126-7; Tudor and Stuart, 24-5, 65;
    wealth and power, 24; attitude to
    trade, 126-7; the small squire, 12-13,
    24, 101, 126-7
Court, the, of Charles II, 118-19
Court Leet (Manor Court), 27, 73
Courteen Association, 78, 79
Cox, Bishop of Ely, 11
Craft-gilds, mediaeval, 49, 59; decline,
    50, 59
Cranmer, Thomas, Archbishop, 33
Cromwell, Oliver, 94, 95, 97, 101, 106,
    115; Imperial development under, 80;
    and protection of English trade, 79;
    and land reclamation, 84-6
Crossbow, the, 28
Cumberland, 14, 16, 140

Dacres, the, 14, 16
Dames' schools, 41
Dearth, times of: Poor Law and food
    supply in, 31

Decoration, 18, 105-6
Deer, 7; hunting of, 138
Defences, before days of standing army,
    28-9. See Military system
Defoe, Daniel, observations of, 133
Deforestation, 46-7, 141, 143
De haeretico comburendo, 114-15
d'Ewes, Simon, 43
Dickens, Charles: Oliver Twist, 51
'Diggers' sect, the, 102
Dissenters (or Nonconformists), Puri-
    tans, 37-8, 92-4, 101, 111-13, 118; per-
    secution of, under the Restoration,
    111-13, 118, 121, 124; the dissenting
    congregations, 113; and the Church
    Establishment, 38. See also under Bap-
    tists, Quakers, Wesleyan
Dodds clan, the, 15
Domestic industry (of the housewife),
    107-8
Dovecots, 7, 108
Drake, Sir Francis, 52-5
Drama, Elizabethan, 62-4
Dress, Elizabethan, 20-1
Drinking glasses, 19
Drury Lane: Theatre Royal, 118
Dryden, John, 119, 120
Duelling, 21
Dugdale, Sir William: Monasticon, 123
Dunning, Richard, 134-5
Dutch, the, 58-9, 66, 73, 76; as allies in
    war, 55, 58; attitude to rivalry of, 130;
    Sea-beggars, the, 53

East India Company, 57, 60-1, 75-80,
    86-7, 130; charter, 57, 75; powers and
    policy, 75-6; trading stations, 76;
    chief articles of trade, 46, 77; Far
    Eastern cloth trade, 77; fleet of, 76,
    87; bullion export, 77; and mono-
    polies, 78; re-established under Crom-
    well, 79; New General Stock, 79
Eastland Company, 60
Ecclesiastical Architecture, 18, 148
Ecclesiastical Court of High Commis-
    sion, 29, 104
Economic Nationalism, Tudor, 50
Edgehill, 100
Education, 23, 123-4; Elizabethan, with-
    out segregation of classes, 23, 41; and
    see Subject Headings
Edward III, 50

Edward VI, 36
Elizabeth, Queen, 2, 3, 11, 36, 37, 38, 52, 55, 56, 77; Chaps. I *and* II *passim*
Elizabethan drama, 61-3
Elizabethan seamen, the, 52-6, 58
Ely Isle, 9-11, 84
Ely Place, Holborn, 11
Emigration and colonisation, 67 *et seq.*
Enclosure, 28, 141
Encyclopaedists, the, 124
English tongue, the, in Seventeenth Century, 95
Erasmus, 1
Erastianism, 34-5
Essex county, 5
Evelyn, John, 64, 103, 120
Eyre, Adam: Yorkshire yeoman, 98-9

FACTORIES, employment in, 31
Fairs, 45
Family life, Seventeenth Century, 107-110
Family prayers, 40
Farm animals; oxen draw the plough, 8-9 *and n.*
Farm labourer. *See* Agricultural labourer
Farquhar, George, 120
Feckenham Forest, Worcestershire, 47
Feldon, the: Warwickshire, 6, 140, 141
Fencing (sword-play), 21
Fenland, 9-11; drainage, 83-6; Windmills, 85
Fenmen, the, 9-10, 84
Fiennes, Celia; *Diary*, 143, 144
Finance and the Crown, 28, 55, 87
Fire of London, 146-7
Firearms, 29
Fiscal assessments of Counties, 139-40
Fish laws, the, 49
Fishermen, 49
Fishing industry, 48-9; cod-fishing, 48; herring fishing, 48-9
Fletchers, the, of Redesdale, 15
Flodden, 66
Floor coverings, 105
Footwear, 8
Foreign immigrants, 50. *See also* Huguenots
Forest laws, the, 136
Forest of Arden, 6, 47, 141
Forty-shilling freeholders, 26

Fowey, 145
Fowling, 10; *and see* Shooting
Fox, George, 93, 124, 125
Foxe, John, 52
Foxhunting. *See* Hunting
France, 67, 88; *noblesse*, the, 23, 87
Franchise, the, 26
Freedom, principle of, 27
French drama, the, 120
French privateers, 143
Frobisher, Martin, 51, 54
Froissart, 28
Fuel, 47-8, 143-4
Fuller, Thomas, 44
Furniture, Jacobean, 105-6

GALLEY slaves, 55*n.*
Game, Game laws, 108, 136-8
Gardens, and garden plants, 106-7
Gentleman, the, status of, 25-6
*Gentlemen's Recreation*, the, 137, 138*n.*
Gentry. *See* Country gentlemen
German workmen in England, 18, 46
Gibbons, Grinling, 123
Gibson, Edmund, Bishop of London, 141; edition of Camden's *Britannia*, quoted, 9-10, 141, 143
Gilbert, Sir Humphrey, 52
Gilds, 50. *See also* Craft gilds
Gilpin, Bernard, 16
Glass, 19; drinking glasses, 19; industry, 19, 46-7
Gold and prices, 187
Goldsmiths of London, the, 81-2; function of, as 'proto-bankers,' 82
Gothic architecture, 17, 18
Grahams clan, of Netherby, 16, 17
Grain, prices, control of, 32
Grammar schools, 1-2, 23, 41
*Grand Cyrus*, 98
Granvelle, 56
Great families and development, 87
Gresham's Royal Exchange, 18
Guise, Duke of, 53
Gunpowder, 46, 77
Gwynne, Nell, 118

HADDON HALL, 18
Hakluyt, Richard, 42, 52, 57
Halls clan, the, 15

Hamburg, 57
Hampden, John, 92
Hanse, towns, the, 57
Harbottle Castle, 15
Hare hunting. *See* Hunting
Harrison, Rev. William, cited or quoted, 3, 6n., 19 *and* n., 22, 43, *passim*
Harrogate, 139
Hatton, Sir Christopher, 11
Hawking, 137
Hawkins, Sir John, 2, 54-6, 70
Hearne, Thomas, 123
Hedleys clan, 15
Henry V, 52
Henry VIII, and break-up of monastic establishments, 91; debasement of coinage, 45; naval policy of, 55
Herb garden, the, 106
Herbert, George, 41
Heresy, death punishment for, 114-15
Herrick, Robert, 97
Herring fishery, 48-9
Highlands, the, and the Highlanders, 15
Highwaymen, 22
Hilliard, Nicholas, 20
Historical research, 123-4
Hobbes, Thomas, 115
Hobson, Cambridge carrier, 45
Hobson's choice, 45
Hobson's Conduit, 45
Holland, 58, 66; *and see* Dutch, the
Homilies, 40
Hooker, Richard, 33, 38; *Ecclesiastical Polity* of, 41
Hopkins, Matthew, 90
Hops, Hop growing, 47
Horse-breeding, 8-9, 109, 139
Horse-racing, 139
Horse transport, 47
House of Commons: powers over business affairs, 129-30
House of Lords, 24
Houses, 105; Tudor, 18-20, 27
Howard, Lord Admiral, 54
Howland, Elizabeth, 86
Howland, John, 86
*Hudibras*, 114, 119, 123
Hudson's Bay Co., 60, 130
Huguenots, 53, 73: in Norwich and London, 106
Hull, 144
Hundred Years' War, the, 67
Hunting, 138-9

INDUSTRIAL Revolution, effect of, on free industry, 78; and application of science, 115; and apprenticeship, 51
Industry, freedom in, 78; domestic system, 31
Inns, Elizabethan 21-3; seamy side of, 22
Inquisition, Spanish, the, 2, 53, 91
Investment of money, 80-1
Ireland: under Tudors, 2, 12; cattle trade, 128; cloth trade, 130
Iron and Steel, 46-8; smelting of iron, 48
Ironsides, the, 101
Italy, trade with, 59; merchant cities of, 58-9; beggars in, 88

JACOBEAN mansion, the, 105-6
Jamaica, 74, 79
James, Duke of York (afterwards King James II), 130
James I of England (and VI of Scotland), 17, 66, 67, 68, 90
James II of England, 104
Jameson's Raid, 60
Jesuit missionaries, the, 2, 13, 40
Jewel, John, Bishop, 34
Joint stock companies, 60, 130
Jonson, Ben, 119
Judicial system, 29-30, 103-4
Jury system, 30, 74
Justices of the Peace: under Tudors, 29-32, 37; under Stuarts, 31, 73, 88, 133; in 1688, 31, 133; Eighteenth Century, 31; functions of, 29-32, 51, 133

KENILWORTH, 18
Kent county, 5
*Killing no Murder*, 97
King, Gregory, 132; his analysis of the nation, 134, 135
King's Lynn, 89n., 145

LANCASHIRE, 100
Landowners, building-up of great estates, 127
Langdale, 146n.
Langland, William, 33
Language, English, the, 95-7
Latitudinarianism, 116
Laud, William, Archbishop, 35, 74, 88

Law: law reform, 104; supremacy of law, 103-4
Lawes, Henry, 97
Lead, 46
Leather industries, 8
Leland, John, 3, 6
Lepanto, 54
Lestrange, Roger, 120
Letters, Letter-writing, 108, 122
Levant (Company or Turkey), 60, 76
Libertines, the, 89-90
Libraries, private, 122; public, 122
Licensing Act (1663). *See* Censorship
Liddesdale, 15
Life, standard of, 20, 47, 133-4, 144
Literacy, 123
Literature and thought, 63-4, 97-8
Liverpool, 77, 144
Local administration, 30-1
Locke, John, 116
Lombard Street, 83
London, Tudor, 4-5; Growth of, 4, 65, 144-5, 147; in Civil War, 4, 78, 92, 99-101; at Restoration, 103, 139-140; self-government, 4; and the Monarchy, 4; the City proper, 4-5;
Westminster, 5
   Apprentices of, 25
   Bridge, 62
   Commerce and industry of, 5, 77-8, 144
   Fire of, 146-7
   Plague of, 145-7
   Population, 4
   Port of, 77, 144
   Tower, The, 5
Longbow, the, 28, 29
Long gun, the, 29
Longleat, 18
Long Parliament, the, 90, 130
Lords Lieutenant, 28
Lynn, 48

MAGISTRATES. *See* Justices of the Peace
Maitland, Prof. F. W., 124
Manchester, Earl of, 101
Manor Court (Court Leet), 27, 73
Manor Houses: Tudor, 18-20, 105; Courtyard, 105; furnishings, 19-20, 105-6
Mansfield, Lord, judgment, 27
Marcher Lords, the 11, 12

Marches, Wardens of the, 14, **17**
Marlborough, Duke of, 130
Marlborough wars, 127, 148
Marlowe, Christopher, 42, 44, 62, 63
Marriage: child marriages, 86-7
Marvell, Andrew, 69, 97, 106-7, 111
Mary, Queen of Scots, 37
Mary Tudor, Queen, 36
Maryland, 69, 70
Massachusetts, 69, 73, 74; university, 72
Massachusetts Bay Co., 68
Matthew, Sir Tobie, 110
*Mayflower,* the, 76n.
Maypoles, 90
Mazes, 106
Meat, in diet, 5, 7, 133; scarcity in winter, 77, 108; spicing of, 77; salted, 108
Medicinal spas, 21, 139
Mendicancy, 31. *See also* Beggars
Merchant, Tudor, the, 26
Merchant Adventurers, the, 59-60
Merchant capitalism, 60
Middle Ages, the, interest in, 123, 124
Middlesex, 139
Milbournes clan, the, 15
Military service, attitude to, 28
Military system, 28-9; the Militia, 28, 29.
*See also* Army
Milton, John, 33, 45, 97, 120, 121; *Comus,* 97; *Il Penseroso,* 47; *Paradise Lost,* 120
Miniature painting, 20
Mining expansion, 46. *See also* Coal
Mogul Empire, 75
Molière, 120
Monasteries, the, dissolution of, in Wales, 13; distribution of the estates, 24, 36. *See also* Pilgrimage of Grace
Money: borrowing, 81; lending, 81-2; interest, 81; investment, 80-1
Money market, 81
Monk, Colonel, 111
Monopolies, 78, 87
Montacute, 18
Moreton Old Hall, Cheshire, 18
Moryson, Fynes, 3,6-7, 22
Mosstrooping, 9, 15-17
Mun, Thomas, 81
Mundy, Peter, 60
Municipal Control in Middle Ages, 49-50. *See also* Local *Administration*
Music, Elizabethan, in Church, 39

NASH, Richard ('Beau Nash'), 139
National consciousness, 67
National control of industrial, commercial and social system, 49-50
Naval tactics, 54, 55
Navigation, 76
Navigation Laws, 49, 74, 130, 145
Navy, the, 53, 54-5, 68, 76; relation to merchant navy and seafaring population, 49, 54-5; development under Elizabeth, 46, 49, 55; in Civil War, 53; under Stuarts, 68; conditions in, 76
Nevilles, the, 14, 16
Newcastle, 17, 144
New England Colonies, the, 67-74
Newfoundland, 48, 52
New Hampshire, 69
Newmarket, 139
New Model Army, 102
Newsletters, 98-9n., 122
Newspapers, 92, 94, 98n., 122
News sheets, 120
Newton, Sir Isaac, 115, 116; Principia, 120, 121, 124
Nicholson, William, 123
Nobility, the, 24-5, 103
Nonconformists. See Dissenters
Norden, John, 5
North, Council of the, 12, 29, 104
Northern counties, 11, 13 et seq.; feudal and religious loyalty in, 14-15; Pilgrimage of Grace, 13, 14; rebellion of (1570), 16, 28
Northern Earls, rebellion of, 16, 28
North Tyne, 14-17
Northumberland, 14 et seq.
Norwich, 4, 48, 144

OATS, 6
Offences, punishment of, 89-90
Open field system. See Agriculture
Osborne, Dorothy, 96, 98, 103
Overseas enterprise, expansion of, 2, 51-61, 67-80; trade, 66-7
Oxen as draught animals, 8-9
Oxford, 143
Oxford University, under Elizabeth, 41-3; Nineteenth and Twentieth Centuries, 44; Christ Church, 43

PAINTERS, painting, 19, 20, 105
Pamphlets, religious and political, 97, 98 and n.

Paradisus, 106
Parish Church, the, Restoration period, 112-13
Parliament, 37
Paston family (the Paston Letters), 109-110
Peasantry, 65
Peel, Sir Robert (2nd baronet), police system initiated by, 89
'Peel towers,' 17
Peers of the Realm, Tudor times, 23-4. See also Nobility
Penshurst, 18
Pepper, 77
Pepys, Samuel, 120; diary, 64, 120, 128; library, 122
Percy family, 14, 15, 16
Perry, Worcestershire beverage, 6
Persia, Persian Gulf, 57, 76
Photography, 20
Pictures for wall decoration, 19, 105
Pilgrimage, custom of, 21
Pilgrimage of Grace, the, 13, 14
Pilgrim Fathers, the, 68
Pinkie Cleugh, 66
Piracy in the Channel, 56
Plague, the, 4, 105; of London, 145-b, 147. See also Black Death
Plays and Players, 61-3, 118-20
Pluralism, 37
Plymouth, 144
Police: no effective system, 89; Peel's police, 89
Political, controversy, 97; democracy, 102
Poor Relief: Tudor and Stuart, 31-2, 72, 88-9, 136; the Privy Council control of, 88-9; in Restoration era and Eighteenth Century, 88-9, 136; the Act of Settlement and, 136
Pope, the, and Henry VIII, 34
Popish plot, the, 119
Population, 3-4, 132, 134, 135; London, 3. See also Birth Rate, Census, Death Rate
Portland stone, 148-9
Portrait painting, 20
Portuguese, the, 76
Potato, the, 106, 108
Prayer Book, the, 33-4, 39
Prerogative Courts, 29, 104
Presbyterian Church, social discipline in, 89
Presbyterians: English, 115; Scottish, 115

Press-gang, the, 136
Prices: rise in, under Tudors and Early Stuarts, 24, 30, 45-6; control under Elizabeth, 30-1, 50
Pride, Colonel, 111
Printing: Printing press, 120-1; restrictions on, under Stuarts, 121-2; the Master Printers, 121; University presses, 121
Privy Council, 29-32, 49, 50, 55, 88; control of the Poor Law, 88; loss of power, 88
Protectorate, the, 91
Protestants, Protestantism, 34, 35, 39-41; ideas and practices of, 34; in Northern counties, 16; the minority of extreme Protestants, 35
Psalms, Psalters, 39
Public conveyances, 109
Publishing trade, 121
Purcell, Henry, 120
Puritan Commonwealth, 91 et seq.
Puritans, Puritanism, 1, 2, 37-41, 91 et seq., 101, 114-16, 120; under Elizabeth, 37-41; persecution of, under the Restoration, 114-16, 120; and orthodoxy, 116; Scripture pedantry of, 38. See also Dissenters
Pym, John, 78, 92

Quakers, the, 113, 124-5; persecution of, 124

Racine, 120
Raleigh, Sir Walter, 42, 51, 52, 68
Reading of books, 123
Redesdale, 14-17
Reeds clan, the, 15
Reformation, the, in England, 11, 16, 33 et seq.
Regicides Republic, 90
Regicide, 111-12
Religion and daily life: Elizabethan, 18, 33-41; Cromwell's time, 92-4
Religious controversy, 97; differences, 33, 37, 114-15; persecution, 38-9
Renaissance, the, 1-2
Reresby, Sir John, 117-18, 125-6, 129; account of a witch trial, 117-18.
Restoration, the, 94, 105, 111; and religious divisions, 112-13
Restoration drama, 118-20

Revenge, the, 57, 76n.
Revolution of, 1688, 91, 104, 116
Rhode Island, 69
Roads, 47, 48
Robsons clan, 15
Roe, Sir Thomas, 75
Roman Catholicism, 13, 16-17, 33-8 passim, 100, 112
Roman law, 30
Roses, Wars of the, 11, 24, 99, 110
Rotherhithe docks, 86
Rotten boroughs, 126
Roundheads, the, 100, 112, 114
Royal Society, the, 115-17, 121
Royalists, the, in Civil War, 100
Rubens, Peter Paul, 105
Rugby, trade, 8
Rupert, Prince, 115, 130
Rural worship, social side, 112-13
Russell family, 82-4, 86-7, 112
Russia, 57
Russia Company, 60
Rye, 6
Rymer, Thomas, 123

Sabbatarianism. See Sunday observance
Saffron Walden, 7
St. Martin-in-the-Fields, 122
St. Paul's Cathedral, 148
Salads, 108
Salamis, battle of, 54
Salt, 46
Sandys, Sir Edwyn, 74
Scholarship, 115-16
Schoolmen, the, 116
Schools. See Charity Schools, Grammar Schools.
Science and Religious belief, 115-16
Scientific enquiry, progress of, 115-18
Scotland: policy of Henry VIII and Edward VI towards, 14; and the border counties, 13-17; in Elizabeth's reign, 14-17; the union of crowns, 17, 66-7; antipathy with the English, 66-7; restricted intercourse, 66; in Stuart times, 66-7; character and religion, 66, 115. Domestic habits, 8
Mines, the 'bondmen' in, 142
See also Edinburgh, Jacobites, Presbyterians
Scott, Sir Walter, 66

Sculpture, 105
Scurvy, 76
Sea-coal, 17, 48, 144, *and under* Coal
Sea-faring population, 49, 53-4
Seamen, Elizabethan, the, 53-7
Sea-power, 53,54, 55
Seaside, the, as resort, 139
Selden, John, 81
Sermon, the: Puritan and Restoration period, 39-40, 123
Sexes, relation of, 63
Sexual offences, 89-90
Shaftesbury, First Earl, 112
Shakespeare, 33, 35, 61-4, 118, 141*n*.; plays of, 2, 35, 61-4, 118, 141*n*.; and seamy side of English inns, 22-3; idiom of, 62; *Hamlet*, 63; *Love's Labour's Lost*, 35
Shakespeare's England, 95; *and* Chapters I and II
Sheep, sheep farming, 8, 9
Shipbuilding, 55, 77
Shipping, 47-9
Shooting, sport, 29
Shot gun, the, 28, 29
Shrewsbury, Earl of, 21
Sidney, Algernon, 111
Sidney, Sir Philip, 42, 44
Silence, Master, 42
Silver and prices, 46, 87
*Sir Bevis of Southampton*, 94
Skin diseases, 108
Slave trade and slavery, negro, 2, 55*n*., 70, 73
Sly, Christopher, 27
Smith, Adam, 136
Smithfield market, 5
Smithfield fires, 35
Smoking, 59
Smuggling, 59
Society, Elizabethan, 24-6
Somersett: runaway slave, 27
Southampton, 59
Southampton, last Earl of, 102*n*.
Spain, 1, 2, 91; war with, 28, 29, 38, 52 56, 58
Spanish Netherlands, 58
Spas, medicinal, 21, 139
Spenser, Edmund, 2, 33, 42
Spice Islands, the, 76, 79
Spices, 77
Spitalfields, 106
Sport, 29, 136-9

Sporting guns, 29
Sprat, Thomas, Bishop of Rochester, 116-17
Squires. *See* Country Gentlemen
Stage coaches, 109
Stag-hunting, 136, 138
Standard of life, 20, 50, 133-4, 142
Star Chamber, the, 12, 29, 104
Statute of Artificers, 30, 51
Statutes of Labourers, 50
Statute: *De haeretico comburendo*, 114-15
Sternhold and Hopkins, 39, 40
Stewponds, 49
Stillingfleet, Edward, Bishop of Worcester, 123
Stock market, 81
Stourbridge Fair, 45
Stow, John, 25
Strafford, Thomas Wentworth, Earl of, 82, 88
Stratford-on-Avon, 6
Stubbs, William, Bishop, 124
Sturdy beggars, 31
Sunday observance, 40-1, 90; and Puritan intolerance, 90
Surrey county, 140
Swords, wearing, of, 20-1

Tables, 106
Tapestry, 19, 105
Taunton, 100
Taxation, 53, 55
Tea, 77
Tenison, Thomas, afterwards Archbishop, 122
Theatre, 62-3, 118-20; in Shakespeare's England, 62-4; Stage, 62, 118; women's parts, 62, 118; touring companies, 62, 118; effects of Puritan bigotry, 119, 120
Thorney monks, 83
Thornton, Alice, 93
Tillotson, John, Archbishop, 123
Timber, 46-7
Tin-mining, 46
Tobacco and smoking, 59, 68, 77
Toleration, 114
Tories, 114, 127
Torture, 104
Town, Towns, the: Elizabethan, 3-4, 50; Seventeenth Century, 99-100
'Town field,' the, 5

Townshend, Lord (Turnip Townshend), 128

Trade: national control of, under Elizabeth, 49-51; external, 57; coastwise, 48; colonial, 75; and royal grant of monopolies, 87

Trading Companies, 57-60, 65, 75 *et seq.*, 130. *See also under names of the Companies*

Travel, 110

Trevelyan, John, 40

Tunbridge Wells, 139

Turf, the, 139

Tusser, Thomas, 9

Tyldesley, Thomas, 138*n*.


Unemployment, 31, 32, 88, 89 *and n.*

Unitarianism, 2, 115

United States, the, 53

Universities, the: the College system, 42; Tudor and Stuart, 41-5; governing class and, 42; private tutoring in 42; age of undergraduates, 43*n*.

University Presses, the, 121


Van Dyck, Sir Anthony, 105

Vehicles, improvement in, 109

Venetian traders, 59

Venison, 6-7

Vermuyden: Dutch engineer, 84

Verney family, the, 93, 100, 107-10

Village, the: characteristics of, in Sixteenth and Seventeenth Centuries, 27-28, 73

Viner, Thomas, 83 *and n.*

Virginia, 52, 67-74; equestrian aristocracy of planters, 73

Virginia Company, 68

Voltaire, 38, 124


Wage-earning class, 27, 132-3

Wages, 49-50, 132-3; and price rise under Tudors and Stuarts, 46; control by law, 50; regulation by J.P.'s, 50-1, 133; local variation, 133; bargaining, 133; Statute of Artificers and, 133; strikes and combinations, 133

Wake, William, Archbishop, 123

Wales and the Welsh, 11-13; parliamentary and administrative union with England, 12; people of, 12-13; religion in, 13; agricultural system, 13; Wales, Council of, 12, 29, 104

Wall decoration, 19

Walsingham, Sir Francis, 42, 57

Walton, Izaak, 94-6

Warfare at sea, 54

Wars, mercantile and colonial, 131

Wars of the Roses, 11, 24, 99, 110

Warwickshire, 6; industrial progress in, 140-1; reactions on agriculture, 140-1

Washington, George, 73

Weapons, 28, 29, 54

Welsh, the. *See* Wales

Wesley, John, 93

Wesleyan movement, 113

West Indian Islands, 67-70

Westminster, municipality of, 118

Wharton, Henry, 112, 123

Wheat, 5, 6

Whigs, the, 103, 112, 114, 127

Whitehall Palace, 5, 118

Whitgift, Archbishop, 38

Wild-fowl, 10

Wilkins, David, 123

William III (of Orange), 121

Williams, Roger, 69

Windows, 19

Wine, 23

Winstanley, Gerrard, 102

Winthrop, John, 63

Witchcraft, belief in, 90; reaction against, 117-18

Witches, witch trials, 2, 90, 117-18

Wood, Anthony, 123

Wool production, 8

Wool trade, 56, 59; raw wool export prohibited, 130

Woollen cloth. *See* Cloth

Wordsworth, William, 33, 94

Wren, Sir Christopher, 120, 123, 148; Churches of, 148

Wrestling, 139

Wycherley, William, 119, 120


Yarmouth, 48

Yeomen, 24, 26-7, 65, 92, 99

York, 4

Young, Arthur, 128

Younger sons, and apprenticeship to trade, 24-5